Pack Prints: Composition II

Third Edition

FOUNTAINHEAD
PRESS

D1472888

Fountainhead Press's green initiatives include:

Electronic Products and Samples. Products are delivered in non-paper form whenever possible via Xample, an electronic sampling system. Instructor samples are sent via a personalized web page that links to PDF downloads.

FSC-Certified Printers and Recycled Paper. All of our printers are certified by the Forest Service Council, which promotes environmentally and socially responsible management of the world's forests. This program allows consumer groups, individual consumers, and businesses to work together hand in hand to promote responsible use of the world's forests as a renewable and sustainable resource. Most of our products are printed on a minimum of 30 percent post-consumer waste recycled paper.

Cover design: Lori Bryan, Fountainhead Press
Cover and title page art: Ross Carroll, Arkansas State University
Book design: John Abernathy and Kerri L. Bennet, Arkansas State University
Book layout: Permafrost Publishing Services

Cover Artist:

Ross Carroll

Interior Layout & Design:

John Abernathy and Kerri L. Bennet

CONTENTS

Sample Student Reflections   271

Primary Research   287

Copyright Acknowledgments   299

ACKNOWLEDGMENTS

A text such as this one does not come together without many contributors and supporters and as our text grows and changes, the number of those involved continues to grow. First and foremost, we must thank Dr. Kristi Costello for not only imagining this text, but for pooling the resources, organizing the committees, and advocating for the conditions needed to make it happen. Without her early guidance this text and the course that it supplements, would not exist.

Next, we thank those at the A-State Faculty Center for approving Dr. Costello's grant proposal and funding our curriculum committee in the summer of 2018. Many of the Writing Program faculty are not guaranteed work through the summer but their voices and pedagogies are an integral part of our course development. These funds made this discussion more accessible to all levels of faculty.

This, naturally, leads us to a special acknowledgment. To those faculty members who, in the heat of an Arkansas July, were dedicated to creating composition courses that reflect the ever-shifting landscape of public and academic discourse and the developing needs of modern university students, thank you: Kristi Costello, Airek Beauchamp, Loren Skye Roberson, Khem Aryal, Leslie Reed, Elizabeth Chamberlain, Tabatha Simpson-Farrow.

We are grateful to our colleagues who've supported this project through encouraging your students to submit work. Without those texts, *Pack Prints* loses what makes it most special; the voices of the students whom it seeks to serve.

Thank you, also, to Leslie Reed, Jesse Matlock, Hans Hacker, and John Artim for providing your disciplinary insight. These peeks behind the curtain help demystify academia for our students.

Thank you to Dr. Janelle Collins, who consistently supports the Campus Writing Program and views our work as a vital aspect of A-State English Department. Additionally, thank you to Dr. Carl Cates and Dr. Gina Hogue who advocate for the Writing Program.

We would be remiss not to thank our co-editor, Jesse Matlock. His insightful commentary and thoughtful additions to this text provided a steady barometer during the drafting process. We are grateful for his patience and ever-readiness to read, revise, write, and bolster any portion of text we sent his way with the loosest of schedules.

Finally, to the team at Fountainhead Press, who saw potential in our work and offered your support and expertise in matters for which we simply are ill-equipped. Thank you. Specifically, Eddie and Peter, for your enthusiastic interest in our vision, and for the pastries. And to Lindsy, our project manager, for your patience and diligence in trying to make our crazy ideas work in print.

Tab's Personal Acknowledgments

In 2016, I re-entered the college classroom for the first time since graduating from A-State just two years prior. I was eager to be back in academia; the buzz of campus life, being nearer to the many memories I had made on these very same sidewalks, in these very same hallways, but mostly, I was afraid. Afraid that I did not know enough about my field to impart the knowledge and skills my students would need to function in the university or their future professions. I was afraid that they would see the "cracks" in my professional armor.

Though I do not remember all of their names, I think about those first students often, and so choose to thank them here. They taught me that a lesson plan does not always fit neatly into the lives of twenty unique individuals, that one student may latch onto a reading while another sees only muddled jargon, and that discounted Halloween candy is a great motivator for classroom discussion. Most notably, though, they proved to me that what I had perceived as imperfections in my ethos are what allowed my students and I to exchange knowledge with each other. Allowing myself to appear human to those students (and every group that came after them) helped us to approach breaking down the invisible barriers of access to knowledge, a theme I hope carries throughout this text.

Airek's Personal Acknowledgments

In the previous edition of this text I thanked many peers and fellow authors, people of authority who have helped me achieve the success that is equated with the ability to co-produce such a text. I do, from the bottom of my heart, want to thank Tabatha and Kristi, but more honestly, and more in the spirit of the pedagogy that scaffolds this edition, I want to thank the students I have been lucky enough to teach so far, especially those who have pointed out my errors and pushed back on admittedly unfair or punitive practices that I picked up like bad habits along my own journey as a teacher. I want to thank all of the students who have called my bluff, called me out, and made me kinder in my approach. I want to thank students who have had the courage to ask *why*. After all, *why* is one of the most important questions a critical thinker can ask, and one that a student in control of her own education not only has the right but the responsibility to ask. Just like writing, teaching is an imperfect art, and just like in writing I learn much from my failures. The important thing to me is that my own failures don't end in punishment for my students, but maybe illustrate a path to becoming more successful for all of us.

BACKGROUND AND SPECIFICS OF THIS EDITION

The first edition of *Pack Prints* began in 2013 as a research and passion project that its creators, Dr. Kristi Costello and then-graduate student Tabatha Simpson-Farrow, imagined would be a supplemental text for First-Year Writing courses at A-State. They researched collections from other universities and learned that what made each of them unique was the voices of the students who those texts represented. The diversity of writing styles in *Pack Prints* provided students with guideposts off of which to build their writing assignments and faculty with opportunities to illustrate what they privileged in their own writing pedagogies.

To quote Dr. Costello from that first edition, "our chief hope is that this text will facilitate learning for Arkansas State University students and teaching for Arkansas State University faculty." As we move toward publication of this third edition, we hope we have maintained a voice that is unique to A-State students and representative of A-State writing faculty. What we know is distinctly new about this third edition, other than the addition of supplemental readings and course materials, is that it exists as the result of a collaborative effort between several faculty members who considered feedback from the Writing Program as a whole to develop the following learning outcomes.

Upon completion of Composition II, students will

- Produce texts that experiment with genre conventions in various rhetorical situations, modes, and technologies;

- Engage with larger ongoing civic, social, and academic conversations;

- Find, evaluate, and synthesize disciplinary and professional sources by integrating that research into their written work through the appropriate use of summary, paraphrase, and direct quotation;

- Understand the significance of intellectual property, academic honesty, and the rhetorical and disciplinary purposes of citation styles of their discipline;

- Practice invention and recursive writing techniques to develop and compose original researched writing projects;

- Revise their writing based on feedback provided by peers, instructors, tutors, and other audiences, and provide constructive feedback to other writers;

- Refine their writing by making rhetorical choices regarding disciplinary, grammatical, and stylistic conventions;

A NOTE TO READERS

Intro to Note to Readers

In the summer of 2018, a group of composition instructors and scholars gathered weekly to look at our previous practices, pedagogies, assignments, and goals. We knew that we were on the right track with where we were going but we still knew that something, or some things, weren't right.

One thing that you come to know when you teach writing at any level is that your course won't be perfect. No course is. Writing requires attention to detail, a willingness to scrap everything and start from scratch, the ability to listen to others, to give and receive honest and supportive criticism. All of these things are difficult, and when you have a group of twenty students, all with different strengths, different approaches, and different backgrounds all attempting to use words to make sense of the world, well, things can, and often do, go very wrong. However, this points to something else that you come to know when you teach writing at any level, and this thing that you come to know—to make peace with, though it is often a cold comfort—is that things going wrong is always instructive. Mistakes are useful. Accidents are opportunities to learn. These sayings are both threadbare clichés designed to calm down those in times of crisis as well as gloriously, radiantly true.

As a means of introduction to the material in this book, and to our composition program in general, the paragraphs above might not fill you with a sense of comfort, or even confidence, in what you are agreeing to, the contract into which you are entering. But what if we told you that we could successfully argue otherwise? What if we told you that nothing went very wrong in our former curriculum? That it was written by faculty who earnestly strive for student success and who used the scholarship and best practices of our field to design assignments that both encouraged students to find their own voices and engage in the written conventions of their chosen majors? What if we told you that the only thing terribly wrong with our previous curriculum was that it wasn't perfect, and though we are all aware that perfection doesn't exist—and that starting things from scratch is the best way to ensure that things go terribly wrong—it is either because of or in spite of the promises of failed perfection and things going terribly wrong that we met that summer to reimagine our composition curriculum?

We invite you now on this new, imperfect journey to work through the results of that summer project, to ask questions, confront your thoughts, and discover new ones. Even if you need to rebuild those things which might go terribly wrong, we hope that you will walk away with something that makes you as proud as this text, and this course, makes us.

And we are proud of this text, and this course. Each time we are able to engage in such a project, with it comes the opportunity to examine our own behaviors, make explicit the changes we have made since the last time, and to discuss clearly and thoughtfully, with colleagues we respect and whose opinions we value, how our teaching has evolved, and hopefully, how we are able to refine our goals and concepts, deliver better instruction, and center the student in the classroom. As teachers of an imperfect craft, we understand very well the need to revise for our audience. We have carefully constructed this book to remain engaged in its multiple purposes at all times. When you work on a project like this, you have to consider who the stakeholders in the project are. In our case, the stakeholders are various and very different from one another, although there is always some overlap. We will be asking you to write academically for public and scholarly audiences, in very different genres and for different purposes, all the while forming persuasive arguments backed by academic research. That leaves us, those helping guide you through the course, responsible to a lot of people—but the groups we hold most valuable are you, the students, and ourselves, as those charged with navigating the process with you.

Note to Readers

We open the book with thoughts on writing in specific disciplines, supplied by specialized faculty and graduate assistants from across campus. First-year composition sees students from all intended majors, including undeclared students who are taking their first year or so to figure out in which direction they feel a calling. The multidisciplinary identity of our classroom also mirrors our field: Rhetoric and Composition itself is a multidisciplinary field that sees scholars approach it from many different disciplinary lenses. The "Writing in the Disciplines" section is designed to help you see inside how disciplines create and shape knowledge, which is reflected in the way scholars of the disciplines research and report their findings. Thinking of disciplines as ways of researching, writing, and contributing to the growth of knowledge in ways that retain disciplinary identity but also situate the disciplines in the larger conversations of academia is one of the first steps to thinking rhetorically. Thinking rhetorically, or in a way that considers speech or writing to always be an attempt to persuade the reader toward one position or another, is an important part of your college experience.

In your general studies coursework, you will encounter several disciplines per semester, and you will be expected to communicate according to their conventions, in their vocabularies, sometimes as experts regardless of your first-year status. Engaging in the rhetoric of the discipline, for example learning the vocabulary and citation style that historians use, can help you not only survive the course, but potentially enjoy it. While not every discipline is represented (yet), we are experiencing more and more positive feedback, and willingness to work with us, from faculty across campus because students who leave our classes are doing so a little more versed in thinking, reading, and writing critically, with rhetorical awareness, than students have before.

You will see this line of thinking throughout this text. We follow the "Writing in the Disciplines" chapter with a citation guide, "Citing in the Disciplines." One of the things we hope to illustrate to you is how citation styles reflect, or become part of, the rhetoric of the discipline. In other words, disciplines cite their research according to particular style guides because these style guides reflect the information that each discipline privileges, information that is vital to the ongoing conversations in which the disciplines engage and, more importantly, indicative of *how* they engage in these conversations.

From there we move on to "Sample Assignment Overviews," in which we discuss the assignments our faculty created for this particular curriculum. Providing these assignment overviews, including the minor, and sometimes major, revisions different instructors have made for their individual courses illustrates several important concepts that we believe are crucial to the Composition II course in general and to our curriculum at large. You can see how different instructors privilege different aspects of the assignments; how these differences in privilege might affect student performance; what this says about the classroom, and the instructor at the head of the classroom, as an individual rhetorical space; and how learning this space will help you better address one of the intended audiences for the course.

Next you will find "A Note on Group Work," which attempts to address one of the most daunting features of this particular curriculum—the group work-intensive nature of it. This is a feature, not a bug, of the course, and our decision to craft the curriculum in such a fashion reflects one of our own goals from Composition II. That writing is inherently a social activity seems to be at once readily apparent to anyone paying attention, yet at odds with traditional academic notions of authorship, which always involves a certain isolation. This is complicated even further in that we ask you to try to form interdisciplinary groups, or to find members who will, according to their intended majors, approach the topics and assignments in the class in different ways, using different research methods, vocabularies, and writing conventions to contribute to your group's research.

From there we will walk you through the assignments of the course, speaking to the different academic and public ways the genres, in practice, have formed, and are evolving. The first assignment, the Proposal, is a public and an academic genre that introduces you to initial research and establishes your ethos both individually and as a group. The Proposal should identify and convince the stakeholders of your project of your dedication to the project, how you intend to conduct your research, what goals you have for the project, and the manner in which you intend to reach these goals. As you might imagine, this assignment will also demonstrate these same aspects of your participation in the course to your group mates and your instructor and set the tone for the rest of your assignments during the semester.

From the Proposal we move on to the Annotated Bibliography. Chances are you have encountered this genre before, and it might have seemed like a waste of your time. Without proper framing, the Annotated Bibliography will appear to be, at best, a genre for the sake of having a genre, when in fact the ways in which crafting this assignment should help you learn several research and study techniques that are crucial to academic success and critical thinking. In this assignment you will engage with critical and rhetorical reading, allowing you to make succinct evaluations of the source material you encounter. Further, you will begin to see the conventions and vocabularies that inform your discipline's most prestigious genre, the scholarly research article. The scholarly research article is an almost entirely academic genre, but hopefully it will also show you how, at least marginally, this genre does affect public opinion, political policy, and how we allocate and distribute resources locally, regionally, and nationally. If you find yourself stumped by your discipline's seeming lack of interaction with the subject of your group's project, do not hesitate to contact your instructor, the writing center, or a research librarian, all of whom might provide a unique angle that isn't readily apparent; but first, try researching with an open critical eye.

The Annotated Bibliography moves directly into the Literature Review, which exists across disciplines, either as a way to situate certain research in the greater disciplinary or academic conversation, or as a genre worthy of publication on its own. The Literature Review will hopefully resolve any lingering questions about the usefulness of the Annotated Bibliography, as you will rely on your annotations, at least in part, to develop and write the review. The genre of the Literature Review is designed to give the reader an insight into the major voices and stances in a particular disciplinary conversation. Sometimes these voices are aligned almost entirely, and sometimes they are deeply at odds. In the Literature Review you should discuss what these voices say, how they say it, and most importantly find any gaps in the research that will allow you to contribute a unique approach to the subject. This assignment is often daunting, and it can be very difficult, as it requires some of the deepest analysis, synthesis, and critical thinking of any of the assignments.

Following the Literature Review, we move into the "Colloquium" chapter. In this chapter, we provide a guide to making research public, what this means, and how to do it. To think of "public genres" is almost dizzying in scope. There seem to be millions of public genres out there, from the Facebook post to the infographic, and all of them relate to different audiences, through different media, in different ways. Further, when you figure in how audience determines the effectiveness of a certain genre, the possibilities, and ways to succeed and fail, multiply further. In this section we ask students to consider to whom they are speaking, who is on their side and who could be, and what genres will do the work of keeping their faithful audience faithful and moving any opposition a little further over to their side. This will require critical reading of genres that we encounter every day as well as a precise navigation of the genres and their particular media. Students might find that the knowledge required in this section has always been implicitly obvious to them, but making it explicit as a justification for following this path will be more difficult than they expect. The important thing is that students understand that this event is an opportunity for them to celebrate the hard work they have done throughout the semester and begin to reflect on their initial proposals, their challenges, and their own successes.

Not surprisingly, the Colloquium is followed by the "Reflection" chapter, where we ask students to think back on their journeys throughout this version of Composition II. Students have researched their own disciplines, the disciplines of those in their group, and written for public as well as for academic audiences in a variety of genres. In other words, they may be so deep into their own work that they are unable to really gauge how much work they have done, what kind of progress they have made, or what their own strengths and weaknesses are, as they have come to learn over the semester. This type of reflection is key for any kind of growth. Rather than just being busy work, this Reflection holds pretty high stakes. As the introduction to the portfolio, the Reflection serves as evidence of the student journey and a catalogue of progress. In other words, this is where the student tells us, either implicitly or explicitly, how we as instructors should evaluate their work.

At the end of the book you will find samples of many student Reflections and samples of full student portfolios. One of the main differences in this edition of *Pack Prints* is that our sample student writing is largely unpolished, presented as-is upon being turned in for the final grade. This was a conscious decision on our part, as we wanted to show evidence of students who worked hard, whose work might look much like your own. In previous editions we would work closely with authors who did exemplary work to polish and refine their writing, but this no longer felt right. Students in any first-year composition course will not always write like experts in their fields, because they are not yet. Expecting future students to relate to such polished work no longer felt honest. Furthermore, as pedagogues and instructors we believed that this set unrealistic expectations for ourselves when it came time to assign grades. We believe that we should evaluate students' journeys, their hard work, and what they learned in the course. We expect that in your classrooms you read these examples in a spirit of compassion, that you relate to any errors and use them as instructive. No writing is ever perfect, not even ours.

Writing in the Disciplines

INTRODUCTION

As we considered in the introduction, each discipline will have its own set of conventions, discourses, boundaries of knowledge and genres. Learning to read these guiding disciplinary dictums is important to your success as a scholar in your chosen field of study. In this section, we have asked professors from across the A-State campus to provide writing guides that you might follow when engaging in their particular scholarly discourses. We have organized this section to flow as follows.

- **Kate Krueger: "Writing in the Humanities"**
  Dr. Krueger breaks down the conventions of literary analysis, revealing the ways in which humanities scholars utilize inductive reasoning to generate novel interpretations of texts.

- **Rebecca Barrett-Fox: "Writing in the Social Sciences"**
  Dr. Barrett-Fox discusses the methods and responsibilities of scholars in the social sciences, going further to explain the attendant genres, audiences, and overall scope of the social sciences.

- **Vicent Moreno: "Writing in a Foreign Language"**
  Building conceptually upon Dr. Krueger's and Dr. Barrett-Fox's essays, Dr. Moreno addresses artifact analysis across different languages. Dr. Moreno articulates the methods, goals, and purpose of the overarching genre of analysis.

- **Steven Weimer and Jacob Caton: "A Guide to Writing in Philosophy"**
  Dr. Weimer and Dr. Caton move from analysis to argument, forwarding the ways in which philosophers persuade their audiences via well-constructed arguments. They stress clarity, organization, and logical reasoning as fundamental elements of good scholarly writing in philosophy.

- **J. Justin Castro: "Writing History"**
  Dr. Castro expands on the writing of his colleagues by addressing not only analysis and argumentation but also the formulation of effective research questions—questions that fruitfully guide research. Dr. Castro illustrates the importance of primary research materials in providing persuasive accounts of the past.

- **Sarah Scott: "Writing for the Field of Communication"**
  Sarah Scott moves the discussion to the importance of research in scholarly writing for communication. Scott shows the rhetorical utility of various style guides in addressing various modes of communication and rhetorical situations.

- **Robert Robinette: "Library and Information Research"**
  Robert Robinette discusses the library as the nexus of research on the Arkansas State campus. Robinette explains the different ways scholars should use library resources effectively.

- **Hans J. Hacker: "Legal Writing"**
  Hans J. Hacker's "Legal Writing" provides a comprehensive approach to student writing for legal purposes. Hacker establishes legal writing as inherently rhetorical, and he guides the reader through an ongoing discussion of the rhetorical aspects of effective legal writing, including audience and purpose, as well as the long-standing conventions of the discipline, from vocabulary to the eternal debate over passive versus active voice.

- **Jesse Matlock: "Writing for Engineering: An Embedded Tutor's Perspective"**
  Jesse Matlock, a graduate student in English and tutor in the campus writing center, prepared for us "Writing for Engineering: An Embedded Tutor's Perspective." Matlock's situated nature is one that we see often: a writing center tutor is assigned to work with a specific discipline so he or she may serve as a point of contact for students in that department. Matlock's unique approach to this situation, though, is that he is able to discuss the writing needs of engineers from the perspective of an outsider to the discipline. Matlock is able to deftly describe the needs, and the potential frustrations, from each point of view and give a clearer and more effective account of writing in engineering than someone writing from either isolated perspective.

- **John M. Artim: "How Biologists Write for Each Other" and "A Scientific Article Annotated"**
  Biologist John Artim closes the discipline-focused unit, authoring both "How "Biologists Write For Each Other" and "A Scientific Article Annotated." In the first piece, Artim frames his argument in the content of biology, a discipline dedicated to unraveling the intricacies of living things, versus the rhetorical construct of biology, a discipline governed by seemingly rigid conventions, genres, and writing practices. Artim furthers this discussion, extending it to science broadly, when he provides us with "A Scientific Article Annotated," in which he breaks the conventions down further and demonstrates how these conventions work together to format and formalize scientific research.

Conceptually, the writing guides move from analysis to argument and argument to research, showing the disciplinary conventions that scholarly writers operate within. Remember that the guides provided herein function as just that, *guides*. Scholars did not find disciplinary conventions etched into stone tablets or sprouting from the wellspring of knowledge. It is important to understand disciplines and their discourses and conventions as social constructions that continue to evolve as scholars participate with one another within the conversations of their prospective fields.

WRITING IN THE HUMANITIES

Kate Krueger
Associate Professor of Literature at Arkansas State University

. . . .

When you open a book, you must begin with an open mind. Whereas in the sciences you might begin with a hypothesis regarding what you might find in your investigation, in the humanities we work via inductive reasoning. This means that we have no preset expectations regarding the meaning of the work. Rather, as we read we make observations about structural patterns and other elements of a text. The term "text" here is important; everything is a text. While in literature courses one might focus on novels, and in history classes one might analyze historical documents, in composition courses texts might include advertisements, film, or even fashion. In the humanities, we understand that textual analysis depends upon our attentiveness to detail and the messages being conveyed by these modes of expression. We examine what we've found and draw conclusions from that information. Those conclusions become the basis of our thesis statements. The last part of our reading experience thus becomes the beginning of the writing process.

Observations are essentially the "what" and "who" of a text. These are concrete details. The argumentation of humanities writing depends upon a grasp of those "whats," but a basic understanding of those elements is not enough. We also have to explain the "why" and "how." Why are those features significant? How do they contribute to or provide broader insight into the meaning of the text or of the topic as a whole? We must explain the nuance and the importance of the material that we've found because others might read it differently. It is not enough to simply point out where you found patterns. Through your analysis, you show the "why" and "how"—you essentially prove that your interpretation of the information is the correct one. Indeed, another reader may overlook the elements that you see as integral to the text.

As a writer, then, you must first be an observant reader. While there is often no single "correct" answer to textual analysis, this does not mean that every interpretation is equally legitimate. Because texts are complicated systems of communication, there is more than one message being conveyed at the same time. One reader's analysis may provide insight into the representation of social categories such as gender, while another reader might focus on the way in which the writer uses a certain tone. But if a reader uses deductive reasoning and makes assumptions about what the text is doing without attending to its actual details, or if the reader misreads, misrepresents, or misinterprets the language, then those analyses are wrong. Inductive reasoning and textual analysis rely on a set of observational skills and an understanding of the makeup of a text. It's up to us as teachers to give you the vocabulary to enable you to see the patterns and make astute observations.

When you have made your conclusions and have an argument in mind, you will regularly use three primary elements to convey messages of your own: ethos, pathos, and logos. You will need to know what you think, who you are, and to whom you are writing. This is your "rhetorical situation." In a composition classroom, you will be asked to consider multiple circumstances in which your writing will attempt to convince an audience. Those circumstances will change the way you approach your writing. How will the particular audience of this work be convinced? First, you will have to establish your ethos, which is a set of techniques that convinces others that you are trustworthy and knowledgeable. This can be created in lots of ways, including the formality or informality of your language, the mention of your credentials or life experience, and your tone. For instance, I'm using the words "we" and "you" because I want you to like me (we're in this together). But I also want to mention that I'm an Associate Professor of English because I want you to respect me (I am an expert in the field). You may use emotional appeals (pathos) to move the readers of a letter to the editor to feel sadness or anger, while in academic writing you might rely on logic and facts (logos). Each of these strategies are vital parts of writing as an act of communication between writer and reader.

Whether you are a first-year student in a composition class or a seasoned literary critic who has published several books, your argumentative writing will contain the same basic elements. Your introduction and thesis statement tell us the topic (the "what" you've been tracking through the text) and your major claim about it (the "why" and "how" of this topic is significant). In your papers, this might all occur in the first paragraph; when you read a work of literary criticism, the introduction might be four or even ten pages depending upon the length of the argument as a whole. A critic will introduce you to the background you need in order to understand the topic and its significance. This may include defining important terms (because words can imply lots of different meanings, it's always a good idea to define your terminology in the beginning of an argument). The structure of an argument is called "signposting" because it's giving a reader a sense of direction—where are you going and how are you going to get there? You orient the reader through these types of sentences, which are strategically placed at the beginning or end of paragraphs and subsections, so your reader doesn't get lost along the way. This is why we need transitions. Topic sentences will make smaller claims that help to build a case that supports the thesis, which is the one big argument to which each paragraph contributes. Conclusions review the minor points that you used to prove your overarching thesis and leave the reader with a clear sense of why all of this matters.

Writers will also acknowledge the arguments of others who have discussed this topic. Why? Because writing is a conversation in print. The bibliography at the end of a work is not just proof that someone has done their homework; it is also a record of the other people to whom the writer is responding. When you read an argumentative article or book, imagine that the writer is in a room with the other people that she mentions in her text. How do they agree? Why and in what way do they disagree? The writer is actually contributing to a long conversation that happens in print, sometimes over decades. When you write an argument, you are participating in that conversation, too.

Your observations, which you gathered the moment you started reading, have been transformed into a unique analysis that expands our knowledge of the topic. In this way, we become part of an intellectual community committed to critical inquiry. In the humanities, we must be open to texts and to the part each of us can play in our collective pursuit of greater knowledge and understanding. Your voice and perspective matter; your writing does make a difference.

Further Resources

Cain, Patricia. "How to do a Close Reading." 1998. Writing Center at Harvard University, http://writingcenter.fas.harvard.edu/pages/how-do-close-reading. Accessed 21 November 2016.

Dollar, Mark. "What Makes a Good Literature Paper." 19 October 2010. Purdue OWL, https://owl.english.purdue.edu/owl/resource/618/01/. Accessed 21 November 2016.

WRITING IN THE SOCIAL SCIENCES

Rebecca Barrett-Fox
Assistant Professor of Sociology at Arkansas State University

. . . .

The term "social sciences" includes an expanse of disciplines—anthropology, education, economics, geography, political science, psychology, social work, and sociology, as well as their sub-disciplines such as archeology, linguistics, genetics, criminology, and gerontology, and area and cultural studies like women's and gender studies, sexuality studies, American studies, and African American studies. Within each discipline, researchers may adopt a "soft" or humanities-like approach that focuses on theories and supports its ideas with qualitative data or a "hard" approach that focuses on experiments and supports its ideas with quantitative (that is, numbers-based) data. Whether they employ qualitative or quantitative research methods or use a mixture of both (called "mixed methods"), social science writers, unlike writers in many other fields, often devote more pages of writing to their methods than to their results. Indeed, some social science writing's biggest contribution to the field is not *what* the authors find but *how* they find it. Indeed, entire journals, such as *International Journal of Social Research Methodology*, *Journal of Methods and Measurement in the Social Sciences*, and *Journal of Mixed Methods Research* are devoted to publishing articles just on research methods, and disciplines and subdisciplines in the social sciences likewise have their own journals that publish work that pioneers new methods of data collection and analysis. However they conduct their research, though, across disciplines and research orientations, writers in the social sciences have responsibilities to three groups of people:

Responsibilities to Research Subjects

By definition, social scientists investigate human behavior rooted in our interactions with others. We ask others to let us examine their lives. In exchange, we promise to protect them from harm as much as possible—including when we write about them. To do that, social science writers must:

1. Subject our research proposal to the scrutiny of others in the field. Before we conduct research on living human beings, we ask an institutional review board (IRB) to review our proposal. Composed of other researchers, the IRB notes any areas of potential harm to research subjects and gives us feedback to improve the research plan.

2. Protect research subjects' privacy as we collect data and write up our findings. We may assign pseudonyms and/or change identifying details about our research subjects, such as the town where they live, so their identities cannot be discerned by readers. We tell our readers that we've made these changes with phrases like *names and identifying details have been changed to protect research subjects' privacy*. We store our notes on a password-protected computer or in a locked file cabinet. When we are finished with our project, we destroy our notes so the information that we have gathered cannot be used against our research subjects in the future.

Responsibilities to Readers

Social science writing is very popular among general readers. News agencies, for example, include social science correspondents who distill the technical details of social science research into journalistic accounts. Self-help books on a variety of topics—being financially savvier, getting along with your spouse, recovering from addiction, or learning tips for success in college—all rely upon social science. Writers ranging from Malcolm Gladwell (author of five *New York Times* bestsellers, including *Tipping Point*, *Blink*, and *David and Goliath*) to Nate Silver (whose subfield is sabermetrics, the study of statistics in baseball) likewise rely on social science when they write. Social science writers show respect for readers when they:

1. State their conclusions at the beginning, often in an abstract of 100–200 words that precedes the main body of text. Readers want to understand *what* you learned in your research before they invest time in reading about the process of *how* you learned it.

2. Avoid jargon. If technical words cannot be avoided, they should be clearly defined.

3. Include only the level of detail necessary to make and support the main point. If, for example, the race of a research subject is important, you should mention it. If it's not, don't.

4. Don't make claims bigger than their research findings indicate. You might have some guesses or hopes that your results mean more, but any conjecture must be clearly marked as such. For example, if you find that one out of four students in your English 102 class fear writing, this does not mean than 25% of all A-State English 102 students fear writing, that 25% of all students at A-State fear writing, or that 25% of college students across America fear writing. It only means that 25% of your particular classmates fear writing. A sample of 20 students in a single

section of a single course at a single university simply isn't sufficient for you to make a larger claim, though it might be a data point that allows you to start theorizing about fear of writing in the college classroom.

Responsibilities to Other Researchers

Social science writers are in conversation with other researchers. They show respect for those whose work they are building on or disagreeing with by citing them, either in APA or Chicago style. (Always check with your professors to see which citation style they prefer!) They work to keep the conversation going by clearly describing their logic and methods. Social science writers show respect to other researchers when they:

1. Articulate how their ideas are similar to or different from other researchers' ideas. This shows that they have read the work of their peers and are willing to consider the perspectives of others, usually in a literature review, a genre that summarizes what has already been written on a topic.

2. Explain their methods in detail. Any researcher who reads your work should be able to repeat your research to verify your results. If you don't adequately describe your methods, future researchers won't know exactly what you did and thus won't be able to repeat your research to see if it still holds true. Your writing should precisely describe who you studied, why you chose them, how you convinced them to join your study, what you asked them to do, how you recorded your data, and how you analyzed it. Describe any tools, such as a survey or list of questions in an interview. If these tools are long, you might include them in an appendix or as a hyperlinked document.

3. Be specific when sharing results, using numbers whenever you can to make your point. If, for example, your research indicates that students who spend more time studying earn higher GPAs, you need to explain how many more hours are necessary for an increase in GPA. And how many points is the corresponding increase? If conducting qualitative research (which does not involve numbers), be specific but not flowery with language. If, for example, you are observing the interactions between mothers and toddlers at the checkout line at the grocery store, it is not enough to characterize their interaction is "positive" or "negative." Instead, provide details about tone of voice, posture, hand gestures, and word choices that mothers use when addressing their young children. Such details help other researchers see if the results of your research might help them understand the problems they are addressing.

Writing in the Disciplines

Social science writing has a real impact on the world. Lawyers consult it when arguing before courts; lawmakers reference it when deciding on public policy; social workers, teachers, nurses, and others in helping professions consult it when trying to assist clients, students, patients, and others they serve. Parents rely on it when they read articles on how to best potty train a toddler, get an unwilling tween to help with chores, or find the best college for their graduating high school senior. In short, it informs many of the decisions people make every day, and social science, perhaps among all scholars, pride themselves on discovering and creating knowledge that is useful to everyday people. Following the basic advice outlined above, you can enter the world of social science writing with confidence.

WRITING IN A FOREIGN LANGUAGE

Vicent Moreno
Assistant Professor of Spanish at Arkansas State University

· · · · · · · · ·

We usually think of language as a vehicle to express or formulate ideas, a vessel with which to communicate our thoughts. While this is true, one important aspect that sometimes is overlooked is the fact that our perception of the world, how we see and experience life, is very much shaped by the language we speak. This is very much noticeable to anyone who starts thinking and writing in a foreign language: words that encapsulate a particular concept and for which we don't have an equivalent in our native tongue; the idiosyncrasies of the syntax in how sentences are constructed; the nuances in evoking pasts and envisioning futures across verbal tenses.

Despite the linguistic and cultural differences, analyzing a literary work in French, for example, will have a similar purpose as an analysis in English: the interpretation of a text. Alternately, writing the review of a film in English or in Spanish will most likely share a number of requirements and purposes that are not imposed by the language *per se* but by the format and the nature of the assignment (or genre). There are important aspects, basic elements of form and content that remain the same (defined thesis and topic statements, distribution of the text in content paragraphs, going beyond the obvious in our analyses, etc.) regardless of the language in which we write. The knowledge of the principles of what constitutes "good writing," which students have already acquired as writers of English, provides a base for writing in a foreign language.

What follows will give you a few tips and guidelines about how to be a successful writer in a foreign language. As mentioned before, the type of writing and its contents will largely be dictated by the nature of the assignment, but there are certain basic elements that are shared across writings. For the sake of clarity, I'll focus here on the specific writing used in the argumentative analysis of a cultural product (a text, a film, etc.), which is one of the most typical forms of academic writing. First, I will provide some details about format, style, and content, or in other words, what is expected of an academic paper; second, I will explain key elements for the proper use of language when producing essays and I will offer some general and useful tips for writing in French and Spanish; finally, you will find some links with more information about some of the aspects mentioned.

1. Format and Content of an Academic Essay

The ultimate purpose of any argumentative academic paper analyzing a cultural product is to provide an interpretation that goes beyond the obvious, creating a new understanding or reading of it. As such, the most important element is the thesis, that is, your claim about the text you are analyzing. The paper, then, will attempt to demonstrate your claim through textual evidence or, to put it more bluntly: you need to make your reader see what you mean—convince her. Your thesis statement will have to be as specific and concrete as possible. For example, saying "This paper will analyze the topic of love and its presence in the film" would be too broad; instead, you should narrow it by focusing on a character or a particular aspect within the film: "In this paper, I will analyze how in this film, the love interests of the protagonist symbolize the ongoing democratic processes that were occurring at the time."

In addition to a well-formulated thesis, you must organize your essay in a way that is clear and cohesive. Typically, essays will have a title that is not merely descriptive, but captures the reader's attention, and a structure that will consist of three parts. First, an introductory paragraph in which you state your thesis and lay out the purpose and organization of the paper. Secondly, a number of paragraphs linked to the thesis with a distinct focus. These paragraphs will include an opening statement and a transitional statement at the end leading to the next paragraph. Finally, there is a conclusion in which, rather than summarizing, you reflect on your previous analysis and how your findings prove your thesis. Note that the conclusion should not present new material.

2. A Few Notes on Foreign Language Writing for an English Speaker

A key element of writing in a foreign language is to try and think in the target language rather than translating it from English. As you formulate your ideas and compose your sentences, think about structures, vocabulary, or expressions that you already know. Literal translations are almost never a good idea because, while the meaning may come across, the grammar is usually very different, resulting in awkward sentences that a non-English speaker might even have difficulty understanding.

As you write your paper, pay extra attention to concordance. Unlike English, many other Indo-European languages like French, Spanish, Portuguese, and even German, have grammatical gender, which, among other things, means that nouns and adjectives have to "agree." While in English the adjective "tall" would stay the same regardless if you're talking about Sarah or John, in Spanish, you will either write "alta" or "alto" depending on who the person is. Something similar happens with verb conjugations, in which the verb ending changes depending on who is performing the action indicated by the verb.

Accent marks are another distinctive trait of many languages that English doesn't have. Because of this, they are easily overlooked in papers, but it is important that you include them when writing in Spanish or French. They are not mere cosmetic elements—they, in fact, can change the meaning of a word.

"Faux amis" (in French) or "falsos amigos" (in Spanish), which translate as "false friends," are literally very dubious and you should stay away from them. They refer to words that look almost the same in both languages, but that, in fact, bear a very different meaning. Consider "constipado" in Spanish, which, contrary to what it looks like, doesn't make reference to your bowel movements (or lack thereof), but simply means you have a cold. As you progress in your learning of a foreign language, you will find many more of these and it is always a good idea to double check before writing a word that looks suspiciously similar in both languages.

Use technology to your advantage. All operating systems have the option to customize your input language. By doing that when you write in a foreign language, you'll find it easier to type in accent marks, umlauts, and other international characters that don't appear on the physical keyboard. Additionally, set your word processor's language to the language in which you are writing and turn on the spell-checking option. This will help you tremendously in noticing mistakes while you write.

3. Useful Online References for Writers Writing in a Foreign Language

3.1. MLA is one of the most common styles for citing and writing papers in the humanities and the style used for writing about literature and culture. The Purdue OWL is a very well composed and always up-to-date website that will help you with any questions you have about formatting and style: https://owl.english.purdue.edu/owl/resource/747/01/

3.2. There are many online bilingual dictionaries. Word Reference is one of the most useful and user friendly, with a number of examples and words in context. http://www.wordreference.com/

3.3. The False Friends Dictionary is another useful reference to learn about and identify "false friends." The website is available in Spanish, http://www.falsefriends.eu/en and French, http://french.about.com/od/vocabulary/a/fauxamis.htm.

3.4. The American Council on the Teaching of Foreign Languages (ACTFL) sets the standard for foreign language education in most schools in the United States. Becoming familiar with their terminologies and their rubrics will help you become a better writer: https://www.actfl.org/publications/guidelines-and-manuals/actfl-proficiency-guidelines-2012/english/writing

3.5. Microsoft Word has several tools to help you write in a foreign language. Learn about them here: https://support.office.com/en-us/article/Customize-language-features-in-Word-2013-and-later-8fec4c7b-150e-4226-8087-d00d5093fade. Also, learn how to change your input language in Windows and Mac at https://support.microsoft.com/en-us/kb/306560 or http://www.macworld.com/article/1147039/os-x/accentinput.html.

A GUIDE TO WRITING IN PHILOSOPHY

Steven Weimer and Jacob Caton
Assistant Professors of Philosophy at Arkansas State University

. . . .

Unlike the fields of English or psychology, there are no widely accepted styles or formats for writing in philosophy. If you took a stroll through our University library and landed in the "B" section of the Library of Congress Classification system (where many philosophy books are located), you would find a variety of styles, formats, and structures.

Despite this diversity, there are a number of helpful general recommendations for writing a successful philosophy paper. First, it is important to remember that writing is about communication. In most cases, you will be attempting to communicate a philosophical idea of some kind to your reader. In order to do this effectively, your paper will need to exhibit the following:

1. **Clarity:** As best as you can, use ordinary language. When using technical terms, make sure to give a definition or characterization of this new term. Do not obfuscate.
2. **Precision:** Help your reader by saying exactly what you mean. If you are attempting to argue that proposition P is true, tell your reader early in your paper that this is your aim.
3. **Conciseness:** Simplicity and economy is often a virtue in philosophical writing. You may find that you can generate page after page on a subject; but ask yourself, for each sentence, whether this has helped progress the aims for your paper. If not, strike the sentence.

Beyond these general recommendations, there are many ways to structure a successful philosophy paper. In many cases you will need to accomplish the following:

4. Carefully lay out the major positions taken on your topic. Explain, in your own words and in detail, what those on both (or more, as the case may be) sides of the issue believe and why.
5. Offer any objections or criticisms that you can think of (or have researched) for *all* of the major positions on the issue.
6. Develop and defend a thesis. This could be either positive (an attempt to develop and defend a position on the issue), or negative (a critique of one or more of the positions taken on the issue). In either case, you will need to defend your thesis with careful, critical argumentation.

7. Respond to possible objections to *your* thesis. Anticipate the strongest arguments against your view and do your best to give reasons why these objections are ultimately not successful.

When laying out the major positions on your topic and when representing your thesis or main argument, it is often helpful to describe these arguments in premise-conclusion form. That is, it is often helpful to explicitly list the premises of the argument and the conclusion of the argument. For example,

(i)   All humans are mortal.
(ii) Socrates is a human.
(iii) Therefore, Socrates is mortal.

Explicitly representing arguments in premise-conclusion form is helpful to your reader because they know what you're arguing for (conclusion) and why (premises). Arguing in premise-conclusion form also helps you as a writer because it forces you to focus on the essential elements of your philosophical idea, and it helps you achieve the clarity, precision, and conciseness described above.

Once you've explicitly represented your argument in premise-conclusion form, give a defense of your argument by providing reasons for your stated premises as well as reasons to think that your premises support your conclusion. That is, attempt to convince your reader that your argument is a good argument. This is a great opportunity to bring to bear all you've learned in your logic class!

The above recommendations presuppose that philosophy is about argumentation. As such, many of the recommendations that are appropriate for good argumentation in general are applicable here. For instance:

8. It is never acceptable to use a fallacy in defending or responding to a claim. Consult an elementary logic or critical thinking textbook for a list and discussion of common fallacies.

9. Use the principle of charity when discussing opposing views and arguments. When describing a rival view, present the strongest version of that view. When interpreting a passage or argument from another author, give the strongest and most plausible interpretation. To refute a weak version of an argument is not an accomplishment, it is a fallacy (namely, the straw man fallacy).

10. Be careful with empirical claims. If you make use of empirical claims in your paper, make sure to support your claim by citing a reliable source.

Last, be sure to properly cite all work that you quote, paraphrase, or draw from. Two rules of thumb: (1) if the idea didn't come from you, cite the source, and (2) when in doubt, cite the source. Citation is about giving proper credit to the source of an idea.

Writing in the Disciplines

WRITING HISTORY

J. Justin Castro
Assistant Professor of History at Arkansas State University

· · · · · · · · ·

There are the humanities. There are the social sciences. And then there is history. Like literature, philosophy, and theatre, history has been around since people have been telling stories. In written form, histories are almost as old as writing itself. The discipline, however, took its current form alongside the social sciences in nineteenth century Europe. Since then, history has borrowed heavily from its cousins in the humanities and the social sciences, taking from each while never fitting completely into either. Unlike most social scientists, historians tend to write narrative stories. The best of them read very much like a good short story or novel. We want the public to be able to enjoy and comprehend our work, even if not as many people read it as we would like. But historians differ from novelists and authors of other forms of fiction in that historical works are nonfiction and are more often than not argumentative and based on a thesis backed by empirical evidence. Historians argue that there are facts and objective truths, and that a serious study of the past can benefit humanity's present and future. It is this empirical component that historians take from the sciences. The fact that we make argumentative cases based on substantial but imperfect evidence is similar to law.

Historical writing varies considerably depending on the medium, individual style, and school of thought, but my goal here is more to provide some nuts and bolts for writing a successful undergraduate history paper than to explore the nuances of style or the philosophy of history. What I am about to suggest, I admit, is a bit formulaic, but I think my advice will prove useful for those of you delving for the first time into the world of professional history. After all, you must nail down the basics before soaring to new heights. So here are the essentials: come up with a viable question, conduct historical research, compose a strong thesis, and write with clear prose and organization.

Selecting a viable research question sounds easy enough, but it can be difficult and time consuming. It is, in many ways, the most important step toward writing a good paper. The question cannot be too broad to answer in a brief essay. It also can't be so esoteric that there are too few sources. You must be sure your question fits within the parameters of your class and that you have access to sufficient sources. For example, a question far too broad and problematic would be: Why did Germany lose World War II? There are too many variables to comprehend within a semester of study. To write a serious and successful essay or book would require that you at least read German, Russian, and French in addition to English. Would you have access to all the necessary German sources? How do we know the outcome of World War II would have been different if German military leaders had made different decisions? There is no way to know for sure. You can write about World War II, but you will need something much more tangible and specific.

As a history student, you have to be aware of the limitations and opportunities within the sources available to you. History is a slave to evidence, especially primary sources—those sources from the period, place, and people you are studying. That is not to say that historians automatically take sources at face value; we do not. Indeed, you will have to develop two other essential skills on your path to mastering historical writing, the capability to contextualize and the ability to spot biases. Despite all the obstacles and potential pitfalls of comprehending material evidence, history requires proof.

Crucial to finding that Goldilocks topic is understanding what sources you have at hand: get to know your librarians; talk to your professors; ask the people that can help you for assistance, and do so now. Many sources can be found in Arkansas State's library databases, including the American Antiquarian Society Historical Periodicals, American Historical Newspapers, and Congressional Publications. There is also an impressive historical archive on the seventh floor of the Dean B. Ellis Library building. Secondary sources, which are more current scholarly accounts in journal articles and books—and which are crucial for understanding your subject and contextualizing your primary sources—are on library shelves, available through inter-library loan, and in databases such as JSTOR and EBSCOhost.

Now, let's go back to developing that research question. After some exploration, you'll find that there are online university databases and microfilm holding historic Arkansas newspapers. There are local sources about World War II in the archive, including letters to congressmen and conversations with German prisoners of war in Arkansas. So, a better question might be: How did residents of northeast Arkansas perceive people of German descent during World War II? It would be a more original topic and there would likely be good materials from which to mold an argument.

Once you obtain a grasp on your sources, you can begin to form your thesis. A thesis states what you are arguing—the point of your paper. In history classes it is important to state the answer to the question that drove your investigation and to place that answer up front in your essay, usually within the first couple paragraphs. Your thesis, once formed, will then dictate much of your paper's organization. This is why the thesis is absolutely critical. It not only states your argument, it lays out how you will argue it. To continue with our hypothetical World War II example, a thesis might end up being something like this: "During World War II, many residents of northeast Arkansas displayed contempt for Germans, but the interaction of local white landowners and German prisoners of war created sympathetic ties between the two populations based on shared notions of hard work and perceived racial similarities." I don't know if this is what the evidence would actually show, but for now, let's pretend.

This thesis provides a roadmap for your essay. Using secondary sources, you will need to provide some contextual information about northeast Arkansas and World War II, especially about the war with Germany and German prisoners of war camps in Arkansas. You will then lay out the evidence you found, perhaps in personal letters and local newspapers, about contempt for Germans. Then you will explore how interactions between white landowners and German prisoners built mutual sympathies, first through conceptions of work, and then through thoughts about race. Perhaps you uncovered most of this evidence in the archive. Your essay will end with a conclusion that reinforces your argument but also stresses the big picture-significance of your essay. Does it say something about race relations more broadly or the complexity of wartime sympathies in local communities? Maybe there are connections between Germans and residents of northeast Arkansas that still exist today. This is where that broader contextualization is important. It will take considerable study and observational skills. Time is essential to history, to its content and its construction.

Lastly, write with intention and revise your work. Love every word. Make sure your topic sentences are clear and that they relate to their paragraphs. Vary your sentence length and style, but in general, write concisely and boldly. Check your work for common errors and have other people provide feedback if possible. It is a common mistake for students entering college to think that history is about memorizing dates, facts, and famous people, but it is much more than that. History is about empathy and understanding our place within the context of space and time. History is about storytelling. History is about sleuthing and using well-researched evidence to construct superbly written argumentative essays. For those of you up for the challenge, history can be an eye-opening and rewarding practice.

WRITING FOR THE FIELD OF COMMUNICATION
Sarah Scott
Instructor of Communication at Arkansas State University

· · · · · · · · ·

Humans are storytelling creatures. Sharing and telling stories is unique to the human experience. To be an effective communicator, it is imperative to be a good storyteller. The field of communication is comprised of students and scholars who use and tell stories to meet a variety of needs. As one of the youngest disciplines on many college campuses, the field of communication is interdisciplinary—meaning that research and scholarship cross borders and borrow concepts from many other traditions, including, but not limited to, history, English, sociology, philosophy, and psychology. The result is a dynamic and diverse field that transcends rigid boundaries to look at the many and varied ways humans communicate.

At Arkansas State University, for instance, the classes in communication, and consequently the faculty who teach them, may have a media, journalistic, strategic communication, social science, interpretative, or rhetorical approach. In contrast to fields where there is a uniform approach to scholarship and writing—such as writing in accordance to the Modern Language Association guidelines for English or in accordance with the American Psychological Association guidelines for psychology—scholars and students in communication do not have a definitive standard. The challenge, then, for the communication student is to know the conventions and expectations for the particular area of communication in which they are working. Most often in an undergraduate class, the course instructor will set clear expectations for the type of writing that is expected, but it is a good idea to know the various styles of writing, as well as when and why to use a particular style. The three most common styles of writing used in communication are: 1) Associated Press, 2) American Psychological Association, and 3) Chicago. Here is a brief discussion of each style, how it affects the way the story is told, and what sub-disciplines might utilize that particular style.

Associated Press

The Associated Press (AP) develop guidelines for writing news content. News writing goes well beyond traditional print newspapers. News outlets may include print, television, online, and multimedia news outlets. However, the AP style is often used in public relations and advertising, in addition to journalism, and expands into more current outlets such as blogs and social media platforms. The AP style should be used anytime providing timely, accurate information to a specific audience is the primary goal. Therefore, AP style is not used in scholarly publications. Creating content for news outlets requires writers to be clear, consistent, correct, and concise. In order to achieve the most effective writing in AP style, the inverted pyramid style of organization is used for news writing.

The inverted pyramid may seem to contradict everything you have been taught about narrative writing. However, with news writing—as opposed to most types of writing—the introduction is not a slow build-up to a synthesizing thesis statement. The first sentence of news writing is the lead and the lead contains the most important information the audience needs to know. The who, what, when, where, and why should be covered as concisely and accurately as possible in this lead sentence. One of the ways to think about news writing is to imagine an audience and how they will read a piece of writing. Whether the writing is a news article, a social media post, or a press release, assume that the audience may not read past the first few sentences. If that is the case, did the audience receive the most important information? With the inverted pyramid, the information in the writing proceeds from most important to least important. This style assures your audience receives the most pertinent information of the story first.

You will use AP style any time you are creating news content. Media, journalism, public relations, and advertising classes at Arkansas State University utilize the AP style.

When creating academic writing, however, the AP style is never used. Instead instructors and students will utilize one of the formats of academic writing. Many disciplines, such as sociology, business, nursing, and psychology will use APA style documentation. Many in the field of communication use this style as well.

American Psychological Association

While the name may seem deceptive, the American Psychological Association (APA) is simply one type of documentation that can be used for academic and scholarly writing. Many scholars outside the field of psychology also use this style. Organization, writing style, and reference citations are priorities of APA. One benefit to using APA style is that readers see similar organizational patterns and source citations across readings. This minimizes confusion on the part of readers by allowing readers to focus on the main ideas expressed in the writing. In communication, this style is primarily used by those writing in media and communication studies, and it is suited for both quantitative and qualitative work.

Students and scholars using APA style writing in media or communication studies can find comfort in an easily identifiable format for academic writing. To avoid bias in writing, APA style avoids using first names in writing—to avoid revealing a person's sex. This style also attempts to remove bias concerning race, disability, and sexuality in writing. Gender-neutral pronouns are used when possible. These conventions are strategic choices in an attempt to write as free from bias as possible. In APA style, in-text citations are used with an author's last name and date of publication. Writing in APA style is always done in past tense. For instance, "A. Smith (1999) stated that . . ." This is a social science approach to communication. Scholars and students who are social science-minded are practicing the scientific study of human communication and human relationships. To that end, the research reads much like that from other fields of science.

Quantitative (objective) research in communication tries to generate information about some aspect of communication phenomenon (answer some communication question) that is generalizable to a larger population. These researchers may utilize survey or poll data to do the analysis. Qualitative (interpretive) researchers in communication are not seeking generalizable data, necessarily, but rather are looking for a more specific and in-depth answer to the communication question asked. Qualitative researchers may use focus groups, case studies, or interviews to gather data. Most students and researchers will find, after taking classes in different styles, a style in which they feel most comfortable.

Communication classes where you might expect to write using APA style include media, research methods, interpersonal communication, and health communication classes. The APA style of documentation is one of the most common in academic writing in the United States. Writing stories in APA style requires creating an effective, scientific argument that is as free from bias as possible. Students will find that they will utilize APA style for a variety of classes during their undergraduate experience at Arkansas State University. However, there is one more style that is found in the communication field at the university, and that is Chicago style.

Chicago Style

Chicago style documentation will be seen most often in the fields of history and rhetoric. Rhetoric is a sub-discipline of communication studies that focuses on persuasion. Chicago's notes and bibliographic style use footnotes or endnotes to contain source citations. This makes the writing easy to read with minimum in-text distractions. The benefit to this style is that unconventional source material may be used that does not have an appropriate citation method in APA. Footnotes and endnotes also allow for authors to include additional information that may seem out of place in the body of the text. Chicago style writes in the present tense and includes author's first names and affiliations, "Angelia Smith, a feminist philosopher, claims . . ." Author information is included in full because Chicago style recognizes that gender, race, nationality, sexuality, and the like are positive starting points for research for many scholars. Students and scholars in this sub-discipline realize that research is never free from bias. Instead of attempting to remove bias, authors utilizing this style embrace the uniqueness of each individual writer and acknowledge the potential biases instead of trying to avoid them.

Chicago style documentation is used for rhetorical analysis in communication studies. Rhetorical scholars and students attempt to tell a story about why some aspect of communication is or is not persuasive or how language and communication function to persuade. Classes in communication studies where a student might use Chicago style documentation include communication theory, research methods, communication criticism, and rhetoric classes.

While having several styles of writing available may, at first, seem confusing, it is useful to be able to find the right style that best suits the needs of the writer. Knowing the purpose of the writing is a crucial step in picking the correct writing style. And finding the best suited writing style will help any student tell an effective story.

LIBRARY AND INFORMATION RESEARCH
Robert Robinette
Student Success Librarian at Arkansas State University

"I don't use the library. I never need it."
–Bertha Bumpkin, sophomore Bellybutton Studies major

This type of comment frustrates librarians, but it has some truth to it. You can hop on Google, misspell a few words, and instantly have millions of results on any topic imaginable. The problem, of course, is that much of what you find is worthless. We are inundated with "fake news," propaganda, disguised advertisements, infotainment, and other misleading or inaccurate sources. In a 2016 Stanford University study, more than 80% of students were unable to identify a story prominently labeled "sponsored content" as an advertisement (Stanford 10). Surrounded by constant social media updates, app notifications, and a 24-hour news cycle, students often fail to take advantage of the library's invaluable research tools and quality information sources. Thus, in this section, you will learn about trustworthy, high-quality information sources available to you through the library.

Scholarly Sources

You will hear the term *scholarly* a lot in college, usually in the context of *scholarly journals*, also known as *academic*, *peer-reviewed*, or *refereed* journals. Scholarly journals contain articles written by expert scholars (usually somebody with an advanced degree in the field) for other expert scholars. These articles almost always undergo peer-review, i.e., they are chosen for publication by other experts in the discipline. They also provide extensive documentation of their sources, i.e., they have a bibliography listing their sources. Along with these key features, scholarly journals typically have one goal in mind: contributing new knowledge to a discipline. Scholarly sources may possess other attributes—for instance, they might use technical language or jargon, assume you have background knowledge of the topic, or use discipline-specific research methods—but these will vary from discipline to discipline. You can find scholarly journal articles and other quality sources by searching the library's many research databases.

Research Databases

The A-State library subscribes to hundreds of research databases[1] that provide access to thousands of information sources, including scholarly journals, e-books, government documents, research reports, and more. Research databases come in a few primary types:

- *General databases*, such as JSTOR,[2] provide sources from a wide variety of disciplines in a wide variety of formats.
- *Specialized databases* focus on a specific discipline or set of disciplines. For example, ABI/Inform[3] focuses exclusively on business sources.
- *Aggregated databases,* such as OneSearch[4] and ProQuest Central,[5] are very large databases that collect several databases into one searchable interface. These are often the best places to begin your research because you can almost always find something on even the most esoteric topic.

Most information research will require you to search several databases, so if you do not find what you need in one database, try another—we have plenty. Something to keep in mind: *If you use the library, you will never have to pay for access to information*! Even if we do not immediately have access to something you need, we can request it from another library for free by using a service called *Interlibrary Loan.*

For some assignments and projects, professors might require *primary sources*, which are information sources without any layer of analysis or interpretation over them. A *secondary source* comments on, critiques, or otherwise analyzes a primary source. In history and other humanities disciplines, primary sources refer to information sources from the time being studied, e.g., a firsthand account of an earthquake. In the sciences, primary sources typically refer to original research articles, e.g., a report on a study of mutant barnacles. Where you search for primary sources will depend on the discipline in question and your research needs. You might use the library's *primary resources databases*[6] or the *library catalog,*[7]

---

1 http://libguides.astate.edu/az.php
2 https://ezproxy.library.astate.edu/login?url=http://www.jstor.org
3 https://ezproxy.library.astate.edu/login?url=https://search.proquest.com/abicomplete/index?accountid=8363
4 http://eds.b.ebscohost.com/eds/search/advanced?vid=0&sid=e17217fd-6785-4a72-89ec-1cd93d221bce%40sessionmgr120
5 https://ezproxy.library.astate.edu/login?url=http://search.proquest.com/central?accountid=8363
6 http://libguides.astate.edu/az.php?t=2023
7 http://dbellis.library.astate.edu/vwebv/searchAdvanced

which is the searchable interface for everything the library owns. You might even need to dig a little deeper and use the *university archives*,[8] which is where we store and preserve rare and fragile research materials.

Conducting Effective Searches

Knowing how to access quality library sources is great, but if you struggle to formulate an effective search, you will never find what you need. Here are some quick tips to improve your searches:

- *Search, search, and search again*: Your first few searches will probably be clumsy and demonstrate your lack of knowledge. As you find new sources and learn more about your topic, you will discover new terms to use and new avenues of research to explore. Trying a different search strategy never hurts.
- *Be specific, but not too specific:* Searching for *medical marijuana* is too broad. Searching for *medical marijuana Arkansas children autism garbanzo beans* is probably too specific. You must strike the right balance.
- *Use Boolean search operators:* The *OR* operator will expand your search (useful for synonyms, e.g., *medical marijuana OR medical cannabis*), the *AND* operator will narrow your search, and the *NOT* operator will exclude certain terms. An effective search commonly uses a combination of Boolean operators.
- *Search for specific phrases:* Most databases will allow you to search for a specific phrase by placing it in quotation marks. For example, *"medical marijuana"* retrieves results with that exact phrase whereas *medical marijuana* might give you results on medical devices and growing marijuana but nothing about the concept of "medical marijuana."
- *Use search limits:* You often find too much information. When this happens, it can be helpful to set search limits. You might set a limit for a specific date range, material type, language, or discipline. Setting limits generally provide a more manageable set of results.

Sometimes you search and search and search to no avail. If you struggle to find what you need, contact a librarian to help get you on the right track.

---

8 http://www.astate.edu/a/library/archives/

The Physical Library

As an undergraduate, you can check out up to twenty of the hundreds of thousands of books, films, government documents, maps, games, and other sources in the library, all of which can be located via the library catalog.[9] In addition, the library contains:

- dozens of computers located throughout the library;
- several printers to use for free printing;
- twenty-three study rooms, many with whiteboards (you can check out markers from the service desk);
- a presentation room with a projector;
- innumerable nooks and crannies to hole up in; and
- librarians and library staff who can help you with your research.

The library is a welcoming, inviting place with an atmosphere highly conducive to research and creativity. We hope to see you around.

---

9 http://dbellis.library.astate.edu/vwebv/searchBasic?sk=en_US

LEGAL WRITING

Hans J. Hacker
Associate Professor of Political Science at Arkansas State University

· · · · · · · · ·

What Does It Mean to "Write Legally"?

Before discussing what is legal writing, let's consider what it is *not*. Legal writing is *not* about using obscure legal and technical language to *hide your argument* behind words that only people who have gone to law school understand. Legal writing is *not* about writing pages and pages of incomprehensible clauses *to shield some corporation from a lawsuit*. For a long time, lawyers defined legal writing in exactly these terms and for these purposes. But beginning in the mid-twentieth century, legislators, government lawyers, law schools, and legal firms all began to move away from a vision of legal writing as unintelligible. Instead they began to consider the *benefit to society* of communicating legal obligations *clearly* to citizens. As it turns out, writing plainly, clearly, simply, and straightforwardly creates greater certainty and faith in government and our legal system. This writing system (sometimes called the "plain language" movement) resides at the heart of our writing process at A-State.

So, what is good legal writing, then? Simply put, legal writing is writing well. Good writing techniques developed while completing law courses at Arkansas State University can help you write well in courses taken in a variety of departments and programs. Learning to write well about the law helps you write clearly about virtually any topic. This is so in part because in your legal courses we ask you to write case briefs, papers, and appellate briefs about a diverse set of legal topics. These include warrantless surveillance of citizens by governments, free speech, religious free exercise, juvenile justice, same-sex marriage, racial equality, economic rights, medical ethics, and a host of other government policies and conflicts between parties.

To make things even more interesting, we will ask you to write in a variety of genres that require different levels of comprehension and analysis. For example, the case brief requires you to summarize the opinions written by judges in a particular case. When writing a case brief you don't write any original arguments of your own. Instead, you define the issue in the case precisely, extract the rule the court applied to the conflict, and summarize the reasoning of the court thoroughly. So case briefs don't require critical thinking, but they do require you to read carefully and summarize thoroughly.

On the other hand, legal memos and appellate briefs require you to think critically and creatively to construct an argument on a unique legal issue. Writing legal memos and appellate briefs requires critical thinking. It forces you to create a solution to a complicated problem governed by a complex body of law using rule-based reasoning while considering the consequences of applying one solution rather than another. And, you have to reason through these complicated problems and rules plainly, clearly, and precisely.

So, how do you go about developing a plain, clear, precise, and well-reasoned writing style given the bewildering diversity of subjects about which you will have to write? The rest of this chapter provides a set of recommendations, techniques, tips and tricks for writing well legally.

Storytelling: Your Job as a Legal Writer

As a legal writer you must (believe it or not) tell a story about the law and the necessity that the judge find in favor of your client based on the facts. To tell your story well, you must avoid jargon-filled sentences and confusing language. Consider the following example in terms of "storytelling."

> *The party of the first part alleges that the party of the second part is in violation of 42 U.S.C. ch. 126 § 12101, The Americans with Disabilities Act (1990).*

This messy sentence makes it difficult to understand the reason the writer wrote it. As a story, it's a pretty bad one. Here is one way to fix it.

> *Wilcox alleges that the Carson Coal Company's actions violate the Americans with Disabilities act.*

This sentence tells part of a story simply and straightforwardly using an active voice and the names of parties, hinting at a conflict the author will explain later. I don't know about you, but after reading this sentence, I really want to know what Carson Coal Company did that allegedly violates the rights of disabled persons!

A good legal writer who strives to relate to the reader a story about the law and the facts will exhibit the following characteristics. First, the writer will use simple sentence structure. Second, the writer will emphasize transitions between paragraphs as a tool allowing the reader to follow and understand the argument easily. Third, the writer will avoid something called passive voice. Finally, a good legal writer will employ a logical style that critically analyzes and applies legal rules to conflicts and questions.

Micro and Macro Writing Styles

This section addresses the first and second characteristics identified above—simple sentence structure and paragraphs that help you make your argument effectively. At Arkansas State University, we divide our legal writing broadly into micro and macro writing styles. By *micro* we mean sentence- and paragraph-level writing. We generally keep our sentence structure simple and use active verbs (see the section on avoiding passive voice below). When constructing paragraphs, we identify the thesis of the paragraph clearly, use the paragraph to develop and support our argument, and then transition from the central point of that paragraph to the central point of the next. In general, we try to write paragraphs that average between five and seven sentences in length. We also vary sentence length to draw the reader's attention to our most important arguments.

Let's be honest, your job as a writer is to manipulate your audience into accepting that your argument is the best one. So, when trying to manipulate your reader, consider varying your sentence length to draw the reader's attention to the most important points, the ones you want him or her to remember. Several ways exist to *draw the reader's attention* by varying sentence length. First, identify your most important argument. Then, use a series of short sentences leading up to that argument. Perhaps use two or three sentences of almost identical length and construction. Finally, when you get to the main point, make the initial statement of your point using a longer, more complex sentence that *bumps* the reader, signaling that he or she has arrived at the most important part of that paragraph.[1] Alternatively, you could simply do the reverse—use several longer sentences, followed by a short, simple sentence or two making your central point.

Think of paragraphs as your most valuable tool for structuring your argument. Some students write papers without any thought for their structure. Worse still, students often submit papers written as one gigantic paragraph! They lose an important tool for guiding the reader through their paper, showing that they thought through what kind of argument they want to make and actually making the argument. As a result, they receive a poor grade.

---

1 By the way, look back at the last four sentences. They exhibit the very same technique I have described.

Besides writing a thesis sentence that clearly defines the topic of a sentence, the most important part of a paragraph is the transition. A sentence containing a transition first references something already discussed and then pivots to a new, but related, topic. Make your transitions smooth and effortless, like a shortstop flipping the ball he just caught to his throwing hand from his glove before making the throw to first base. Because of its importance, I have employed many transitions to guide you through the organization of the chapter you are reading![2] Consider the final sentence of paragraph three (*"And, you have to reason through these complicated problems and rules plainly, clearly, and precisely"*) and the first sentence of paragraph four (*"So, how do you go about developing a writing style that is plain, clear, precise, and well-reasoned..."*). Here, I have replicated the words "plain," "clear," "precise," and "reason" to link the two paragraphs together. The restatement of words or ideas provides a clear link across paragraphs and helps the reader follow your logic.

By *macro* we mean the overall structure of a written assignment. *Overall structure* refers to the thesis or primary purpose of a paper, how we divide the assignment into manageable sections, and how those sections relate to each other. Here, a table of contents or a well-developed thesis paragraph included close to the beginning of a paper will come in handy. At Arkansas State University, we employ a complex overall structure that flows from the table of contents/thesis paragraph to the sections of our appellate brief or paper. Thus, while we use simple sentence structure and transitions across paragraphs at the micro level, we pay careful attention to the critical and analytical structure of our argument across sections at the macro level. The arguments we make flow logically across sections of our written work leading to a well-developed, organized, thoughtful product.

Whatever You Do, Eliminate Passive Voice!

We now turn to the third (and, perhaps, most important) characteristic of good legal writing—eliminating passive voice. To improve your writing in any discipline, eliminate passive voice in favor of active verbs and voicing. When you write "passively" it means that you have constructed a sentence in which the subject receives the action (i.e., the subject is acted on, rather than doing the action). Consider this example of a sentence written in passive voice: "The ball *was* kicked by the girl." Notice that the subject of this sentence (the ball) is acted upon by the

---

2 I'm so sneaky.

actor (the girl). This actor, however, comes at the very end, not at the beginning, of the sentence. To eliminate passive voice in your sentences, first determine what is the actor in the sentence, then move that actor up to the beginning of the sentence: "The girl kicked the ball." Now, we have an active voice sentence. The subject ("The girl") acted. She "kicked" something. That something is the direct object of her action ("the ball").

In the previous paragraph, I provided a very simple initial example. Let's consider another simple one, followed by a passively voiced sentence presenting a more difficult problem: "Last summer our house *was* painted by me. First, the exterior *was* washed using mild detergent and warm water." We can fix the first sentence easily by moving the subject to the front, changing "me" to "I": "Last summer, I painted our house." The problem with the second sentence is this—it has no actor. The person who wrote this sentence writes so badly that he engineered the actor right out of the sentence altogether.[3] So, ask yourself this question—who is acting? In this case, who washed the house? Once you answer that question, it becomes easy to write an active sentence: "First, I washed the exterior using mild detergent and warm water."

As it turns out, you can solve the vast majority of your problems with passive voice by eliminating "to be" verbs. Notice that all of the examples of passive voice include the verb "was" (I have italicized them in the sentences above). Conjugations of the English verb "to be" include the following: *Is, am, are, was, were, being, been, have been.* We use "to be" verbs in two ways. The first involves drawing an equivalency. "The ball is red." That's not a great sentence, but it is not passive. The second turns otherwise good, strong, active sentences into weak, apathetic, wordy, horrible sentences by shifting the actor to the end of the sentence or eliminating the actor altogether. I provide weak, wordy, unclear, horrible sentences as examples of passive voice above.

Let me provide some ideas for writing with an eye toward eliminating passive voice. First, just write a draft of your paper assignment. Don't worry about eliminating passive voice, or anything else really! Just get your thoughts down on paper.[4] After completing a first draft, conduct a search on every conjugation of "to be," above. Find every single instance in your draft in which you used a conjugation of "to be." Then,

---

3 I wrote this sentence.
4 My dissertation adviser at Ohio State, Larry Baum, told me repeatedly "if you haven't written a bad first draft, you haven't done your job!" But then, you have to fix it. That's the next step. So do not put pressure on yourself to write a perfect first draft. Do your job. Write a bad first draft! But don't turn that in for a grade. Instead, fix it! We call fixing a bad draft "editing."

try very hard to eliminate those words from your draft. Once you have eliminated passive voice, your paper will read more clearly, simply, and straightforwardly.

Logical Legal Style

The final characteristic of good legal writing relates to employing a logical style that critically analyzes and applies legal rules to conflicts and questions. This style requires that the writer structure his or her argument using what we call a syllogism. An ancient argument form, the syllogism includes three parts—a major premise, a minor premise, and a conclusion.[5] Syllogistic reasoning (for our purposes) resides at the sentence and paragraph levels (so, this section refers to micro-level style). In legal writing, we modify the standard syllogism to include a conclusion at the beginning and end of your paragraph, and not one, but two, minor premises. A paragraph written using this formula should include at least five sentences arranged like this:

- ☐ **Conclusion (topic sentence):** You start your paragraph with what you want the court to do. Thus, your thesis is the conclusion you want the court (or, your instructor) to draw.

- ☐ **Major Premise (The Rule):** A rule drawn from a previous case.

- ☐ **Minor Premise 1:** A fact or facts important to the outcome of that previous case.

- ☐ **Minor premise 2:** A factual link between that case and the one you are discussing.

- ☐ **Restatement of the conclusion:** Close by saying what you want again!

Let's consider the writing of an actual Arkansas State University student who submitted the following for a grade in our *Legal Research, Writing, and Advocacy* course. In this example, the student wrote about a fictitious case in which the FBI investigated a man named Comerford for running an internet chat room in which people discussed plans to assassinate the president. The FBI used something called an administrative subpoena to acquire the records of these conversations. An administrative subpoena does not require judicial oversight—the FBI issued it, approved it, and then executed it. The student argued for Mr. Comerford, and asked the court to conclude that the FBI conducted an

---

5 Consider this example of a syllogism: All men are mortal (major premise). Socrates is a man (minor premise). Therefore, Socrates is mortal (conclusion).

illegal search. In asking the court to arrive at that conclusion, the student relied on a real case called *Katz v. United States*. In that case, the Court considered FBI surveillance of a man named Katz while he used a phone booth. The FBI attached microphones to the outside of the booth and recorded Katz' side of his phone conversations. But, no one was sure if the FBI could do this, or if the Fourth Amendment prohibition against unreasonable searches applied to phone booths. The Supreme Court decided that the Fourth Amendment did protect Katz because he closed the door to the phone booth before calling (once upon a time, there were these things called phone booths, and they had doors). Applying the logical structure I just outlined above, my student made the following argument.

First, he stated his conclusion, the thing he wanted from the court: *This Court should resolve the issue before it by excluding the evidence gathered using an administrative subpoena*. Next, he stated the major premise, which is the rule drawn from a previous case: *In Katz v. United States, this Court stated that the 4ᵗʰ Amendment protects persons not places when people attempt to keep their conversations private*. The only way to know what rule a court announced in a case is to actually read that case. Maybe you haven't read *Katz*, but we can understand this rule. People enjoy protection wherever they are, not only in certain places.

Then he stated his first minor premise, an important fact that the court in *Katz* relied upon in making its decision. He took two sentences to do this: *Mr. Katz intended to exclude the listening ear when he closed the door to the phone booth. Because he asserted a privacy interest, this Court applied the Katz doctrine to protect his speech from government intrusion without a warrant*. The second minor premise drew a comparison between the facts in *Katz* and the facts of our case involving Mr. Comerford: *Similarly, in the case before us today, Mr. Comerford "closed the door" by putting in place a series of software locks and rotating password codes*.

Finally, my student concluded by asking the court one more time to protect Mr. Comerford and exclude evidence against him gathered by the FBI: *Thus, Comerford's speech within the chat room should receive 4ᵗʰ Amendment protection because he asserted a privacy interest, and society willingly recognizes it as legitimate*. His complete paragraph of six sentences (without my interjections) looked like this:

> This Court should resolve the issue before it by excluding the
> evidence gathered using an administrative subpoena. In Katz
> v. United States, this Court stated that the 4ᵗʰ Amendment
> protects persons not places when people attempt to keep

> *their conversations private. Mr. Katz intended to exclude*
> *the listening ear when he closed the door to the phone booth.*
> *Because he asserted a privacy interest, this Court applied the*
> *Katz doctrine to protect his speech from government intrusion*
> *without a warrant. Similarly, in the case before us today, Mr.*
> *Comerford "closed the door" by putting in place a series of*
> *software locks and rotating password codes. Thus, Comerford's*
> *speech within the chat room should receive 4th Amendment*
> *protection because he asserted a privacy interest, and society*
> *willingly recognizes it as legitimate.*

Using this formula, a student can write every single paragraph in a paper as a logical argument, supported by appeal to a general rule and supporting evidence of how that rule has worked in the past. The paragraph above contains a clearly defined line of reasoning. The reader can understand what the writer wants and why the writer wants it. This particularly fine example captures the essence of legal writing.

When Writing Case Briefs, Define the Issue

I conclude this chapter on legal writing with a word to the wise about briefing cases. Primarily, we see the kind of writing in the example about Mr. Comerford and Mr. Katz in appellate briefs and essays on law. However, I usually start students on their journey to good legal writing by asking them to brief cases. A case brief outlines and summarizes a previously decided case. We call these previously decided cases precedents. We call one technique for briefing cases the IRAC method. It includes four sections—a statement of the *Issue*, statement of the *Rule*, the *Application* of the rule to the facts of the case you are briefing, and a *Conclusion*. Here, I focus on defining the issue.

A student of legal writing must first learn to define a legal issue properly. Without question, the statement of the issue constitutes the most important part of the IRAC—if you do not understand the issue before the court, then the rest of your brief is useless. Being able to define the issue properly is an art, a skill. You would be surprised at how many attorneys can't do it very well.

First, begin your issue statement with the word "whether." The most important element of stating the issue (besides getting it right) is stating it precisely and specifically. Here is an example of a really poorly worded, horribly vague statement of an issue:

*Whether the policy of the university in excluding religious
groups violates the US Constitution.*

I call this a horribly vague issue statement because you cannot
resolve the issue with the information it gives you. What part of the US
Constitution? Is the university violating the Preamble? The Commerce
Clause? Excluding religious groups from where? The cafeteria?! This
statement does not define the issue adequately, and I would assign it a
grade of F. The next example tries to do better, but still fails:

*Whether the policy of the university in excluding religious
groups violates the First Amendment to the US Constitution.*

We now know which part of the Constitution! But, the First
Amendment contains lots of clauses. So, which one *specifically* is it that
the university is violating? Here is yet a better example:

*Whether the policy of Ohio State University in excluding
the Conservative Catholics Against Abortion student-led
organization from a university created speech forum violates
the members' rights to expression and religious freedom found
in the First Amendment to the US Constitution.*

We now enjoy a much better understanding of this conflict. We
know what Ohio State did to what group, and we know what part of the
Constitution the group says Ohio State violated. Furthermore, a court
can actually decide this issue. It raises a clear and precise constitutional
question.

If you think about it, I have really made clarity the theme of this
chapter. To write legally, you have to write clearly. To write clearly, you
must write use simple language, simply constructed sentences, active
verbs, transitions across paragraphs, and a critical analytical style. You
must also plan your writing and spin a story across sections of your paper
so that your reader can understand what is the point of your paper, the
problem you want to resolve, and the reasons for resolving it the way you
want. If you follow these basic rules of legal writing, and strive for clarity
and precision, you can write well in almost any discipline, including the
law.

WRITING FOR ENGINEERING: AN EMBEDDED TUTOR'S PERSPECTIVE

Jesse Matlock

. . . .

"Gah, [Instructor's Name Redacted] is such a stickler about these progress reports. I don't get it; I'm supposed to be designing and building this project, but I have to spend so much time working on this stupid report. Why?!"

"Our students can design and fabricate all sorts of incredible projects, but we keep finding that they get out into the business world and can't write a coherent email or memorandum. That's a deficiency in our program, and one that we have to address as we go into reaccreditation with ABET [Accreditation Board for Engineering and Technology]."

These are the poles between which I, as an embedded tutor for the College of Engineering, find myself. Students that hated high school English and decided to become engineers in order to do something "real" see no point in documenting their process and logging their progress, as long as they produce timely results. Instructors, on the other hand, seasoned in real-world experience, are reacting to feedback from employers about students who have graduated, entered the workforce, and have been found lacking in what is commonly regarded as a "basic" skill: writing.

That is not to say that engineering students are unable to compose intelligible expositions. Most, if not all, of them are prolific text messengers and social media posters, demonstrating that they have a firm grasp of concepts such as multimodal composition; they are simply inexperienced in the genres relevant to the business of engineering. After all, how often does a high school graduate, entering directly into college, have occasion to write a lab report, never mind a serious proposal for a project that will directly affect the infrastructure of their community or a business in that community as well as progress reports for that project? What qualities should that writing exhibit? What is the proper format for a lab report or progress report as a business memorandum? And how should these students know these genres, formats, and qualities when the majority of "formal" writings they have composed have been for humanities courses, if not solely for English classes?

Science involves the use of precise information in the simple execution of direct processes. Scientific writing operates by the same principles. Clear understanding of materials, methods, processes, results, and obstacles is paramount; therefore, simple, direct language that precisely details those categories is necessary for the uniform repetition of an experiment or to decide what process or method will be safest, least costly, and/or produce the most desired result.

As an embedded tutor, it is my job to serve as something of a liaison between student and instructor, requirements and execution of an assignment. I am not an expert; I came into this position with no special experience in engineering. What I can do, however, is let you talk about the work *you* are doing. I can listen as you explain to me the nature of your work or assignment, ask questions that help you clarify assumptions, and help you consult and decode the Department of Engineering Course Standards in accordance with the rubric of the writing assignment with which you have been tasked, be it a project proposal, progress report, lab report, or other documentation related to course work. I can provide feedback on what you produce within the context of those course standards and my communication with instructors.

You, the student, though, are the subject matter expert; I am your sounding board and test audience. What you do not see is what is happening beneath the surface that benefits both of us: you—in explaining your work to me, answering my questions, and clarifying jargon, concepts, and processes for someone outside your chosen discipline—are self-clarifying and solidifying your own knowledge; simultaneously, you are helping me to gain knowledge and experience in a genre or discourse that I might have otherwise never had a reason to practice, but can now add to my own rhetorical repository. In this ideal situation, we have surpassed the "transaction" of meeting arbitrary assignment requirements and achieved the "interaction" of real learning.

The most important thing that you can remember as a student—regardless of discipline—seeking help with a writing assignment from a Writing Center tutor: this is not a subservient, teacher-student situation; this is a collaboration—your tutor *needs* your input, to know your concerns and help you address them. What good is forty-five minutes spent discussing your work if we never address why you are nervous about turning it in? Beyond sincerely encouraging you to seek out feedback for any writing you do, I implore you to not be afraid of honest feedback and to believe that your input is valuable in a tutoring session. The writing, the work, is *yours* after all, so it behooves you to take fullest advantage of the tools at your disposal.

Writing in the Disciplines

HOW BIOLOGISTS WRITE FOR EACH OTHER
John Artim

. . . .

Biologists—as with most all humans—are storytellers. In order to better understand our lives— and all life—we tell each other stories. When we are telling our stories to the public, our storytelling is loose and often colorful. We ladle in a large dollop of anecdote so that we are not only telling stories about living creatures and how those creatures go about their lives, we are also making those creatures more understandable to the public. In telling our stories this way, we are also sharing with our audience a little about how we discovered that story and who we are as scientist-storytellers. In this way, humanizing ourselves is an important aspect of our public storytelling. But when we are telling stories to other scientists, we focus closely on life's story and downplay our own role in the discovery. When we teach, our goal is mixed—we both want to humanize the process of discovery so that our students see themselves in our acts of discovery, while at the same time going into great detail on how life itself works. In this essay, we focus on how biologists write for each other.

In biology journal articles, the topic of the writing will be some question that has been preventing biologists from better understanding how life works. Science writing is always very structured, with named sections that always appear in the same order. The first part of the paper—the *Introduction*—tells how the problem addressed by the article is relevant to other biologists and the problems those biologists work on. The author begins by describing the context their work fits into, describing this context as a broad area of connected questions and prior results from the author and from selected work by other researchers. The author uses citations to carefully call out where this prior work was published and how to find the corresponding papers. The *Introduction* ends with a problem statement—usually one or two sentences summarizing the question the current research is going to answer. The middle of the article is broken into two named parts: first *Methods*, then *Results*. In the *Methods* section, the authors tell other biologists how they collected evidence to address their problem statement. If the authors used methods that are described in earlier work, the authors will cite that earlier work. In this way, biologists keep the *Methods* section from getting long and cookbook-like. The *Results* section describes the evidence the authors have collected, but must only describe their data and never draw conclusions based on that data. The last part of the article is called the *Discussion*. The *Discussion* first draws on the evidence the authors collected to conclude an answer to their problem statement, then goes on to describe how this conclusion changes our shared understanding of how life works. Throughout the *Discussion*, citations to existing papers help the reader understand how the conclusions in this new work extend or overturn the worldview expressed in the articles in the current literature.

The flow and the structure of a biology story is shown graphically in the upper portion of Figure 1. Start with the *Introduction* which is meant to engage the reader, drawing her into the paper. The *Introduction* starts with a hook, a writing device that provides the user with a ready-made perspective on a problem or idea and serves to actively engage the reader. The *Introduction* is shown in Figure 1 as largely-flat because this is the context from which the article rises up, the stable ground from which the author is about to ask the reader to leap up.

The middle of the paper—the *Methods* and *Results*—must maintain interest. The *Methods* section is the reader's assurance that she can trust the evidence reported in this paper. If the *Methods* succeed in convincing the reader the work was properly done, the reader should be carried downward by the data reported in *Results* as inexorably as a ball rolling down a hill.

This leads to the *Discussion* where the reader first sees the answer to the problem statement. If the middle section of the paper has done its job, this conclusion concerning the problem statement should be easy for the reader to accept—the ball running down the *Results* hill rolls on through the first part of the *Discussion*. If there are any uncertainties in the evidence the writer has presented, the writer should bring up these uncertainties here in the early part of the *Discussion* and immediately diffuse those concerns. By explicitly admitting to any uncertainty in their evidence, the writer is clearing a path for the user to proceed to the authors' conclusions. This final part of the *Discussion* brings the reader back to the context the paper's problem statement fits into and helps the reader understand how the paper's conclusion alters her view of the world. The *Discussion* portion of the story line shown in Figure 1 is elevated above the level of the *Introduction* because the altered perspective at the end of the paper should elevate the reader to a new world view.

We can also look at a biology article in terms of how the focus of the article widens or narrows throughout the article (see the bottom of Figure 1). A good *Introduction* starts with a focus as broad as the interests of the readers of a journal. By the end of the *Introduction* the reader is taken to the narrow focus of the paper's problem statement. Throughout the middle part of the paper—*Methods* and *Results*— the reader stays at this narrow focus. This narrow focus is the day-to-day work all scientists share in common, but focused on the specific work of the authors. The final section of the paper—the *Discussion*—takes the user from the narrow focus of the problem statement back out to the wide focus of all of the readers of the article. In this way, biologist storytellers tie their own story to the web of all the science stories that have ever been told. In turn, the readers influenced by an article will later cite that article when they themselves publish their own story. This is how each new published science article expands the web of science!

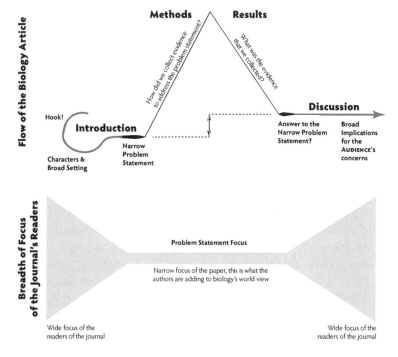

Figure 1. *This figure depicts the structure of a biology journal article. The top graphic shows how the focus of the article flows from the wide focus of the journal, down to the narrow problem addressed by the article, and back out to the wide focus of the journal's readers. The bottom graphic shows the flow of the reader's energy and interest in the storyline.*

A SCIENTIFIC ARTICLE ANNOTATED
John Artim

• • • • • • • •

Key to Annotations	
S	Structure—points out the conventions of the scientific academic article genre as expressed in this article
D	Description—highlights important aspects of the authors' contribution
A	Argument—rhetorical constructs intended to persuade or to convey a generalization or distinction
C	Context—highlights where the authors tied their work into the broader web of scholarly work

The thesis of the article is underlined in the article abstract and body.

A heavy horizontal bar is shown between the introductory and middle content and between the middle and end content.

Fish mucous cocoons: the 'mosquito nets' of the sea[1]

Alexandra S. Grutter, Jennifer G. Rumney, Tane Sinclair-Taylor, Peter Waldie and Craig E. Franklin

Abstract[2]

Mucus performs numerous protective functions in vertebrates, and in fishes may defend them against harmful organisms, although often the evidence is contradictory[3]. The function of the mucous cocoons that many parrotfishes and wrasses sleep in, while long used as a classical example of antipredator behaviour, remains unresolved. Ectoparasitic gnathiid isopods (Gnathiidae), which feed on the blood of fish, are removed by cleaner fish during the day; however, it is unclear how parrotfish and wrasse avoid gnathiid attacks at night[4]. <u>To test the novel hypothesis that mucous cocoons protect against gnathiids, we exposed the coral reef parrotfish Chlorurus sordidus (Scaridae) with and without cocoons to gnathiids overnight and measured the energetic content of cocoons.</u> Fish without mucous cocoons were attacked more by gnathiids than fish with cocoons[5]. The energetic content of mucous cocoons was estimated as 2.5 per cent of the fish's daily energy budget fish[6]. Therefore, mucous cocoons protected against attacks by gnathiids[7], acting like mosquito nets in humans, a function of cocoons and an efficient physiological adaptation for preventing parasite infestation that is not used by any other animal[8].

S Titles are vital to attracting scientific readers. Whether the reader is browsing a journal or performing a web search, good titles convey an article's focus and catch the eye.

D 1.) This provocative **Title** draws the reader in and encourages further exploration. It effectively uses metaphor in a way not often done in scientific writing. It also illustrates one of the limited uses of pathos in formal scientific genres. This paper is well-accepted—at this writing it has more google scholar citations than any other 2011 article retrieved using the terms fish and **mucous**.

S 2.) The **Abstract** attracts readers using a summary of the paper's thesis, evidence, conclusion, and the context into which the work fits. This restatement of the content in the body of the article has a different purpose. This abstract has just enough information to convince most readers who would benefit from the work to continue on and read it. It is well-written and the cost to the reader to continue is not excessive.

C 3.) The wide context of this work is described first followed by the specific context. The contradictory nature of the specific context alerts the reader that this area of uncertainty will be the focus of the paper.

D 4.) The authors list the characters for this story: parrotfish and wrasses are the protagonists, cleaner fish are the heros, and gnathiids are the enemy as are morray eels.

D The thesis—the scientists' hypothesis—is stated in minimal form.

D The evidence (5) supports the hypothesis and (6) verifies it is a feasible mechanism.

D 7.) The authors interpret their results in this positive statement. This sentence is most likely to draw readers and future citations.

C 8.) The authors delineate the generality of their conclusion.

1. INTRODUCTION

The functions of the thin layer of mucus covering fishes include osmoregulation, reducing friction and protection from abrasions, pollutants and desiccation [1], as well as ultraviolet radiation [2][9]. The role of mucus in protecting fish from harmful organisms, however, is uncertain [1][10]. One of the most notable nocturnal behaviours of coral reef fishes, mainly some wrasses and parrotfishes, is the large mucous cocoons that they envelop themselves in at night [3–5][11]. The function of mucous cocoons remains unresolved. In an early study, showing that spotted moray eels (*Gymnothorax moringa[12]*) ate more of three species that do not secrete cocoons (*Sparisoma radians*, *Sparisoma chrysopterum* and *Cyprinodon* sp.) than a parrotfish species that does (*Scarus croicensis*), Winn & Bardach [6] 'tentatively' (p. 298) concluded that cocoons reduce predation by the spotted moray eel. However, the effect of species differences was not controlled for nor was mucous cocoon presence manipulated, and many individuals of the cocoon-producing species were still eaten during the experiment[13]. Indeed, the role of mucous cocoons in large wrasse as defence against predators while wedged in crevices or buried in sand has been questioned [7,8][13]. Alternative functions proposed include protection against settling silt [4] and bacteria [9], and as a warning system upon contact [9][13]. Despite limited empirical support, the function of cocoons as defence against nocturnal predators remains regularly cited [10,11].

Gnathiid isopods attack many coral reef fishes, especially at night [12 – 14]. During the day, parrotfish repeatedly seek cleaner fish [15], which only control gnathiid infestations during the day

S This paper flows from a broad context in the introductory content to narrow focus in the middle content and back to a broad context in the end content. Using this structure authors place their work—the narrow focus in the middle content—within the web of scientific work performed to date—the broader context. Think of this as the authors helping their readers to understand how this work relates to the readers' work.

This structure works well with the scientific article genre's overarching dependence on ethos.

D 9.) This article begins by placing the work into a wider context.

D 10.) The sentence, "The role of mucus ..." acts as a narrative hook drawing the reader to continue with the narrative.

D 11.) The article then goes on to cite an unusual fish behavior and its currently-accepted function.

S Where organisms are discussed, their official binomial name is used at least once and indicated using italic text or underline. This is a necessary part of the discourse and reduces ambiguity when discussing organisms.

D 12.) 'Moray eel' is a common name while Gymnothorax moringa is the species name.

A 13.) The earlier assertion concerning mucous cocoons and predatory fish is called into question by pointing out logical flaws: an experiment that allows for alternative explanations, evidence that is equivocal, and alternative explanations.

S The analysis of the function of mucous cocoons, though written in impeccable formal technical language, is structured in a story-like way. The main characters are parrotfish, the protagonist, and their adversaries, gnathiid isopods. The daytime alliance between parrotfish and cleanerfish is identified as protective of parrotfish. The authors suggest that mucous cocoons are the story element that tips the balance of power towards parrotfish. The narrative hook was previously identified.

Writing in the Disciplines

[13] but it is not clear how parrotfish control gnathiids at night. <u>Here, we tested the hypothesis that the production of a mucous cocoon in the bullethead parrotfish (*Chlorurus sordidus*) is an energetically efficient and effective means to reduce nocturnal attacks by gnathiids, parasites that harm fish in various ways [16,17].</u>

S The flawed assertion pointed out by this argument becomes a foil for introducing the authors' hypothesized novel mucus function.

S The final sentence of the Introduction, shown underlined here for emphasis, provides the paper's problem statement. This problem statement sets the scope of the middle content of the paper that follows.

S The **Introduction** describes the context, the authors' thesis, and the placement of this thesis within the wider context. The reader exits this section precisely knowing the scope of work for the middle content.

2. MATERIAL AND METHODS

Chlorurus sordidus were collected with a barrier net at Lizard Island Great Barrier Reef held singly in 65 × 40 × 36 cm plastic bins, and supplied with a shelter (11 diameter × 13 cm pipe), constant sea water and aeration. Mucous cocoon production began at the mouth and progressed backwards to surround the body in a solid gelatinous mass in 45–60 min. In order to test whether cocoons defend against gnathiids, fish were placed singly in the bins on their first night of captivity (15–19 March 2004) and randomly assigned to a cocoon presence treatment. At midnight, when all fish had produced a cocoon, the cocoon was removed from half of the fish by gently pushing the fish out of its cocoon and scooping out the mucus with a scoop. Fish remained asleep during this procedure. Twenty, cultured [14][14], unfed third stage gnathiids *Gnathia aureusmaculosa* were then added to each bin. Fish were exposed to gnathiids for 4.5 h, this is sufficient time for the gnathiids to feed off the fish *Hemigymnus melapterus* [14]. Flow-through water was not supplied from 18.00 to 06.00 h to contain gnathiids in bins. Beginning at 04.30 h, quiescent fish were gently rubbed to remove

S MATERIALS AND METHODS and RESULTS form the middle content and objectively describe the paper's evidence and only that evidence.

S This MATERIALS AND METHODS section only discuss how evidence is collected. This section is organized logically and reflects the order in which results will later be reported, the order that later helps build to the conclusion. That this order is also chronological is coincidence and not reflective of the genre.

This section is as concise as possible while easily supporting replication of the described activities by the reader. Limiting this section to a description of procedures for evidence collection is a rigorously-enforced aspect of this genre.

D 14.) Activities that are already described elsewhere such as culturing gnathiids are documented by citation to the primary literature—in the case of gnathiid culturing, reference [14]. This reduces the text needed to describe the collection of evidence and, more importantly, credits earlier work and authors for pioneering earlier similar efforts.

any attached gnathiids and fish were removed with a hand net. Gnathiids in the bin were collected with a sieve (62 mm) and preserved in 10 per cent formalin. Fed gnathiids were identified by their engorged red gut [14]. Gnathiid feeding success was expressed as the number of fed gnathiids relative to the total number recovered (14−20).Trials in which the fish had abandoned or damaged its cocoon (n = 5) or produced a second cocoon after the first one was removed (n = 7) were omitted from the analyses[15].

The mucous cocoons removed above were dried to a constant mass at 70°C in an oven. Organic content was determined by then burning the cocoon in a muffle furnace (500°C) for 24 h, and subtracting the mass after combustion from the pre-combustion dry mass. Gross energy (GE) values of mucous cocoons, obtained from fish collected in September 2009, were obtained using a bomb calorimeter (IKA—WERKE, C2000, GMSBH & CO. KG, Staufen, Germany), which had been standardized using benzoic acid. Since individual cocoons contained extremely low energy and would not combust alone, they were mixed with a known amount of sunflower oil (0.4g) of a known energy content (mean±s.e., 39 586 ± 1 J g^{-1}, n = 3). GE was measured individually for three similar-sized fish (146 ± 16.3 g)[16]. The mean of two to four replicates per sample was used.

3.   RESULTS

Significantly, more fish from which the cocoon had been removed (94.4%), compared with fish with cocoons not removed (10%), were attacked by gnathiids (likelihood ratio test, χ^2 = 31.9, p < 0.001). The median proportion of gnathiids that

D 15.) The first piece of evidence directly tests the article's hypothesis (thesis statement).

D 16.) The second piece of evidence tests the energetic efficiency of the hypothesized mechanism providing a test of whether or not this is hypothesis conforms to broader biological theory. This secondary evidence strengthens the author's argument by demonstrating conformance not just with the author's narrow hypothesis, but with this broader body of biological theory.

This is especially important in biological writing genres. The discipline of Biology places enormous weight on a handful of central theoretical principals—tying back to these principals ties a paper into the discipline.

S This RESULTS section presents evidence for the authors' hypothesis. The evidence consists of the observations collected when executing the methods. The authors' refrain from any interpretation of these observations in the results. Exclusion of interpretation from results is a rigorously-enforced aspect of this genre.

had fed on fish was higher on fish without than fish with cocoons (Wilcoxon rank sum test, S = 519.5, Z = 5.25, p < 0.0001; figure 1)[17]. Many fish (60%) produced a second cocoon after the first one was removed at midnight. The mass per

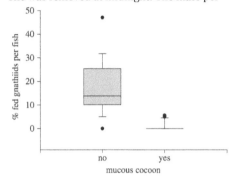

Figure 1[18]. The percentage of fed gnathiids in trials with (n = 20) and without mucous cocoons (n = 18). Box and whisker plot: centre line denotes the median value, box encloses the inner two quartiles, error bars indicate the 90th and 10th percentiles and the closed circles indicate outliers.

cocoon, estimated using organic content, increased with fish body mass with a mass exponent of 0.29 (cocoon mass (mg) = 0.107 $Mb^{0.29}$, where Mb = body mass (g)), thus indicating a relatively higher cost of cocoon production for smaller fish. The energetic content (mean±s.e.) of cocoons with a mass of 146±16.3 g was 861±42 J per cocoon; when adjusted to the mass of dried cocoon (which included much salt) it was 469±123 J g^{-1}. Although the daily energy budget is not available for *C. sordidus*[19], the daily energy assimilation is for the parrotfish *Scarus vetula* [18]; this measure, however, does not include costs like basal metabolic rate, foraging and digesting food. Using this measure (34 000

D 17.) The first piece of evidence uses two different but related measures to support the authors' hypothesis. By using two measures, the authors provide complementary tests of their hypothesis which may help persuade additional readers.

S Not strictly part of the narrative, the use of graphics is essential to good scientific discourse. Graphics like this provide a more compelling depiction of numeric evidence than words alone convey.

D 18.) This graphic visualizes this article's hypothesis: that the proportion of fed gnathids on fish without a mucous cocoon is greater than on fish with a cocoon. The graphic visualizes how variable the results were for the fish in each of these two groups, showing the degree of overlap between the groups.

Using the figure and its caption, we can determine that 90% of fish with no mucous cocoon had 1 or more fed gnathiids on it and 50% of the these fish had (on average) ~2.8 or more gnathiids. Of the fish with a cocoon, 90% had 1.0 or fewer fed gnathiids and none had more than 1.2 gnathiids. The reader can also determine that fish with no cocoon had from 0.0 to ~9.4 gnathiids that fed on it—more variability than fish with a cocoon which had from 0 to ~1.2 gnathiids that fed on them.

For the practiced reader, a short inspection of the graphic yields all of the information from the preceding paragraph.

S 19.) When a species' Latin binomial name is used more than once and doing so will not be ambiguous, the convention in scientific writing is to abbreviate the first part of the species name, the genus, to a single letter.

J d^{-1}) for *S. vetula* with a mass of 134 g as a proxy for the daily energy budget, and the average energetic content per cocoon of the above *C. sordidus*, we estimated that it cost *C. sordidus* 2.5 per cent of their daily energy budget to produce a cocoon.

**Writing in the Disciplines

D The second piece of evidence verifies the energetic feasibility of the hypothesis and so demonstrates conformity with biological theory.

4. DISCUSSION

By remaining in a mucous cocoon at night, parrotfish *C. sordidus* may avoid being attacked by gnathiids, which regularly attack fish at night [13] and possibly other parasitic isopods, of which there is a wide range on coral reefs [19]. This anti-ectoparasitic protective function differs from Winn & Bardach's [6] tentative proposal that cocoons defend against predatory moray eels, but the two functions need not be mutually exclusive. Cocoons may prevent infestation by masking olfactory cues used by gnathiids to find fish or act as a physical or chemical barrier [20]. Gnathiids can be harmful when in large numbers [16], and have been implicated as vectors of haemogregarines, blood parasites found in a few coral reef fishes, including parrotfishes [17].

How fishes that do not produce mucous cocoons prevent nocturnal isopod attacks is unclear; however, some gobies have toxic skin cells that prevent gnathiid attacks on certain body areas [20], many wrasses and some parrotfish bury themselves in the sand [5,21], a parrotfish (*Sparisoma aurofrenatum*) that does not produce cocoons sleeps in open areas away from the reef

S The **DISCUSSION** section is the falling part of the story narrative where the authors interpret evidence reported in the **METHODS** and **RESULTS** sections and relate these interpretations to the body of existing primary literature. This section starts with specific and often less controversial conclusions and uses these to drive towards broader conclusions of interest to the widest audience. It is this section that often determines how widely-cited a paper becomes.

A 20.) The authors assert that their hypothesis is true. This assertion is tempered by conceding that an alternative explanation is not mutually exclusive. The authors describe how the two functions may result from the same underlying mechanism, suggesting an area of further study.

This is both pragmatic in that it points to a pressing question that will require future work and identifies forward connections in the literature. But it is also an invocation of ethos as the authors delineate the limits of interpretation of their work.

A 21.) The authors raise the question of how fish that cannot create a mucous cocoon defend against gnathiids. They raise a number of alternative strategies that have been cited in the literature. This is the beginning of a comparison and contrast of a mucous cocoon defense with these alternatives. This line of argument helps to specifically place this work into its broader context. The **A** annotation on the bottom of this page concludes this comparison.

[22]; alternatively, fish may use nocturnal cleaner organisms. While noxious compounds occur in fish mucus [1], whether they do in cocoons is unclear[21].

The larger allocation of organic content to cocoons by smaller fish suggests it costs these more to produce cocoons and also that cocoons may have a minimum thickness around the fish. The moderate investment in cocoon production, estimated at 2.5 per cent of their daily energy budget, by using the daily assimilation rate of *S. vetula* [18] as a proxy may explain why fish can produce cocoons nightly and also could produce a second cocoon on the same night if needed[22]. Despite the differences in feeding behaviour between members of these genera [23], the assimilation rate estimated by Bruggemann is a useful starting point for implying daily costs in similar-sized species.

▲ 22.) This discussion of energetics appeals to broader biological theory further demonstrating the practicality of the author's hypothesis. This is driven home by the point that even constructing a second cocoon in one night is still easily feasible.

Anti-parasite behaviours fish can engage in, including seeking cleaner organisms, avoiding infectious habitats and infected individuals [24], chafing along a substrate, reducing activity and shoaling [25] are relatively energetically costly. Using mucous cocoons, however, circumvents this limitation by deterring parasites in a moderately energetically efficient way[23]. While aestivating frogs, salamanders and lungfish produce cocoons, this is to prevent desiccation [26][24].

▲ 23.) By stating that other anti-parasite behaviors are not as energetically efficient as mucous cocoons, this paragraph closes out the ▲ annotation that was started two paragraphs previous to this one by contrasting the protective mechanism discussed in this article with the alternative mechanisms described and cited in the literature for other fish taxa.

▲ 24.) The paragraph closes by citing literature that assigns a different function to cocoons in other vertebrates, implying that the defensive function they tested in a fish does not appear in other vertebrate taxa. This further delineates the context by limiting the generalizability of their results to other taxa while also highlighting the uniqueness of their results.

In contrast to the astonishingly diverse behavioural adaptations [24] and the use of toxic compounds in other animals [27], parrotfish use a physiological adaptation to deter parasites. This involves large highly specialized glands in the gill cavity and/or under the operculum [3], which secrete a structure that not only protects the whole fish but also allows the fish to sleep, a combination of features not known to occur in any other animal. Physiological adaptations to control ectoparasites and other fouling organisms in animals are relatively rare and tend to involve chemical compounds [27]. Mucous cocoons, in contrast, are more reminiscent of the barriers, such as mosquito nets, constructed by humans to control biting arthropods [28]. This adaptation shows the tremendous selective pressure that parasites can impose on fish[25].

Acknowledgements

Many thanks to G. Muñoz, C. Jones, J. Pickering, L. Curtis, J. Marshall, N. Raihani, J. Oates, R. Bshary, C. Newport and Lizard Island Research Station staff for their help in the field or on the manuscript, H. Bruggeman for discussions on this project, X. Li for the bomb calorimetry and the Australian Research Council for funding (A.S.G.).

References [26]

1. Shephard, K. L. 1994 Functions for fish mucus. *Rev. Fish Biol. Fish.* 4, 401–429. (doi:10.1007/BF00042888)
2. Zamzow, J. & Losey Jr, G. S. 2002 Ultraviolet radiation absorbance by coral reef fish mucus: photo-protection and visual communication. *Environ. Biol. Fish.* 63, 41–47. (doi:10.1023/A:1013846816869)
3. Casimir, M. J. 1971 Zur Morphologie, Histochemie, Tagesperiodik und Biologie der Operculardruse bei Labriden und Scariden (Pisces). *Mar. Biol.* 8, 126–146. (doi:10.1007/BF00350928)
4. Winn, H. E. 1955 Formation of a mucous envelope at night by parrot fishes. *Zoologica* 40, 145–148.
5. Randall, J. E., Allen, G. R. & Steene, R. C. 1997 *Fishes of the Great Barrier Reef and Coral Sea*, 2nd edn. Bathurst, Australia: Crawford House Publishing.
6. Winn, H. E. & Bardach, J. E. 1959 Differential food selection by moray eels and a possible role of the mucous envelope of parrot fishes in reduction of predation. *Ecology* 40, 296 – 298. (doi:10.2307/1930041)
7. Potts, G. W. 1973 The ethology of Labroides dimidiatus (Cuv. & Val.) (Labridae, Pisces) on aldabra. *Anim. Behav.* 21, 250 – 291. (doi:10.1016/S0003-3472(73) 80068-5)

S The authors widen their discussion back out in the final paragraph by discussing the implications of their work and how it informs a broad range of issues. Overall, this article was structured so that it started out discussing a wide context, narrowed the focus down to a thesis statement, discussed the evidence collected in support of this hypothesis, then broadened the discussion back out to the wider implications of the work. This pattern is seen in many well-written scientific papers and is especially good at leaving the reader with no doubt as to the conclusions reached by the authors or the connections with the broader literature.

▲ 25.) The final sentence broadens the context out to its fullest by stating the generalized conclusion that parasites can drive the evolution of fish in the context of their communities.

S The final sentence delivers the paper's take-home message and closes the story by returning to a wide context.

S For scientific papers based on field work, **Acknowledgements** often reflect substantial work that does not rise to the level of coauthorship. Recognizing these contributions is an important aspect of the discourse in these fields.

S 26.) This short paper cites 28 primary sources. Secondary sources are rarely used in scientific articles. Note that papers are often found by tracing forward from the references they cite.

S Note that ultimately every citation within an article describes how the work fits into the broader context of the web of prior work. This article's carefully justified citations make it more likely that other scientists will seriously consider the work and later cite it.

Writing in the Disciplines

8. Wiley, J. W. 1974 Observations on the use of mucus envelopes by the California sheephead, *Pimelometopon pulchrum*, on Southern California rock reefs. *Copeia* 1974, 789 – 790. (doi:10.2307/1442700)

9. Videler, H., Geertjes, G. J. & Videler, J. J. 1999 Biochemical characteristics and antibiotic properties of the mucous envelope of the queen parrotfish. *J. Fish Biol.* 54, 1124 – 1127. (doi:10.1111/j.1095-8649.1999. tb00864.x)

10. Langerhans, R. B. 2007 Evolutionary consequences of predation: avoidance, escape, reproduction, and diversification. In Predation in *organisms*, pp. 177 – 220. Berlin, Germany: Springer.

11. Smith, R. J. F. 1997 Avoiding and deterring predators. In *Behavioural ecology of fishes* (ed. J. G. Godin), pp. 163 – 190. Oxford, UK: Oxford University Press.

12. Grutter, A. S. & Poulin, R. 1998 Intraspecific and interspecific relationships between host size and the abundance of parasitic larval gnathiid isopods on coral reef fishes. *Mar. Ecol. Prog. Ser.* 164, 263 – 271. (doi:10. 3354/ meps164263)

13. Grutter, A. S. 1999 Cleaner fish really do clean. *Nature* 398, 672–673. (doi:10.1038/19443)

14. Grutter, A. S. 2003 Feeding ecology of the fish ectoparasite, *Gnathia* sp. (Crustacea: Isopoda), from the Great Barrier Reef, Australia and its implications for fish cleaning behaviour. *Mar. Ecol. Prog. Ser.* 259, 295 – 302. (doi:10.3354/meps259295)

15. Grutter, A. S. 1995 The relationship between cleaning rates and ectoparasite loads in coral reef fishes. *Mar. Ecol. Prog. Ser.* 118, 51 – 58. (doi:10.3354/meps118051)

16. Jones, C. M. & Grutter, A. S. 2005 Parasitic isopods (*Gnathia* sp.) reduce haemocrit in captive blackeye thick- lip (Labridae) on the Great Barrier Reef. *J. Fish Biol.* 66, 860–864. (doi:10.1111/j.0022-1112.2005.00640.x)

17. Smit, N. J., Grutter, A. S., Adlard, R. D. & Davies, A. J. 2006 Hematozoa of teleosts from Lizard Island, Australia, with some comments on their possible mode of transmission and the description of a new hemogregarine species. *J. Parasitol.* 92, 778 – 788. (doi:10.1645/ GE-756R.1)

18. Bruggemann, J. H. 1994 *Parrotfish grazing on coral reefs*. Wageningen, The Netherlands: Posen & Looijen bv.

19. Jones, C. M., Miller, T. L., Grutter, A. S. & Cribb, T. H. 2008 Natatory-stage cymothoid isopods: description, molecular identification and evolution of attachment. *Int. J. Parasitol.* 38, 477 – 491. (doi:10.1016/j.ijpara. 2007.07.013)

20. Munday, P. L., Schubert, M., Jones, G. P., Caley, M. J. & Grutter, A. S. 2003 Skin toxins and external parasitism of coral-dwelling gobies. *J. Fish Biol.* 62, 976 – 981. (doi:10. 1046/j.1095-8649.2003.00078.x)

21. DeLoach, N. 1999 *Reef fish behavior: Florida, Caribbean, Bahamas*. Jacksonville, FL: New World Publications, Inc.

22. Dubin, R. E. & Baker, J. D. 1982 Two types of cover-seeking behavior at sunset by the princess parrotfish, *Scarus taeniopterus*, at Barbados, West-Indies. *Bull. Mar. Sci.* 32, 572 – 583.

23. Bellwood, D. R. 1994 A phylogenetic study of the parrot-fishes family Scaridae (Pisces: Labroidei), with a revision of genera. *Rec. Aust. Mus. Suppl.* 20, 1 – 86. (doi:10.3853/j.0812-7387.20.1994.51)

24. Loehle, C. 1995 Social barriers to pathogen transmission in wild animal populations. *Ecology* 76, 326 – 335. (doi:10.2307/1941192)

25. Wisenden, B. D., Goater, C. P. & James, C. T. 2009 Behavioural defenses against parasites and pathogens. In *Fishes defenses* (eds G. Zaccone, M. A. Perrie`re & B. G. Kapoor), pp. 151 – 168. Enfield, NH: Science Publishers.

26. Secor, S. M. & Lignot, J. H. 2010 Morphological plasticity of vertebrate aestivation. In *Aestivation: molecular and physiological aspects* (eds C. A. Navas & J. E. Carvalho), pp. 183 – 208. Berlin, Germany: Springer.

27. Williams, C. R., Smith, B. P. C., Best, S. M. & Tyler, M. J. 2006 Mosquito repellents in frog skin. *Biol. Lett.* 2, 242 – 245. (doi:10.1098/rsbl.2006.0448)

28. Kitchen, L. W., Lawrence, K. L. & Coleman, R. E. 2009 The role of the United States military in the development of vector control products, including insect repellents, insecticides, and bed nets. *J. Vector Ecol.* 34, 50 – 61.

D Even something as mundane as the use of mosquito nets warrants its own citation of the primary literature—see [28].

Writing in the Disciplines

CONCLUSION

Just as each discipline will have its own set of conventions (as demonstrated by the previous disciplinary style guides) so will each course you take (be it a Gen. Ed. course or a course specifically for your field). As such, Composition II, as taught on the A-State campus, does not follow a set curriculum—that is, not all instructors will teach the same lessons and assignments the same way. It is up to you to adapt to the particulars of the Composition II course you find yourself within. Indeed, your adaptation to Composition II will, in many ways, mirror your work of adapting to the writing within your larger scholarly career.

In the next chapter, we provide you with a guide to citation in the various style formats. As Sarah Scott discussed at length, each style is crafted by experts in the disciplines to fulfill specific rhetorical purposes. Citation is not just a means of making sure you aren't accused of plagiarism; citation also demonstrates your awareness of the mechanisms that drive the scholarship in your disciplines. Clear and correct citation practices help develop your ethos as a scholar in your field. As such, it is important to pay attention to the rules and understand why they are in place.

Citing in the Disciplines

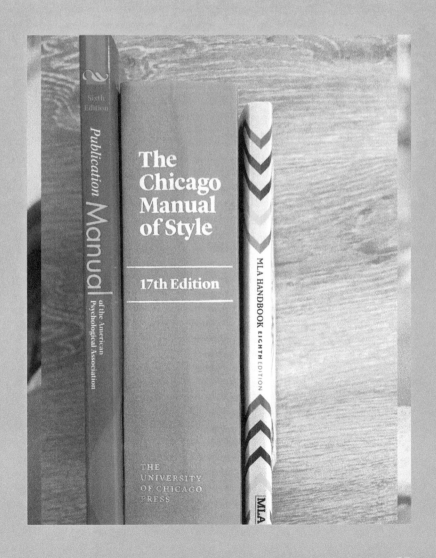

CITING IN THE DISCIPLINES

Kristi Murray Costello
Former Director of the A-State Writing Program

• • • • • • • • •

When and Why We Cite

You have likely heard a collective groan anytime the professor at the front of the room explains that the paper she's just assigned needs to be in a specific style, such as APA (American Psychological Association), AP (Associated Press), CMS (Chicago Manual of Style), MLA (Modern Language Association), or Turabian, but universities require students to cite sources for several reasons:

- To give credit to others for their ideas
- To provide information to readers so they can find the sources themselves
- To lend credibility to the author's claims
- To distance themselves from someone else's ideas

While it is a good practice to give credit to anyone whose words or ideas you share, it is especially important in institutions of higher learning because faculty and students are held accountable for their work. In higher education, one's writing and research can help them obtain publication, tenure, grants, and prestige. However, more importantly, when shared with others, one's ideas, writing, methods, and research can lead to new and improved ideas, writing, methods, and research. This process of sharing and building on one another's ideas has led to life-changing scientific advancements, new perspectives on canonical texts, policy reforms, and social and political movements. In Kenneth Burke's *The Philosophy of Literary Form,* he describes this process as an ongoing conversation. He writes:

> Imagine that you enter a parlor. You come late. When you arrive, others have long preceded you, and they are engaged in a heated discussion, a discussion too heated for them to pause and tell you exactly what it is about. In fact, the discussion had already begun long before any of them got there, so that no one present is qualified to retrace for you all the steps that had gone before. You listen for a while, until you decide that you have caught the tenor of the argument; then you put in your oar. Someone

answers; you answer him; another comes to your defense; another aligns himself against you, to either the embarrassment or gratification of your opponent, depending upon the quality of your ally's assistance. However, the discussion is interminable. The hour grows late, you must depart. And you do depart, with the discussion still vigorously in progress. (110-111)

Thus, if you think about knowledge and the generation of knowledge as unending conversation, it becomes clear that everyone who had a voice in the conversation deserves to be heard and know they were heard. Even when we're refuting their ideas, research, or methods, they still deserve credit for being a part of the conversation because it may have been their finding or mistake that led to the next improvement or advancement. It is also equally important to interrogate the conversation, asking yourself whose voices have been left out and why.

In sum, any time you bring someone else's ideas or work into your writing, you should cite the source. The only time you need not cite is when the information is common knowledge. For example, you would not need to cite that Thomas Jefferson was the third president of the United States of America, but you would want to cite that President Jefferson gave of more than 6,000 of his own books to replenish the Library of Congress after arson perpetrated by British soldiers depleted the library's holdings ("10 things you didn't know about Thomas Jefferson"). When in doubt as to whether information should be cited, cite it. It is always better to over-cite than under-cite. To see essays formatted according to each style guide, please see the examples provided for you later in the book.

Works Cited

"10 things you didn't know about Thomas Jefferson." *The Washington Post,* 30 June 2011. www.washingtonpost.com/lifestyle/kidspost/10-things-you-didnt-know-about-thomas-jefferson/2011/04/12/AGGLlWsH_story.html?utm_term=.03d87ec3f8a9#comments. Accessed 6 Feb. 2017.

Burke, Kenneth. *The Philosophy of Literary Form.* University of California Press, 1941.

WRITE about an instance in which someone was accused of plagiarism. It can be your own experience or that of a friend, politician, or celebrity. What do you recall about the story? Was it plagiarism? How did people react? What impact did the allegation have on the accused?

MLA STYLE

The Modern Language Association of America, or MLA, developed a style guide to establish rules and bring consistency to written academic works. The *MLA Handbook* is most often used in the language arts and humanities disciplines, including literature, literary criticism, English studies, and cultural studies. The most recent publication, the 8th edition, was published in 2016.

MLA Guidelines for Formatting Papers

An MLA essay follows the following formatting guidelines:

- The essay should be typed, double spaced in 12-point font size without additional spacing between paragraphs, in an easy-to-read font (such as Times New Roman) on 8.5-inch by 11-inch paper, with 1-inch margins on all sides.
- Do not include a title page unless required to do so. The first page of the essay should include the author's name, instructor's name, course information, and the date the essay is due. This information should be double spaced and placed in the upper left corner of the page, beginning one inch from the top.
- The title should follow the author and course information and should be centered, in title case (uppercase and lowercase letters), with no underlining, italicizing, or bolding.
- Starting on the first page, each page should have a running header in the right corner, 1/2 inch from the top margin and flush with the right margin, which includes the author's last name and the page number.
- Use the tab key or your ruler to indent the first line of each paragraph 1/2 inch from the left margin.
- Use only one space after periods or other punctuation marks.
- Commas and periods go inside the quotation marks, not outside: "Chapter 1," rather than "Chapter 1", for example.
- Use em dashes (—) and ellipses (...) and replace hyphens (-) with en dashes (–) where appropriate, and make consistent.

MLA General In-Text Citation Rules

Including source information in parentheses after a quote or paraphrase is known as parenthetical citation or an in-text citation, and it is required when using MLA style.

In MLA, it is important to provide a lead-in or introductory phrase for source quotations, paraphrases, or summaries in the text, especially the first time the source is used. Lead-ins introduce the sources to the audience and provide a smooth transition from the student author's writing to quotes, summaries, and paraphrases within the text. When the author's name is mentioned in the signal phrase, you do not need to include it in the in-text citation; rather, use the page number alone, if the source is paginated. However, you will need to continue to include the author's last name in subsequent uses.

Example: Introducing Sources with a Lead-In
As Glenn and Ratcliffe explain in Silence and Listening as Rhetorical Arts, we "can more productively discern and implement actions that are more ethical, efficient, and appropriate when all parties agree to engage in rhetorical situations that include not only respectful speaking, reading, and writing, but also productive silence and rhetorical listening" (3).

In-Text Citation: Print Sources

A Work by a Single Author
The author's last name and the page numbers (when available) from the source material should appear in the text. The relevant page numbers appear in the parenthetical citation, not in the text.

Examples:
Shor argues that basic writing is "a containment track below freshman comp, a gate below the gate" (94).

Basic writing is "a containment track below freshman comp, a gate below the gate" (Shor 94).

Block Quotations
Begin quotations more than four lines in length on a new line that is indented one inch from the left margin. Place the whole quote, double spaced, within the new margin. Do not use quotation marks. Note that the parenthetical citation comes after the end punctuation.

Example:
As a builder, Lubbers was tasked to determine the most effective method for ensuring the safety and integrity of structures in a variety of climates. Lubbers's study found the following:

> The prevailing wind being forecast for January 2 will be from the southwest, and will reach speeds of up to 50 miles per hour. This wind has the potential to cause significant damage

to the current construction. The building should be braced
heavily to avoid collapse. (202)

Unknown Author

When the author it not known, use an abbreviated title of the source in
the parenthetical citation. Use quotation marks for titles of short works
(articles, chapters, episodes, songs) and italics for titles of longer works
(movies, books, television shows), and include a page number.

Example:
The results of the study on multitasking showed that switching from one
task to another actually takes more time than giving attention to one task
at a time ("Is Multitasking More Efficient?" 6).

Authors with Same Last Name

If two or more cited authors have the same last name, include both
authors' first initials. If different authors share the same first initial,
provide the authors' full names.

Example:
Although some researchers have found that multitasking is actually
counterproductive and inefficient (K. Jones 12), more and more students
are employing multitasking in their daily lives (P. Jones 46).

Two Works by the Same Author

To cite two or more sources by the same author, include the title (or
abbreviated title) in the parentheses, preceding the page number.

Example:
Bartholomae states that to be successful, college students must invent a
language they feel places them in the realm of academia ("Inventing the
University" 146), and argues that basic writing programs both preserve
and attempt to bridge cultural differences in the classroom ("The Tidy
House" 87).

A Work by Two or Three Authors

If a source has two or three authors, provide the authors' last names in the
text or in parentheses.

Examples:
Collins and Blum outline the way socioeconomics and politics outside the
university also play a role in instigating the division between "basic" and
"normal" writers (14).

The authors outline the way socioeconomics and politics outside the university also play a role in instigating the division between "basic" and "normal" writers (Collins and Blum 14).

A Work by More than Three Authors

For more than three authors, include the first author's last name followed by et al., or give the last name of each author.

Examples:
Cincotta et al. assert that the launch of Sputnik expanded the competitive arena between the U.S. and the Soviet Union (68).

Historians assert that the launch of Sputnik expanded the competitive arena between the U.S. and the Soviet Union (Cincotta et al. 68).

Cincotta, Brown, Burant, Green, Holden, and Marshall assert that the launch of Sputnik expanded the competitive arena between the U.S. and the Soviet Union (68).

Indirect Sources

It may sometimes be necessary to use a work that has been cited in another source. For such indirect or secondary sources, use "qtd. in" to indicate the primary source.

Example:
According to Harvey Graff, "We do not know what we mean by literacy" (qtd. in Lunsford 252).

Encyclopedia/Dictionary Entry

Use the term being cited in quotation marks for the parenthetical citation of this type of source.

Example:
A citation is a "quotation from or reference to a book, paper, or author." ("Citation").

In-Text Citation: Electronic Sources

For electronic sources, include the first item (author name, title, etc.) in the Works Cited entry that corresponds to the citation. Do not include URLs in the text unless absolutely necessary; if included, make the URL as brief as possible, such as npr.org rather than http://www.npr.org.

Website

A similar study determined that subjects lost more time when switching from a familiar task to an unfamiliar task ("Is Multitasking").

Film

Big Fish, directed by Tim Burton, details the extraordinary life of Edward Bloom (2003).

Television

In *Criminal Minds*, a suspect awakens from a coma with no memory of having committed the crimes of which he is accused ("Tabula Rasa").

MLA Works Cited Page

A Works Cited must be included at the end of the paper. Each source cited in the text must have a corresponding Works Cited entry.

Begin the Works Cited on a separate page, formatted with one-inch margins and running header that contains a last name and page number which continues from the last page of the essay. Center the words "Works Cited" as the title at the top of the page. Do not use italics, bolding, underlining, or quotation marks.

List entries alphabetically by the author's (or editor's) last name, using last name, first name format. Do not list titles (e.g., Dr.) or degrees (e.g., PhD), but include suffixes such as "Jr." (e.g., Gates, Henry Louis, Jr.).

Use a hanging indent for each entry that is more than one line in length. Double space all citations, and do not add extra spaces between entries.

Capitalize each word in the title, with the exception of conjunctions, prepositions, or articles (such as a, an, the) unless it is the first word of the title or subtitle: *Everything Is Illuminated*, *The Art of War*, *For Whom the Bell Tolls*.

List page numbers efficiently. For example, if referencing a work that appeared on pages 136 through 153, list the page numbers as 136–53.

Use italics for larger works (books, movies, magazines) and quotation marks for shorter works (articles, songs, essays, poems).

MLA 8: The Works Cited List

Given that new media are being introduced constantly and some publication types now include more than one medium or blur the lines between traditional mediums, MLA 8 included a general list to follow for citing sources to ensure that any source can be cited in MLA—even those that have not yet been created. Note that the punctuation that follows each element is the punctuation that should be included in your Works Cited, though your Works Cited entry will always end with a period.

1. Author.
2. Title of source.
3. Title of container,
4. Other contributors,
5. Version,
6. Number,
7. Publisher,
8. Publication date,
9. Location (if important).

Example 1: Citing the Full Book

Allen, Jason. *A Meditation on Fire: Poems*. Southeast Missouri State UP, 2016.

Example 2: Citing Part of the Book

Allen, Jason. "Uncle Jeff Jumped Out a Window." *A Meditation on Fire: Poems*, Southeast Missouri State UP, 2016, p. 25.

Rodrigueź, Jose Antonio. "The Little Rooms." *The Shallow End of Sleep*, Tiá Chucha Press, 2011, pp. 76-77.

Note that because Allen's poem, "Uncle Jeff Jumped Out a Window" is only one page, we use "p. 25" in the Works Cited entry. Since Rodrigueź's poem is two pages, we use "pp. 76-77."

MLA 8 uses the term "container" to indicate the site of a given source, such as the website that houses the article or the journal from which an article came. If a source has multiple containers (e.g., the article came from a journal found in ProQuest), your citation may extend beyond the directions above. Consult the chart below for assistance with sources with more than one container.

1. Author.
2. Title.
3. Title of container,
4. Other contributors (translators or editors),
5. Version (edition),
6. Number (vol. and/or no.),
7. Publisher,
8. Publication date,

9. Location.
10. Second container's title,
11. Other contributors,
12. Version,
13. Number,
14. Publisher,
15. Publication date,
16. Location (if necessary).

Print Sources: Books

One Author

When a book has one author, list the author's name in last name, first name format.

Example: Sedaris, David. *Barrel Fever*. Little, Brown, 1994.

Two or Three Authors

Use the last name, first name format for the first author; then list other author names by first name and last name.

Example:
Ward, Geoffrey, Ken Burns, and Kevin Baker. *Baseball: An Illustrated History*. Alfred A. Knopf, Inc., 1996.

Three or More Authors

For more than three authors, you may include each author's name, or you may list only the first author followed by et al., rather than listing the additional authors' names. The et in et al. should not be followed by a period.

Example:
Barnes, Sonya, et al. *Image Power: Top Image Experts Share What to Know to Look Your Best*. PowerDynamics Publishing, 2008.

Two or More Works by the Same Author

For more than one work by the same author, list the entries alphabetically by title, and use three hyphens rather than the author's name for each entry after the first.

Example:
Bartholomae, David. "Inventing the University." [...]

---. "The Tidy House: Basic Writing in the American Curriculum." [...]

Work by an Unknown Author

Works by an unknown author should be alphabetized by their title.

Example: Beowulf. [...]

Author with an Editor

Begin with the author, then include the editor after the title.

Example:

Fielding, Henry. *Tom Jones.* Edited by Sheridan Baker, W. W. Norton &
Company, Inc., 1973.

Editor with no Author

Begin with the title of the piece, then provide the editor name.

Example:

Che: The Life, Death, and Afterlife of a Revolutionary. Edited by Joseph
Hart, Thunder's Mouth Press, 2003.

Author with a Translator

List the entry by author name, then include the translator after the title.

Example:

Gide, André. *Lafcadio's Adventures.* Translator Dorothy Bussy, Vintage
Books, 1953.

A Work in an Anthology

Begin with the author name, then the title of the article or chapter in
quotation marks. List the anthology title in italics, followed by the editor's
name.

Example:

Bartholomae, David. "Inventing the University." *When a Writer Can't
Write*, Editor Mike Rose, Guilford, 1985, pp. 134–65.

Encyclopedia/Dictionary Entry

For entries in reference works, cite the entry by the term being referenced.
Do not include publisher information or page number.

Example: "Citation." *The Shorter Oxford English Dictionary.* 5th ed.,
2002.

List the author of the article first, then include the article title in quotation marks and the periodical title in italics. Follow with the date of publication, and abbreviate all months.

Article in a Magazine

Example:

Miller, Jeremy. "The Tyranny of the Test: One Year as a Kaplan Coach in the Public Schools." *Harper's Magazine*, 2 Sept. 2008, pp. 35–46.

Article in a Newspaper

Example:

Timson, Judith. "Stop All That Multitasking, Study Suggests." *The Toronto Star*, 7 Aug. 2001, p. E2.

Article in a Scholarly Journal

Provide issue numbers, when available.

Example:

Collins, Terence, and Melissa Blum. "Meanness and Failure: Sanctioning Basic Writers." *Journal of Basic Writing*, vol. 19, no. 1, 2000, pp. 13–21.

Electronic Sources

Because websites are often updated and the same information may not be available later, it is a good practice to list your date of access, even though MLA 8 does not require it.

Website

List the name of the organization hosting the website, followed by the name of the site. Include the DOI or Permalink if available; otherwise, include the URL (without http://), followed by the date of access.

Example:

National Public Radio. Morning Edition. NPR, 14 Jan. 2014. www.npr. org/programs/morning-edition. Accessed 26 Apr. 2014.

Web Page

List the author if known, followed by the information required for websites.

Example:

Abdullah, Mardziah Hayati. "The Impact of Electronic Communication on Writing." *EricDigests.org. ERIC Clearinghouse on Reading, English, and Communication*, Dec. 2003. www.ericdigests.org/2004-1/impact.htm. Accessed 13 Oct. 2004.

Online Book

List the entry by author name, title of book in italics, followed by the organization hosting the page.

Example:

Austen, Jane. *Pride and Prejudice*. Project Gutenberg, 2013. www.gutenberg.org/files/1342/1342-h/1342-h.htm. Accessed 14 Apr. 2014.

Article in an Online Magazine

Start with the author name, followed by the article name in quotation marks, title of the online magazine in italics, publisher name, publication date, medium, and date of access.

Example:

Remnick, David. "Putin and the Exile." *New Yorker*. NewYorker.com, 28 Apr. 2014. www.newyorker.com/magazine/2014/04/28/putin-and-the-exile. Accessed 28 Apr. 2014.[KLB1]

Article in an Online Scholarly Journal

Use the same format as a scholarly journal in print, but include the DOI or permalink and list the date of access.

Example:

Soliday, Mary. "From the Margins to the Mainstream: Reconceiving Remediation." *College Composition and Communication*, vol. 47, no. 1, 1996, pp. 85–100. www.jstor.org/stable/358275. Accessed 14 Jan. 2014.

Films

List films by their title in italics, followed by the director's name, then list performer names if relevant. Follow with the distributor and release year.

Example:

The Wolf of Wall Street. Directed by Martin Scorsese, performances by Leonardo DiCaprio, Jonah Hill, Matthew McConaughey, Kyle Chandler, and Jon Favreau. Paramount, 2013.

Broadcast Program

Begin with the title of the episode in quotation marks, then the name of the program in italics. Include the network name, call letters of the station and the city, and broadcast date.

Example:

"Unsolvable." *Brooklyn Nine-Nine.* Fox. WXMI, Grand Rapids, 19 Mar.
      2014.

Recorded Episode

List the entry by episode name in quotation marks, followed by the series name in italics, the distributor name, and the date of distribution.

Example:

"Tabula Rasa." *Criminal Minds: Season 3*, written by Jeff Davis, Dan
      Sworkin, and Jay Beattie, directed by Steve Boyum, Paramount,
      2010.

Music or Sound Recording

Begin with the artist name, then put song titles in quotation marks and album names in italics. If relevant, list composer or performer information after the album title. Include the recording company and publication date.

Examples:

The Beatles. *Revolver.* EMI, 2009.

Beyoncé. "Pray You Catch Me." *Lemonade,* Parkwood Entertainment,
      2016, www.beyonce.com/album/lemonade-visual-album/.
      Accessed 6 Feb. 2017.

Yo-Yo Ma. *Yo-Yo Ma Plays Ennio Morricone,* composed by Ennio
      Morricone, Sony Masterworks, 2010.

MLA Works Cited Page Example

Works Cited

Austen, Jane. *Emma*. Edited by George Justice, 4th Norton
    Critical Edition, W.W. Norton & Company, 2011.

---. *Mansfield Park*. Edited by Claudia L. Johnson, Norton
    Critical Edition. W. Norton & Company, 1998.

---. *Northanger Abbey: A Norton Critical Edition*. Edited by
    Susan Fraiman, W.W. Norton & Company, 2004.

---. *Persuasion*. Edited by Patricia Meyer Spacks, 2nd Norton
    Critical Edition, W.W. Norton & Company, 2012.

---. *Pride and Prejudice*. Edited by Donald Gray and Mary A.
    Favret, 4th Norton Critical Edition, W.W. Norton &
    Company, 2016.

---. *Sense and Sensibility*. Edited by Claudia L. Johnson, Norton
    Critical Edition, W.W. Norton & Company, 2001.

"Deconstructing Jane Austen." *On Story*. Season 7, episode
    16, PBS, 09 July 2017, www.pbs.org/video/
    deconstructing-jane-austen-p2hrdr/. Accessed on 03
    March 2019.

Fashioning the Victorians: A Critical Sourcebook. Edited by
    Rebecca N. Mitchell, Bloomsbury, 2018.

JASNA: Jane Austen Society of North America. 2019, jasna,org,
    Accessed on 03 March 2019.

Johnston, Freya. "Jane Austen's Past Lives." *The Cambridge Quarterly,* vol. 39, no. 2, 2010, pp.103-121. *JSTOR,* www.jstor.org/stable/43492506. Accessed on 03 March 2019.

This is an example of a journal article from a database.

Use stable links or DOIs when listing articles from databases.

Mitchell, Rebecca N. "Before and After: Punch, Steampunk, and Victorian Graphic Narrativity." *Drawing on the Victorians: The Palimpsest of Victorian and Neo-Victorian Graphic Texts*. Edited by Anna Maria Jones and Rebecca N. Mitchell. Ohio UP, 2017, pp 237-268.

This is an example of a chapter from a book with editors.

Peterson, Linda H. *Becoming a Woman of Letters: Myths of Authorship and Facts of the Victorian Market*. Princeton UP, 2009.

This is an example of a typical book.

CHICAGO STYLE (CMS)

The *Chicago Manual of Style*, or CMS, is a style guide created by the University of Chicago Press in the early twentieth century to establish formatting rules and bring consistency to their publications. Chicago style is most often used in the social sciences, arts, and humanities disciplines, such as history, art, philosophy, music, theatre, and religious studies. The most recent version, the 17th edition, was published in 2017.

CMS Guidelines for Formatting Papers

- The essay should be typed, double spaced in 12-point font size, in an easy-to-read font (such as Times New Roman) on 8.5-inch by 11-inch paper, with 1-inch margins on all sides.
- Include a title page, with the title centered a third of the way down the page, and the author's name and any other relevant information centered a few lines down from the title.
- Paginate the essay with a header in the top right corner of the page, beginning with the first page of the text (not the title page).
- Change underlining to italics. However, some underlining may need to be preserved, depending on the original material.
- Fix commas and periods relative to quotation marks (commas and periods go inside the quotation marks, not outside: "Chapter 1," rather than "Chapter 1", for example).
- Use em dashes (—) and ellipses (…) where appropriate, and make consistent.
- Replace hyphens (-) with en dashes (–) where appropriate.
- Leave one character space, rather than two spaces, between words and sentences and after colons.
- Use double spacing for text, except in block quotations. Use single spacing for footnotes and bibliography/reference lists, with a line to separate entries.
- The bibliography should begin on a new page, separate from the essay.

CMS General In-Text Citation and Footnote Rules

Note Numbers

Note reference numbers in text are superscripted. In the notes themselves, they are full size and followed by a period.

Example: Sedaris recalls, "We rode round and round the block on our pony, who groaned beneath the collective weight of our rich and overwhelming capacity for love and understanding."[1]

    1. David Sedaris, *Barrel Fever* (New York: Little, Brown, 1994), 9–10.

Notes should be numbered consecutively, beginning with 1, throughout the essay. A note number should generally be placed at the end of a sentence, a clause, or a quotation. The number follows any punctuation mark except for the dash, which it precedes.

Example: Many students argue that they work better when multitasking[5]— but research suggests this may not be the case.

Bibliographic citations are provided in footnotes (which appear at the bottom of a page), supplemented by a bibliography at the end of the work. Footnotes are numbered (but not superscripted) and correspond to superscripted note reference numbers in the text.

Full Footnote Citation

1. David Sedaris, *Barrel Fever* (New York: Little, Brown, 1994), 36–37.

Short Footnote Citation

1. Sedaris, *Barrel Fever*, 36–37.

Entry in a Bibliography

Sedaris, David. *Barrel Fever*. New York: Little, Brown. 1994.

If the same source is used consecutively in the text, the source should be formatted as usual for the first entry, and shortened citations should be used for each subsequent entry, until a different source is used within the text.

    1. David Sedaris, *Barrel Fever* (New York: Little, Brown, 1994), 36.

    2. Sedaris, 36.

    3. Sedaris, 37.

    4. David Bartholomae, "Inventing the University," in *When a Writer Can't Write*, ed. Mike Rose (New York: Guilford, 1985), 146.

Shortened Citations

Because the complete citation information is available in the corresponding bibliography, using the short footnote citation is acceptable in Chicago style.

The short form of a citation should include enough information to lead readers to the appropriate entry in the bibliography. The short form consists of the last name of the author, the main title of the work cited (usually shortened if more than four words), and the page number indicating where the information is located.

1. David Bartholomae, "Inventing the University," in *When a Writer Can't Write*, ed. Mike Rose (New York: Guilford, 1985), 146.

2. Bartholomae, "Inventing the University," 146.

Using In-Text Sources

It is important to provide a lead-in to source quotations, summaries, or paraphrases in the text, especially the first time the source is used. Lead-ins introduce the sources to the audience and provide a smooth transition from the author's writing to quotes, summaries, and paraphrases within the text.

Block Quotations

For quotations that are more than four lines in length, add an extra line space and indent 1/2 inch from the left margin. Place the whole quote, double spaced, within the new margin. Do not use quotation marks. The note number should come after the end punctuation.

Example:

As a builder, Lubbers was tasked to determine the most effective method for ensuring the safety and integrity of structures in a variety of climates. Lubbers's study found the following:

> The prevailing wind being forecast for January 2 will be from the southwest, and will reach speeds of up to 50 miles per hour. This wind has the potential to cause significant damage to the current construction. The building should be braced heavily to avoid collapse.[3]

Because the formatting for footnotes is consistent regardless of the medium being cited, not all areas that follow will include in-text citation examples.

Books

One Author

In-Text Citation

*Example: S*edaris recalls, "We rode round and round the block on our pony, who groaned beneath the collective weight of our rich and overwhelming capacity for love and understanding."[1]

Short Footnote Citation

Example: 1. Sedaris, Barrel Fever, 9–10.

Two to Three Authors

In-Text Citation

Example: Collins and Blum outline the way socioeconomics and politics outside the university also play a role in instigating the division between "basic" and "normal" writers.[3]

Short Footnote Citation

Example: 3. Collins and Blum, "Meanness and Failure," 14.

More than Three Authors

In-Text Citation

Example: Cincotta et al. assert that the launch of Sputnik expanded the competitive arena between the U.S. and the Soviet Union.[2]

Short Footnote Citation

Example: 2. Howard Cincotta et al., *An Outline of American History* (Washington DC: United States Information Agency, 1994).

Unknown Author

In-Text Citation

Example: A study determined that subjects lose time when switching from task to task.[4]

Short Footnote Citation

Example: 4. "Is Multitasking," 3.

Editor as Author

This type of source includes information written by the editor of an anthology, as in a foreword, introduction, afterword, or editor's notes. In these cases, the editor should be treated as the author of the source being used.

In-Text Citation

Example: Historian Joseph Hart asserts, "Ernesto Che Guevara's death at the hands of Bolivian troops last October enhanced a legend that began when he was Fidel Castro's right-hand man in Cuba."[5]

Short Footnote Citation

Example: 5. Hart, *Che,* 3.

Bibliography Entry

Example:

Hart, Joseph, ed. *Che: The Life, Death, and Afterlife of a Revolutionary.* New York: Thunder's Mouth Press, 2003.

Work in an Anthology

Please note that in these cases, the author of the work being quoted will be the primary reference in the text, the footnote, and the bibliography; the anthology editor(s) will also be included in the bibliography entry. A bibliography entry is included here as an example.

In-Text Citation

According to David Bartholomae, students who were less successful at this "invention" were considered basic writers; those who were more successful were not.[6]

Long Footnote Citation

Example: 6. David Bartholomae, "Inventing the University," in *When a Writer Can't Write,* ed. Mike Rose (New York: Guilford, 1985), 134–65.

Short Footnote Citation

Example: 6. Bartholomae, "Inventing the University," 146–47.

Bibliography Entry

Example:

Bartholomae, David. "Inventing the University." In *When a Writer Can't Write*, edited by Mike Rose, 134–65. New York: Guilford, 1985.

Periodicals

Article in a Journal
In-Text Citation

Example: Teacher-researchers Terence Collins and Melissa Blum pointed to the ways that socioeconomics and politics outside of the university also played a role in instigating the division between "basic" and "normal" writers.[7]

Short Footnote Citation

Example: 7. Collins and Blum, "Meanness and Failure," 14.

Article in a Magazine
Short Footnote Citation

Example: 8. Miller, "The Tyranny of the Test," 39.

Article in a Newspaper
Note that Chicago style does not require newspaper articles to be included in the bibliography, as long as they have been included in the text and footnotes. In these cases, however, the long footnote citation should be used.

Long Footnote Citation

Example: 9. Eric Pianin, "Use of Arsenic in Wood Products to End," *Washington Post,* February 13, 2002, final edition.

Entry in an Encyclopedia/Dictionary
Though cited in the footnotes, well-known reference materials are typically not cited in the bibliography, and the publication information is often omitted. If the publication is not the first edition, the edition number must be included.

Footnote Citation

Example: 10. *The Shorter Oxford English Dictionary,* 5th ed., s.v. "citation."

Electronic Sources

Article from an Online Periodical
Follow the same guidelines as those for printed articles and include the
URL or, if available, the digital object identifier (DOI).

Scholarly Journal
Example: 11. Adler-Kassner and Harrington, "Responsibility
and Composition's Future," 77. http://www.jstor.org/
discover/10.2307/27917885?uid=3739728&uid=2129
&uid=2&uid=70&uid=4&uid=3739256&sid=21104117601803

Article in a Popular Magazine
Example: 12. Remnick, "Putin and the Exile." http://www.newyorker.
com/talk/comment/2014/04/28/140428taco_talk_remnick

Online Newspaper Article
Remember that Chicago style does not require newspaper articles to be
included in the bibliography. Additionally, a URL need not be included
for online newspaper sources; however, the long footnote citation must be
used.

Long Footnote Citation

Example: 13. Felicia R. Lee, "Trying to Bring Baldwin's Complex Voice
Back," *New York Times,* April 24, 2014.

Online Encyclopedia/Dictionary Entry
Example: 14. Merriam-Webster Online, s.v. "citation," accessed April 26,
2014, http://www.merriam-webster.com/dictionary/citation.

Film
Example: 15. *Big Fish,* directed by Tim Burton. (2003; Culver City, CA:
Sony Home Pictures Entertainment, 2004), DVD.

Single Episode of a Television Series
Example: 16. Jeff Davis, Dan Sworkin, and Jay Beattie, "Tabula Rasa."
Criminal Minds, season 3, episode 19, directed by Steve Boyum, aired May
14, 2008. (Los Angeles, CA: Paramount, 2010), DVD.

Music or Sound Recording

Album

Example: 17. The Beatles, *Revolver,* EMI, 2009, CD.

Song

Example: 18. Miranda Lambert, vocal performance of "Heart Like Mine," by Travis Howard, Miranda Lambert, and Ashley Monroe, recorded 2009, on *Revolution,* Columbia Nashville, CD.

CMS Bibliography Page

A bibliography must be included at the end of the essay when using footnotes. All sources to be included—books, articles, websites—are arranged alphabetically by the last names of the authors (or, if no author or editor is given, alphabetically by the title or other identifying word or phrase).

- Entries should have a hanging indent—all lines after the first line of each entry should be indented one-half inch from the left margin.
- Bibliography entries should be alphabetized by the last name of the first author of each work, and the author should be listed in last name, first name format.
- List entries for multiple articles by the same author in chronological order, from earliest to most recent.
- Include the complete title, maintaining the capitalization and punctuation used in the original title.
- Italicize titles of longer works, such as books and journals, and put quotes around the titles of shorter works, such as journal articles or essays in edited collections. Do not italicize or underline them.

Formatting Bibliography Entries

Books

Information to include:
- Full name(s) of author(s) or editor(s)
- Complete title (including subtitle) of book and edition, if not the first
- Publication information (city, publisher, date)
- Page reference for a chapter, essay, or other section of a book. Complete book sources do not include page numbers in the bibliography.
- DOI or URL for online books

One Author

Sedaris, David. *Barrel Fever*. New York: Little, Brown, 1994.

Two Works by the Same Author

To list two or more works by the same author in the bibliography, use three em-dashes followed by a period in place of the author name for each entry after the first.

Example:

> Sedaris, David. *Barrel Fever*. New York: Little, Brown, 1994.
> ———. *Me Talk Pretty One Day*. New York: Little, Brown, 2000.

Two to Three Authors

Example:

Ward, Geoffrey, Ken Burns, and Kevin Baker. *Baseball: An Illustrated History*. New York: Alfred A. Knopf, Inc., 1996.

More than Three Authors

Example:

Barnes, Sonya et al. *Image Power: Top Image Experts Share What to Know to Look Your Best*. San Francisco: PowerDynamics Publishing, 2008.

Unknown Author

Example: Beowulf. New York: Farrar, Straus and Giroux, 2000.

Author with an Editor

Example:

Fielding, Henry. *Tom Jones*, edited by Sheridan Baker. New York: W.W. Norton & Company, Inc., 1994.

Editor with no Author

Example:

Hart, Joseph, ed. *Che: The Life, Death, and Afterlife of a Revolutionary*. New York: Thunder's Mouth Press, 2003.

Author with a Translator

Example:

Gide, André. *Lafcadio's Adventures*. Translated by Dorothy Bussy. New York: Vintage Books, 1953.

Work in an Anthology
Example:

Bartholomae, David. "Inventing the University." In *When a Writer Can't Write*, edited by Mike Rose, 134–65. New York: Guilford, 1985.

Periodicals

Information to Include:
- Full name(s) of author(s)
- Complete title (including subtitle) of article
- Title of periodical
- Volume number, issue number, date
- Page reference. Please note that if a page number is not available, a chapter or paragraph number or section header may be included.
- DOI or URL for online periodicals

Article in a Magazine
Example:

Miller, Jeremy. "The Tyranny of the Test: One Year as a Kaplan Coach in the Public Schools." *Harper's Magazine,* September 2008.

Article in Journal Paginated by Issue
Because journals are paginated by issue, begin with page one for each issue and include the issue number in the citation.

Example:

Collins, Terence and Melissa Blum. "Meanness and Failure: Sanctioning Basic Writers." *Journal of Basic Writing* 19, no. 1 (2000): 13–21.

Article in Journal Paginated by Volume
Journals paginated by volume begin with page one in issue one, and page numbers continue in issue two where issue one left off. Therefore, it is not necessary to include an issue number.

Example:

Sledd, Andrew. "Readin' not Riotin': The Politics of Literacy." *College English* 50 (1998): 495–508.

Electronic Sources

Include all available relevant publication information, including the URL or, if available, the DOI.

Website
Example:
National Public Radio. Morning Edition. http://www.npr.org/programs/
    morning-edition/

Web Page
Example:
Abdullah, Mardziah Hayati. "The Impact of Electronic Communication
    on Writing." *ERIC Clearinghouse on Reading, English, and
    Communication.* http://www.ericdigests.org/2004-1/impact.htm

Online Book
Example:
Austen, Jane. *Pride and Prejudice.* London, 1813.
    http://www.gutenberg.org/catalog/world/readfile?fk_files=3381939

Article from an Online Periodical
Example:
Soliday, Mary. "From the Margins to the Mainstream: Reconceiving
    Remediation." *College Composition and Communication 47,* no.
    1 (1996): 85–100. Accessed January 14, 2014. http://www.jstor.
    org/stable/358275

Popular Magazine
Example:
Remnick, David. "Putin and the Exile." *New Yorker,* April 28, 2014,
    accessed April 28, 2014, http://www.newyorker.com/talk/
    comment/2014/04/28/140428taco_talk_remnick

Scholarly Journal
Example:
Soliday, Mary. "From the Margins to the Mainstream: Reconceiving
    Remediation." *College Composition and Communication 47,* no.
    1 (1996): 85–100. Accessed January 14, 2014. http://www.jstor.
    org/stable/358275

Video/Film

Example:

Ewan McGregor, Ewan, Albert Finney, Jessica Lange, Billy Crudup, and
      Marion Cotillard. *Big Fish*. DVD. Directed by Tim Burton. Culver
      City: Sony Home Pictures Entertainment, 2003.

Broadcast Program

Begin with the writer(s), followed by the name of the program in italics.
Also include the director's name, broadcast date, distribution city and
company, and publication medium (e.g., Television, Radio).

Example:

Door, Daniel, and Michael Schur. *Brooklyn Nine-Nine*. Directed by Ken
      Whittingham. 2014. Los Angeles: NBCUniversal Television
      Distribution.

Television Episode

Begin with the writer(s), followed by the name of episode in quotation
marks and the program title in italics. Also include the season number,
episode number, director's name, original broadcast date, distribution
city and company, release date, and publication medium (e.g., Television,
Radio).

Example:

Davis, Jeff, Dan Sworkin, and Jay Beattie, "Tabula Rasa." *Criminal Minds*,
      season 3, episode 19, directed by Steve Boyum, aired May 14,
      2008. (Los Angeles: Paramount, 2010), DVD.

Sound Recording

List artist, title of album in italics, city and name of distribution company,
medium, and date of original release.

Example:

Lambert, Miranda. *Revolution*. Nashville: Columbia Nashville, CD.
      Recorded 2009.

CMS Bibliography Page Example

Bibliography

Door, Daniel, and Michael Schur. *Brooklyn Nine-Nine*. Directed by Ken Whittingham. 2014. Los Angeles: NBCUniversal Television Distribution.

Hart, Joseph, ed. *Che: The Life, Death, and Afterlife of a Revolutionary*. New York: Thunder's Mouth Press, 2003.

Remnick, David. "Putin and the Exile." *New Yorker*, April 28, 2014, accessed April 28, 2014, http://www.newyorker.com/talk/comment/2014/04/28/140428taco_talk_remnick

Soliday, Mary. "From the Margins to the Mainstream: Reconceiving Remediation." *College Composition and Communication 47*, no. 1 (1996): 85–100. Accessed January 14, 2014. http://www.jstor.org/stable/358275

APA STYLE

The *Publication Manual of the American Psychological Association*, or APA, is a style guide created by the American Psychological Association to establish formatting rules and bring consistency to their publications. Academic disciplines such as psychology, sociology, economics, business, and nursing, typically use APA style. The most recent publication, the 6th edition, was published in 2009 and updated in 2016.

APA Guidelines for Formatting Papers

- The essay should be typed, double spaced in 12-point font size, easy-to-read font (such as Times New Roman) on 8.5-inch by 11-inch paper, with 1-inch margins on all sides.
- Include a title page, with the title (in title case—upper- and lowercase letters) centered in the upper half of the page, with the author's name and any other relevant information centered below the title.
- Paginate the essay in a header in the right corner of the page, beginning with the title page.
- In a running header in the left corner of the page, include the essay title in all capital letters, beginning with the title page.
- Change underlining to italics. However, some underlining may need to be preserved, depending on the original material.
- Fix commas and periods relative to quotation marks (commas and periods go inside the quotation marks, not outside: "Chapter 1," rather than "Chapter 1", for example).
- Use em dashes (—) and ellipses (…) where appropriate, and make consistent.
- Replace hyphens (-) with en dashes (–) where appropriate.
- The second printing of the 6th edition of the APA style guide recommends, but does not require, using two spaces after the end punctuation of a sentence, for ease of readability.
- The reference page should begin on a new page, separate from the essay.

APA General In-Text Citation Rules

It is important to provide a lead-in to source quotations, summaries, or paraphrases in the text, especially the first time the source is used. Lead-ins introduce the sources to the audience and provide a smooth transition from the author's writing to quotes, summaries, and paraphrases within the text.

When referencing the title of a source in the text, capitalize all words that are four letters long or more in length: *Pride and Prejudice*. Short words that are verbs, nouns, pronouns, adjectives, and adverbs are exceptions to this rule: *Everything Is Illuminated*, *Brave New World*.

Italicize the titles of longer works such as books, movies, anthologies, television series, or albums: *American Idol*; *Anchorman*. Put quotation marks around the titles of shorter works within a text, such as journal articles, essays in anthologies, and song titles: "Red"; "Inventing the University."

In titles, capitalize both words in a hyphenated compound word: "The Tell-Tale Heart." Also capitalize the first word after a colon or dash: *The World Is Flat: A Brief History of the Twenty-First Century.*

Block Quotations

Begin quotations longer than 40 words on a new line, indented 1/2 inch from the left margin. Place the whole quote, double spaced, in the new margin. The parenthetical citation follows the end punctuation. Do not use quotation marks.

Example:

As a builder, Lubbers was tasked to determine the most effective method for ensuring the safety and integrity of structures in a variety of climates. Lubbers's (2013) study found the following:

> The prevailing wind being forecast for January 2 will be from the southwest, and will reach speeds of up to 50 miles per hour. This wind has the potential to cause significant damage to the current construction. The building should be braced heavily to avoid collapse. (p. 202)

Print Sources

A Work by a Single Author

If quoting directly from a work, include the author, year of publication, and the page number (preceded by "p.").

Example: Sedaris (1994) recalls, "We rode round and round the block on our pony, who groaned beneath the collective weight of our rich and overwhelming capacity for love and understanding" (p. 9–10).

Example: "We rode round and round the block on our pony, who groaned beneath the collective weight of our rich and overwhelming capacity for love and understanding" (Sedaris, 1994, p. 9–10).

Two Authors
List both authors whenever the work is cited. In the signal phrase, "and" should be used between the authors' names, while an ampersand should be used in the parentheses.

Example: Research by Collins and Blum (2000) outlines the way socioeconomics and politics outside the university also play a role in instigating the division between "basic" and "normal" writers (p. 14).

Example: Researcher scholars outline the way socioeconomics and politics outside the university also play a role in instigating the division between "basic" and "normal" writers (Collins & Blum, 2000, p. 14).

Three to Five Authors
List all the authors by last name the first time the source is cited. In later citations, use the first author's last name followed by "et al." The et in et al. should not be followed by a period.

Example: Ward, Burns, and Baker (1996) note, "The game varied from state to state, town to town, but town ball was the most popular" (p. 4).

Example: (Ward et al., 1996, p. 4)

Six or More Authors
Use the first author's last name, followed by et al.

Example: Cincotta et al. (1994) assert that the launch of Sputnik expanded the competitive arena between the U.S. and the Soviet Union (p. 68).

Unknown Author
If the author of a source is unknown, cite it using the title in the lead-in, or include an abbreviated version of the title in the parenthetical citation.

Example: A similar study determined that subjects lose time when switching from task to task ("Is Multitasking," 2001).

Authors with the Same Last Name

Include first initials with the last names to distinguish between the authors.

Example: (R. Jones, 2012; A. Jones, 2003)

Anthology

Example: According to David Bartholomae (1985), students who were less successful at this "invention" were considered basic writers; those who were more successful were not (p. 136).

Encyclopedia/Dictionary Entry

Example: A citation is a "quotation from or reference to a book, paper, or author." (Citation, 2002).

Indirect Sources

It may be necessary to use a work that has been cited in another source. For such indirect or secondary sources, use "as cited in" to indicate the primary source.

Example: According to Harvey Graff, "We do not know what we mean by literacy" (as cited in Lunsford, p. 252).

Electronic Sources

Web Sources

When possible, cite a web document the same as any other document.

Example: Bianchi (2007) suggests […]

If no author or date is given, cite the source using the title in the lead-in, or an abbreviated version of the title in the parenthetical citation, and use the abbreviation "n.d." ("no date").

Example: A similar study determined that subjects lost more time when switching from a familiar task to an unfamiliar task ("Is Multitasking," n.d.).

If no page number is available, include information that will help readers find the material being cited. If the paragraphs are numbered, use "para." and follow with the paragraph number.

Example: (Hubbard, 2014, para. 3).

Video/Film

Example: Big Fish, directed by Tim Burton, details the extraordinary life of Edward Bloom (2003).

Television

Example: In *Criminal Minds,* a suspect awakens from a coma with no memory of having committed the crimes of which he is accused ("Tabula Rasa").

APA Reference Page

The reference list, including all sources cited in the text, should appear on a separate page at the end of the text. The reference page should include the title References centered at the top of the page, with no bolding, underlining, italicizing, or quotation marks. All text in the reference section should be double spaced, with no additional spaces between entries.

- Entries should have a hanging indent—all lines after the first line of each entry should be indented 1/2 inch from the left margin.
- Reference list entries should be alphabetized by the last name of the first author of each work.
- For multiple articles by the same author, or authors listed in the same order, list the entries in chronological order, from earliest to most recent.
- Include the complete journal title, maintaining the capitalization and punctuation used in the original title.
- When referring to books, chapters, articles, or web pages, capitalize only the first letter of the first word of a title and subtitle, the first word after a colon or a dash in the title, and proper nouns. Do not capitalize the first letter of the second word in a hyphenated compound word.
- Italicize titles of longer works (books, films); do not italicize, underline, or put quotes around the titles of shorter works (articles, songs).

Single Author

Use the last name, initials format.

Example:

Shor, I. (1997). Our Apartheid: Writing instruction and inequality. *Journal of Basic Writing, 16*(1), 91–104.

Two Authors

List using the last name, initials format and use the ampersand (&) instead of "and."

Example:

Collins, T., & Blum, M. (2000). Meanness and failure: Sanctioning basic writers. *Journal of Basic Writing, 19*(1), 13–21.

Three to Seven Authors

Use the last name, initials format, separate authors' names using commas, and precede the final author name with an ampersand.

Example:

Rubenstein, J., Meyer, D., & Evans, J. (2001). Executive control of cognitive processes in task switching. *Journal of Experimental Psychology: Human Perception and Performance, 27*(4), 763–797.

More Than Seven Authors

Follow the same rules as a source with three to seven authors, but after the sixth author's name, use an ellipses rather than listing authors' names. Then list the final author name. In other words, there should not be more than seven names listed in the citation.

Example:

Barnes, S., Buchanan, W., Chenn, H., Elrick, H., Graham, J. A., King, D., . . . Law, K. (2008). Web site usability for the blind and low-vision user. *Image Power: Top Image Experts Share What to Know to Look Your Best*. San Francisco, CA: PowerDynamics Publishing.

Two or More Works by the Same Author

Use the last name, initials format for all entries and list the entries by the year, earliest first.

Example:

Child, L. (2007).
Child, L. (2010).

Unknown Author

When a source does not include an author's name, use the source's title (abbreviated, if the title is long) rather than an author's name.

Example:
Beowulf. (2000). New York, NY: Farrar, Straus and Giroux.

Books

For the publication location information, include the city and the two-letter state abbreviation (New York, NY).

Basic Format
Example: Sedaris, D. (1994). *Barrel fever*. New York, NY: Little, Brown.

Author with an Editor
Example:
Fielding, H. (1973). *Tom Jones*. S. Baker (Ed.). New York, NY: W. W.
      Norton & Company, Inc.

Editor as Author
Example:
Hart, J. (Ed.). (2003). *Che: The life, death, and afterlife of a
      revolutionary*. New York, NY: Thunder's Mouth Press.

Author with a Translator
Example:
Gide, A. (1953). *Lafcadio's adventures*. (D. Bussy, Trans.). New York, NY:
      Vintage Books. (Original work published 1914).

Work in an Anthology
Example:
Bartholomae, D. (1985). Inventing the university. In M. Rose (Ed.), *When
      a writer can't write* (pp. 134–165). New York, NY: Guilford.

Encyclopedia/Dictionary Entry
Example:
Citation. (2002). In *The shorter Oxford English dictionary* (5th ed.).
      Oxford, UK: Oxford University Press.

Periodicals

Authors are listed in last name, initial format, followed by the publication year in parentheses. The title of the article is in sentence case (only the first word and proper nouns are capitalized, with the exception of any proper nouns in the title). The title of the periodical is in title case and is followed by the volume number, both of which are in italics.

Article in a Magazine

Example:

Miller, J. (2008, September 2). The tyranny of the test: One year as a
　　　　Kaplan coach in the public schools. *Harper's Magazine*, 35–46.

Article in a Newspaper

Precede page numbers with p. (for a single page) or pp. (for more than one
page).

Example:

Timson, J. (2001, August 7). Stop all that multitasking, study suggests. *The
　　　　Toronto Star*, p. E2.

Article in Journal Paginated by Issue

Because journals paginated by issue, begin with page one for each issue,
and include the issue number in the citation. The parentheses and issue
number are not italicized or underlined.

Example:

Collins. T., & Blum, M. (2000). Meanness and failure: Sanctioning basic
　　　　writers. *Journal of Basic Writing, 19*(1), 13–21.

Article in Journal Paginated by Volume

Journals paginated by volume begin with page one in issue one, and page
numbers continue in issue two where issue one left off. Therefore, it is not
necessary to include an issue number.

Example:

Sledd, A. (1998). Readin' not riotin': The politics of literacy. *College
　　　　English, 50*, 495–508.

Electronic Sources

Follow the same guidelines for printed articles, and include all
available relevant information. Because websites are often updated and
the same information may not be available later, the DOI should be used
rather than the URL whenever possible.

Website

Example:

National Public Radio. (2014, January). Morning edition. Retrieved from
　　　　NPR website http://www.npr.org/programs/morning-edition/

Web Page
Example:

Abdullah, M. H. (2004, October). The impact of electronic communication on writing. *ERIC Clearinghouse on Reading, English, and Communication.* Retrieved from http://www.ericdigests. org/2004-1/impact.htm

Online Book
Example:

Austen, J. (1813). *Pride and prejudice.* Retrieved from http://www. gutenberg.org/catalog/world/readfile?fk_files=3381939

Article from an Online Magazine
Example:

Remnick, D. (2014, April 28). Putin and the exile. *New Yorker.* Retrieved from http://www.newyorker.com/talk/ comment/2014/04/28/140428taco_talk_remnick

Article from an Online Periodical
Example:

Soliday, M. (1996). From the margins to the mainstream: Reconceiving remediation. *College Composition and Communication, 47*(1). Retrieved from http://www.jstor.org/stable/358275

Video/Film
Example:

Cohen, B., Zanuck, R., & Jinks, D. (Producers), & Burton, T. (Director). (2003). *Big fish* [Motion picture]. USA: Sony Home Pictures Entertainment.

Broadcast Program
Example:

Goor, D. & Schur, M. (Writers), & Whittingham, K. (Director). (2014, March 19). Unsolvable. *Brooklyn nine-nine.* [Television series]. In D. Goor & M. Schur (Producers). Los Angeles, CA: NBCUniversal Television Distribution.

Television Episode
Example:

Davis, J., Sworkin, D., & Beattie, J. (Writers), & Boyum, S. (Director). (2008). Tabula rasa [Television series episode]. In E. A. Bernero (Producer), *Criminal minds.* Los Angeles, CA: Paramount.

Music or Sound Recording

Example:

Howard, T., Lambert, M., & Monroe, A. (2009). Heart like mine [Recorded by Miranda Lambert]. On *Revolution* [CD]. Nashville, TN: Columbia Nashville.

APA Reference Page Example

References

Davis, J., Sworkin, D., & Beattie, J. (Writers), & Boyum, S. (Director). (2008). Tabula rasa [Television series episode]. In E. A. Bernero (Producer), *Criminal minds*. Los Angeles, CA: Paramount.

Hart, J. (Ed.). (2003). *Che: The life, death, and afterlife of a revolutionary*. New York, NY: Thunder's Mouth Press.

Howard, T., Lambert, M., & Monroe, A. (2009). Heart like mine [Recorded by Miranda Lambert]. On *Revolution* [CD]. Nashville, TN: Columbia Nashville.

Soliday, M. (1996). From the margins to the mainstream: Reconceiving remediation. *College Composition and Communication, 47*(1). Retrieved from http://www.jstor.org/stable/358275

CITATION CHART

In-Text Citations

Print Sources	
Author Named in a Signal Phrase	
MLA	Sedaris recalls, "We rode round and round the block on our pony, who groaned beneath the collective weight of our rich and overwhelming capacity for love and understanding" (9–10).
CMS	Sedaris recalls, "We rode round and round the block on our pony, who groaned beneath the collective weight of our rich and overwhelming capacity for love and understanding."¹ 1. David Sedaris, *Barrel Fever* (New York: Little, Brown, 1994), 9–10.
APA	Sedaris (1994) recalls, "We rode round and round the block on our pony, who groaned beneath the collective weight of our rich and overwhelming capacity for love and understanding" (p. 9–10).
Author Not Named in a Signal Phrase	
MLA	"We rode round and round the block on our pony, who groaned beneath the collective weight of our rich and overwhelming capacity for love and understanding" (Sedaris 9–10).
CMS	"We rode round and round the block on our pony, who groaned beneath the collective weight of our rich and overwhelming capacity for love and understanding."¹ 1. David Sedaris, *Barrel Fever* (New York: Little, Brown, 1994), 9–10.
APA	"We rode round and round the block on our pony, who groaned beneath the collective weight of our rich and overwhelming capacity for love and understanding" (Sedaris, 1994, p. 9–10).

Two or Three Authors	
MLA	Collins and Blum outline the way socioeconomics and politics outside the university also play a role in instigating the division between "basic" and "normal" writers (14). The authors outline the way socioeconomics and politics outside the university also play a role in instigating the division between "basic" and "normal" writers (Collins and Blum 14).
CMS	Collins and Blum outline the way socioeconomics and politics outside the university also play a role in instigating the division between "basic" and "normal" writers.³
APA	Research by Collins and Blum (2000) outlines the way socioeconomics and politics outside the university also play a role in instigating the division between "basic" and "normal" writers (p. 14).
More Than Three Authors	
MLA	Cincotta et al. assert that the launch of Sputnik expanded the competitive arena between the U.S. and the Soviet Union (68). Historians assert that the launch of Sputnik expanded the competitive arena between the U.S. and the Soviet Union (Cincotta et al. 68). Cincotta, Brown, Burant, Green, Holden, and Marshall assert that the launch of Sputnik expanded the competitive arena between the U.S. and the Soviet Union (68).
CMS	Cincotta et al. assert that the launch of Sputnik expanded the competitive arena between the U.S. and the Soviet Union.² 2. Howard Cincotta et al., *An Outline of American History* (Washington D.C.: United States Information Agency, 1994).
APA	For the first use in text, list all author names: Cincotta, Brown, Burant, Green, Holden, and Marshall (1994) [...] For subsequent entries, use et al.: Cincotta et al. (1994) assert that the launch of Sputnik expanded the competitive arena between the U.S. and the Soviet Union (p. 68).

Unknown Author	
MLA	A study determined that subjects lose time when switching from task to task ("Is Multitasking" 3).
CMS	A study determined that subjects lose time when switching from task to task.[4] Short citation: 4. "Is Multitasking," 3.
APA	A similar study determined that subjects lose time when switching from task to task ("Is Multitasking," 2001, p. 3).
Work in an Anthology	
MLA	According to David Bartholomae, students who were less successful at this "invention" were considered basic writers; those who were more successful were not (136).
CMS	According to David Bartholomae, students who were less successful at this "invention" were considered basic writers; those who were more successful were not.[6] 6. David Bartholomae, "Inventing the University," in *When a Writer Can't Write*, ed. Mike Rose (New York: Guilford, 1985). 134–65.
APA	According to David Bartholomae (1985), students who were less successful at this "invention" were considered basic writers; those who were more successful were not (p. 136).
Encyclopedia/Dictionary	
MLA	A citation is a "quotation from or reference to a book, paper, or author." ("Citation").
CMS	A citation is a "quotation from or reference to a book, paper, or author."[10] Use footnote only; does not appear in bibliography. 10. *The Shorter Oxford English Dictionary*, 5th ed., s.v. "citation."
APA	A citation is a "quotation from or reference to a book, paper, or author." (Citation, 2002).

Electronic Sources	
Web Sources	
MLA	For electronic sources, include the first item (author name, title, etc.) in the Works Cited entry that corresponds to the citation. Do not include URLs in the text unless absolutely necessary; if included, make the URL as brief as possible, such as npr.org rather than http://www.npr.org.
CMS	When possible, follow the same guidelines for printed materials. Include all available information, including the URL or, if available, the digital object identifier (DOI), and use the long footnote citation format.
APA	When possible, cite a web document the same as any other document. If no author or date is given, cite it using the title in the lead-in, or include an abbreviated version of the title in the parenthetical citation, and use the abbreviation "n.d." ("no date"). If no page number is available, include information that will help readers find the material being cited. If the paragraphs are numbered, use "para." and follow with the paragraph number.
Film	
MLA	*Big Fish*, directed by Tim Burton, details the extraordinary life of Edward Bloom (2003).
CMS	*Big Fish*, directed by Tim Burton, details the extraordinary life of Edward Bloom.[15] 15. *Big Fish*, directed by Tim Burton (2003; Culver City, CA: Sony Home Pictures Entertainment, 2004), DVD.
APA	*Big Fish*, directed by Tim Burton, details the extraordinary life of Edward Bloom (2003).
Television	
MLA	In *Criminal Minds*, a suspect awakens from a coma with no memory of having committed the crimes of which he is accused ("Tabula Rasa").

CMS	In *Criminal Minds*, a suspect awakens from a coma with no memory of having committed the crimes of which he is accused.[16] 16. Jeff Davis, Dan Sworkin, and Jay Beattie, "Tabula Rasa." *Criminal Minds*, season 3, episode 19, directed by Steve Boyum, aired May 14, 2008. (Los Angeles, CA: Paramount, 2010), DVD.
APA	In *Criminal Minds*, a suspect awakens from a coma with no memory of having committed the crimes of which he is accused ("Tabula Rasa").

Source Citations

Books	
General Book Format	
MLA	Sedaris, David. *Barrel Fever*. Little, Brown, 1994.
CMS	Sedaris, David. *Barrel Fever*. New York: Little, Brown, 1994.
APA	Sedaris, D. (1994). *Barrel fever*. New York, NY: Little, Brown.
Two or Three Authors	
MLA	Ward, Geoffrey, Ken Burns, and Kevin Baker. *Baseball: An Illustrated History*. Alfred A. Knopf, Inc. 1996.
CMS	Ward, Geoffrey, Ken Burns, and Kevin Baker. *Baseball: An Illustrated History*. New York: Alfred A. Knopf, Inc., 1996.
APA	Ward, G., Burns, K., & Baker, K. (1996). *Baseball: An illustrated history*. New York: Alfred A Knopf, Inc.
More Than Three Authors	
MLA	Barnes, Sonya, et al. [...]
CMS	Barnes, Sonya et al. [...]
APA	Three to seven authors: Rubenstein, J., Meyer, D., & Evans, J. (2001). [...] More than seven authors: Barnes, S., Buchanan, W., Chenn, H., Elrick, H., Graham, J. A., King, D., . . . Law, K. (2008). [...]

Unknown Author	
MLA	*Beowulf*. Farrar, Straus and Giroux, 2000.
CMS	*Beowulf*. New York: Farrar, Straus and Giroux, 2000.
APA	*Beowulf*. (2000). New York, NY: Farrar, Straus and Giroux.
Author with an Editor	
MLA	Fielding, Henry. *Tom Jones*. Ed. Sheridan Baker. [...]
CMS	Fielding, Henry. *Tom Jones*, edited by Sheridan Baker. [...]
APA	Fielding, H. (1973). *Tom Jones*. S. Baker (Ed.). [...]
Editor with no Author	
MLA	*Impossibly Funky: A Cashiers du Cinemart Collection*. Ed. M. White. [...]
CMS	White, M., ed. [...]
APA	White, M. (Ed.). (2010). *Impossibly funky: A Cashiers du Cinemart collection*. [...]
Author with a Translator	
MLA	Gide, André. *Lafcadio's Adventures*. Trans. D. Bussy. [...]
CMS	Gide, André. *Lafcadio's Adventures*. Translated by Dorothy Bussy. [...]
APA	Gide, A. (1953). *Lafcadio's adventures*. (D. Bussy, Trans.). [...]
Work in an Anthology	
MLA	Bartholomae, David. "Inventing the University." *When a Writer Can't Write*, edited by Mike Rose, Guilford, 1985, pp. 134–65.
CMS	Bartholomae, David. "Inventing the University." In *When a Writer Can't Write*, edited by Mike Rose, 134–65. New York: Guilford, 1985.
APA	Bartholomae, D. (1985). Inventing the university. In M. Rose (Ed.), *When a writer can't write* (pp. 134–165). New York: Guilford.
Encyclopedia/Dictionary Entry	
MLA	"Citation." *The Shorter Oxford English Dictionary*. 5th ed., 2002.
CMS	In footnotes only.
APA	Citation. (2002). In *The shorter Oxford English dictionary*. (5th ed.).

Articles in Periodicals	
Magazine	
MLA	Miller, Jeremy. "The Tyranny of the Test: One Year as a Kaplan Coach in the Public Schools." *Harper's Magazine*, 2 Sept. 2008, pp. 35–46.
CMS	Miller, Jeremy. "The Tyranny of the Test: One Year as a Kaplan Coach in the Public Schools." *Harper's Magazine* September 2008.
APA	Miller, J. (2008, September 2). The tyranny of the test: One year as a Kaplan coach in the public schools. *Harper's Magazine*, 35–46.
Newspaper	
MLA	Timson, Judith. "Stop All That Multitasking, Study Suggests." *The Toronto Star*, 7 August 2001, p. E2.
CMS	In footnotes only.
APA	Timson, J. (2001, August 7). Stop all that multitasking, study suggests. *The Toronto Star*, p. E2.
Journal	
MLA	Collins, Terence, and Melissa Blum. "Meanness and Failure: Sanctioning Basic Writers." *Journal of Basic Writing*, vol. 19, no. 1, 2000, pp. 13–21.
CMS	Collins, Terence, and Melissa Blum. "Meanness and Failure: Sanctioning Basic Writers." *Journal of Basic Writing* 19, no. 1 (2000): 13–21.
APA	Collins, T., & Blum, M. (2000). Meanness and failure: Sanctioning basic writers. *Journal of Basic Writing*, 19(1), 13–21.
Electronic Sources	
Entire Website	
MLA	National Public Radio. *Morning Edition*. NPR, 14 January 2014. www.npr.org/programs/morning-edition. Accessed 14 Jan. 2014.
CMS	National Public Radio. *Morning Edition*. http://www.npr.org/programs/morning-edition/
APA	National Public Radio. (2014, January). *Morning edition*. Retrieved from NPR website http://www.npr.org/programs/morning-edition/

Page from a Website	
MLA	Abdullah, Mardziah Hayati. "The Impact of Electronic Communication on Writing." EricDigests.org. *ERIC Clearinghouse on Reading, English, and Communication*, 2003. www.ericdigests.org/2004-1/impact.htm. Accessed 13 Oct. 2004.
CMS	Abdullah, Mardziah Hayati. "The Impact of Electronic Communication on Writing." *ERIC Clearinghouse on Reading, English, and Communication.* http://www.ericdigests.org/2004-1/impact.htm
APA	Abdullah, M. H. (2004, October). The impact of electronic communication on writing. *ERIC Clearinghouse on Reading, English, and Communication.* Retrieved from http://www.ericdigests.org/2004-1/impact.htm

Online Book	
MLA	Austen, Jane. *Pride and Prejudice.* Project Gutenberg, 2013. www.gutenberg.org/catalog/world/readfile?fk_files=3381939. Accessed 14 Apr. 2014.
CMS	Austen, Jane. *Pride and Prejudice.* London, 1813. http://www.gutenberg.org/catalog/world/readfile?fk_files=3381939
APA	Austen, J. (1813). *Pride and prejudice.* Project Gutenberg. Retrieved from http://www.gutenberg.org/catalog/world/readfile?fk_files=3381939

Article in an Online Magazine/Newspaper	
MLA	Remnick, David. "Putin and the Exile." *New Yorker.* NewYorker.com, 28 Apr. 2014. www.newyorker.com/talk/comment/2014/04/28/140428taco_talk_remnick. Accessed 28 Apr. 2014.
CMS	Remnick, David. "Putin and the Exile." *New Yorker*, April 28, 2014, accessed April 28, 2014, http://www.newyorker.com/talk/comment/2014/04/28/140428taco_talk_remnick
APA	Remnick, D. (2014, April 28). Putin and the exile. *New Yorker.* Retrieved from http://www.newyorker.com/talk/comment/2014/04/28/140428taco_talk_remnick

Article in an Online Journal	
MLA	Soliday, Mary. "From the Margins to the Mainstream: Reconceiving Remediation." *College Composition and Communication*, vol. 47, no. 1, 1996, pp. 85–100. www.jstor.org/stable/358275. Accessed 14 Jan. 2014.
CMS	Soliday, Mary. "From the Margins to the Mainstream: Reconceiving Remediation." *College Composition and Communication 47*, no. 1 (1996): 85–100. Accessed January 14, 2014. http://www.jstor.org/stable/358275
APA	Soliday, M. (1996). From the margins to the mainstream: Reconceiving remediation. *College Composition and Communication, 47*(1). Retrieved from http://www.jstor.org/stable/358275
Film	
MLA	*Big Fish*. Directed by Tim Burton, performances by Ewan McGregor, Albert Finney, Jessica Lange, Billy Crudup, and Marion Cotillard, Columbia, 2003.
CMS	Ewan McGregor, Ewan, Albert Finney, Jessica Lange, Billy Crudup, and Marion Cotillard. *Big Fish*. DVD. Directed by Tim Burton. Culver City: Sony Home Pictures Entertainment, 2004.
APA	Cohen, B., Zanuck, R. & Jinks, D. (Producer), & Burton, T. (Director). (2003). *Big fish* [Motion picture]. USA: Sony Home Pictures Entertainment.
Television Program	
MLA	"Tabula Rasa." *Criminal Minds: Season 3*, written by Jeff Davis, Dan Sworkin, and Jay Beattie, directed by Steve Boyum, Paramount, 2010.
CMS	Davis, Jeff, Dan Sworkin, and Jay Beattie, "Tabula Rasa." *Criminal Minds*, season 3, episode 19, directed by Steve Boyum, aired May 14, 2008. (Los Angeles: Paramount, 2010), DVD.
APA	Davis, J., Sworkin, D., & Beattie, J. (Writers), & Boyum, S. (Director). (2008). Tabula rasa. In E.A. Bernero (Producer), *Criminal minds*. Los Angeles, CA: Paramount.

Sound Recording	
MLA	Miranda Lambert. "Heart Like Mine." *Revolution*. Sony, 2009.
CMS	Lambert, Miranda, *Revolution*, Nashville: Columbia Nashville, CD. Recorded 2009.
APA	Howard, T., Lambert, M., & Monroe, A. (2009). Heart like mine [Recorded by Miranda Lambert]. On *Revolution* [CD]. Nashville, TN: Columbia Nashville.

Citing in the Disciplines

CONCLUSION

The guidelines presented in this chapter were put together by style experts in different fields as a means of organizing and codifying secondary research. They differ, as Sarah Scott exhibited in her essay "Writing for the Field of Communication," not only as technical devices but also as rhetorical moves to cue the reader in what has come from outside of the author's own knowledge. Citation styles are important to moving the reading along in an efficient way that also engages the ongoing conversation of the discipline. You will find in your Composition II courses that we privilege disciplinary writing but often we ask you to cite in MLA style. This is simply because, while you will be uncovering the rhetorical conventions and discourses of your discipline, you will be doing so in an English class. As you will see in the next chapter, though, we have designed Composition II assignments to better help you situate yourself in your discipline and move forward as a scholar in that field.

In the following chapter, we walk you through different project overviews used for various assignments by Composition II instructors. Learning to read the genre of the assignment sheet is important to your success as a Composition II student, and your success in this course will determine how prepared you are to enter upper-level classes in your field to engage and produce scholarship. Each of the project overviews presented in the following chapter includes the instructor's notes on the pedagogical imperatives that informed the instructors as they composed the overviews, as well as their own goals for the assignments.

SAMPLE PAPERS IN DIFFERENT STYLES

In this section we provide you with examples of argumentative papers in three different formatting and documentation styles, APA (American Psychological Association), MLA (Modern Language Association), and CMS (Chicago Manual of Style). The goal is not only to provide you with models for citation in the different styles, but also to demonstrate the rhetorical and stylistic conventions of each. As you read through the samples, take time to notice the nuances of each style. Ask yourself how the varied parenthetical citations affect your reading. How does the use of footnotes allow the author to present information? Why are dates used in parenthetical citations in APA, but not in MLA? How do the requirements of each style represent what the field values most? Keep in mind that the conventions of each style were decided on by a board of experts in the field who believe that the current models (i.e., APA 6, CMS 17, MLA 8) are the best ways for research in their disciplines to be presented to readers. As you become more familiar with documentation styles, ask yourself if you agree with their choices.

WRITE a list of the courses you've taken so far in college. Which formatting and documentation style was used in each? Or, if you didn't write a paper in the course, which style is most commonly associated with the discipline? In which field and/ or style do you feel most comfortable writing and why?

Citing in the Disciplines

SAMPLE ESSAY IN MLA STYLE (8TH EDITION): ARGUMENTATIVE ESSAY

Amber Hatcher

Written for Geoffrey Clegg's Composition II class

. . . .

Amber Hatcher is a sophomore at Arkansas State University from Trumann, AR. When she is not in class or working, she enjoys reading, writing, and spending time with her husband.

Ever since she was four years old, she knew that her purpose in life was to write. She loves writing, not only to escape this world herself, but to let others escape as well. A quote from the Harry Potter *character Albus Dumbledore best describes how she feels about writing: "Words are, in my not-so-humble opinion, our most inexhaustible source of magic."*

The Assignment: Argumentative Essay

An argumentative essay is a formal piece in which the student demonstrates the ability to present a strong argument with attention to the rhetorical appeals, acknowledgement of and response to counterargument, and the ability to select, evaluate, and incorporate sources alongside original ideas.

This type of essay can cover anything from local or national politics to views on pop culture or issues currently in public discussion, but it also requires the author to go in search of evidence to support his or her views. This use of outside sources and research should strengthen and enhance the author's position. Authors should also investigate and discuss the views which oppose his or her argument, as this will bring clarity and a well-roundedness to the paper that allows the reader to judge the strength of the author's thesis.

Amber Hatcher

Mr. Clegg

ENG 1013

November 12, 2014

Muggles and Mudbloods and Creatures, Oh My!:

Racism in the Wizarding World

Racism has been a major problem in society for centuries. As a result, it has become a key theme in various works of literature, including the *Harry Potter* series. J.K. Rowling gives a clear insight into how racism has affected the world of humans by illustrating it through a world of magic. She divides the racism in the wizarding world into three major categories throughout the series.

The first category concerning racism in the *Harry Potter* series is the distinction between purebloods and non-purebloods. Lord Voldemort belonged to the Slytherin House while he attended Hogwarts School of Witchcraft and Wizardry. Out of all four houses (Gryffindor, Hufflepuff, Ravenclaw, and Slytherin), Slytherin housed several students who turned evil. The founder of the Slytherin House, Salazar Slytherin, only wanted pureblood students to attend Hogwarts. He did not think half-bloods or Muggle-borns were worthy enough to attend. He was outnumbered, however, as the other founders disagreed. Salazar Slytherin then built the Chamber of Secrets, killing students who were not pureblood. The other founders quickly discovered it, closing the Chamber and banishing Salazar Slytherin from Hogwarts. Years later, Tom Riddle, Salazar Slytherin's heir, reopened the Chamber and continued his legacy.

J.K. Rowling compares Lord Voldemort to Hitler. Both believed in racial purity, although they themselves were not what they believed to be pure. Hitler had Jewish blood, and Tom Riddle was a half-blood. Because of this, their killing people of their own blood "might have been an attempt to eliminate the part of himself he loathed" (Whited 3). She also says that the reopening of the Chamber "coincides with the opening of the Nazis' death chambers" (Whited 3). Racism transpired to the modern times of the wizarding world but not to the same extent, at first. Although the Chamber was once again reopened by Tom Riddle, racism dealt more with verbal abuse. This can be seen by Draco Malfoy's constant comments towards Hermione Granger, such as when he called her a "filthy little Mudblood" (*Chamber of Secrets* 112), which is a cruel name pureblood wizards use to describe Muggle-borns. It can also be seen by the portrait of Mrs. Black, Sirius' mother, who shouts obscenities like, "FILTHY HALF-BREEDS, BESMIRCHING THE HOUSE OF MY FATHERS" (*Order of the Phoenix* 179) and "MUDBLOODS! SCUM! CREATURES OF DIRT!" (*Order of the Phoenix* 180) whenever the Order of the Phoenix meets at Number Twelve, Grimmauld Place. However, after Dumbledore's death, Voldemort's followers, the Death Eaters, took over. The Ministry of Magic was going through drastic changes, including the addition of a new department called the "Muggle-Born Registration Commission". The proceedings to determine whether a witch or wizard was a Muggle-born were very much like the Salem Witch Trials. A witch or wizard would be accused of being a Muggle-born, even if they were half-bloods. At the hearing of Mary Cattermole, Yaxley, the new Minister of Magic, states, "The brats of Mudbloods do not stir our sympathies" (*Deathly* Hallows 259), and Dolores Umbridge tells her, "Wands only choose witches or wizards. You are not a witch" (*Deathly Hallows* 261). If any witch or wizard had Muggles in their family, they were registered as a Muggle-born.

The next manner of racism in the wizarding world is between wizards and magical creatures. There are several wizards who are kind to the magical beings (house-elves, werewolves, etc.), but there are others who treat them as though they are nothing. During the times of slavery in America, slaves were not viewed as equals. This is also the case for house-elves. Dobby, a house-elf, is a slave to the Malfoys. When Dobby arrives at the Dursleys, Harry suggests that Dobby sit down. Dobby bursts into tears, stating, "Dobby has *never* been asked to sit down by a wizard—like an equal" (*Chamber of Secrets* 13). Also like the slaves, house-elves are beaten whenever they do something wrong. Dobby tells Harry, "Dobby is always having to punish himself for something...Sometimes they reminds me to do extra punishments" (*Chamber of Secrets* 14).

Some wizards did not like werewolves or giants. In *Prisoner of Azkaban*, the first werewolf in the series is introduced as the new Defense Against the Dark Arts professor, Remus Lupin. While talking to Harry in the Shrieking Shack, he tells him that "other parents weren't likely to want their children exposed to me" (*Prisoner of Azkaban* 353). He also tells Harry "I have been shunned all my adult life, unable to find paid work because of what I am" (*Prisoner of Azkaban* 356). Even though he stayed away from people during the one week a month when he turned into a werewolf and started taking the Wolfsbane Potion so he could still have his human thoughts, people still feared him. Dolores Umbridge is one of the more racist wizards concerning magical creatures, which is seen when she calls the centaurs "Filthy half-breeds!...Beasts! Uncontrolled animals!" (*Order of the Phoenix* 755). These magical creatures are part-human or have human characteristics, but because they are a different race than the majority of wizards, they are prejudiced against.

The third and final type of racism in the Harry Potter series is between wizards and Muggles. Wizards know that Muggles exist, but "only a very limited number of Muggles know about Wizards" (Bertilsson 5). The ones that do typically consider them strange or fear them. The Dursleys are one of the groups of Muggles that hates wizards. This is why they ignore anything unusual and try to keep Harry from attending Hogwarts. Whenever they took him in, they "had hoped that if they kept Harry as downtrodden as possible, they would be able to squash the magic out of him" (*Prisoner of Azkaban* 2). Their attempts were unsuccessful, however. When Harry first received his acceptance letter into Hogwarts, Vernon tells Petunia, "I'm not having one in the house, Petunia! Didn't we swear when we took him in we'd stamp out this dangerous nonsense?" (*Sorcerer's Stone* 36). Harry cannot even say the word "magic" in their house without being yelled at. When Uncle Vernon tells Harry to give him a pan, Harry asks for the magic word. Uncle Vernon becomes angry, yelling "WHAT HAVE I TOLD YOU ABOUT SAYING THE 'M' WORD IN OUR HOUSE?" and "I WILL NOT TOLERATE MENTION OF YOUR ABNORMALITY UNDER THIS ROOF!" (*Chamber of Secrets* 2).

Some wizards, like Mr. Weasley, who works for the Misuse of Muggle Artifacts department in the Ministry of Magic, find Muggles fascinating. Other wizards, such as the Malfoys, look down upon Muggles and upon those Wizards who think there is nothing wrong with Muggles. Lucius Malfoy looks pointedly at Hermione's parents after Mr. Weasley states, "We have a very different idea of what disgraces the name of wizard" (*Chamber of Secrets* 62). Then, while talking about Mr. Weasley, Pius Thicknesse says, "If you ask me, the blood traitors are as bad as the

Citing in the Disciplines

Mudbloods" (*Deathly Hallows* 247). This goes back to the concept of Slytherins only believing that purebloods should be allowed an education at Hogwarts.

The same problems that were seen in our world during the Holocaust and during the times of slavery are also seen in J.K. Rowling's *Harry Potter* book series. Although Muggles and Wizards are both human, and although non-purebloods and magical creatures share the same magical powers as Wizards, they are looked down upon in the wizarding world. They are not seen as equals by many, even though they make up the majority of the population. J.K. Rowling reminds us that racism is still a problem today through her unforgettable world of characters.

However, some people suggest that J.K. Rowling is a racist herself. The main support for this claim is the fact that the majority of the characters in the *Harry Potter* series are white. According to a 2001 census of the United Kingdom, where the series takes place, "it puts the total of white people in the UK at 92.14%" (Adam). Harry would have graduated a few years before this, so it makes sense that white people form the bulk of the student body and staff. However, that is not the problem. The problem is that the characters who are of a different race are only minor characters. Take Dean Thomas and Angelina Johnson, for instance. They are both black students, but barely get any recognition. Angelina Johnson is only referred to when talking about Quidditch, the Wizarding sport, and Dean is best known as his role as Ginny Weasley's boyfriend before she finally ends up with Harry.

Another character is Cho Chang. She first appears in *Harry Potter and the Goblet of Fire*, when Harry develops a crush on her. They are together briefly in the next book, *Harry Potter and the Order of the Phoenix*. Rachel Rostad, a poet, rants in her video "To J.K. Rowling, From

Cho Chang" about four things. The first thing she rants about is how the non-white characters do not develop throughout the story. She even goes so far as to call the character "worthless" ("Rachel Rostad..."). The second is the way J.K. Rowling stereotyped Cho Chang. Most of the time, when someone hears the word "Asian," they automatically think of the word "nerd." At Hogwarts, the "nerdy" house is Ravenclaw, which coincidentally is the house that Cho Chang belongs to. The next point she brings up is the fact that students of other races make up a minority and that those students are only minor characters in the series whereas the main characters are white. In the video, she states "Between me, Dean, and the Indian twins, Hogwarts has like...five brown people? It doesn't matter; we're all minor characters. Nah, you're not racist!" ("Rachel Rostad..."). The last thing she rants about is her name. Cho Chang is a Chinese character whose name is made up of two Korean last names. Rachel Rostad compares this to "a Frenchman being named 'Garcia Sanchez'" ("Rachel Rostad..."). However, this is untrue as "Chang" is actually one of the fifty most common Chinese surnames. Additionally, it is not a fault in the story that the character wasn't developed. Rowling only developed the characters who were essential to the plot. Sure, Cho Chang could have been more developed, but she was only Harry's love interest for two out of seven of the books, so why would she have been?

One more character is often brought up when people start debating whether or not J.K. Rowling is racist. That character is Lavender Brown. In the first few films, where her character is of little significance, she is portrayed as black. Then, comes Harry Potter and the Half-Blood Prince. In that book/film, she becomes Ron Weasley's girlfriend. However, she is no longer black. Instead, she is played by a white actress. This does not necessarily mean that J.K. Rowling is racist. If anybody could be considered racist in this situation, it would be the person who selects the cast, because Rowling is not in charge of that, but that is only the case if the casting director did not actually want Lavender to be black. Since interracial relationships are typically looked down upon in today's society, that is semi-understandable. Most of the interracial relationships in movies I have seen are abusive, where the black boyfriend beats up his white girlfriend and goes to jail. Movies like those show interracial relationships in a negative way, corrupting a lot of minds into thinking that they are wrong. So, is that why Lavender Brown jumps from being black to white? Another, more plausible, explanation would just be that they needed a replacement. Maybe the actress that had played her in the first few movies just did not want to be her anymore, and the casting directors held auditions for a new Lavender. In situations like these, people tend to jump for the racist card rather than thinking through it rationally.

None of these characters make J.K. Rowling a racist. She was trying to create a semi-realistic aspect to her fantasy world. She made most of the students attending Hogwarts white, because the majority of the United Kingdom is white. She did not develop the minor characters because they weren't a part of the bigger picture, not just because they weren't white. That is a pure coincidence. In her novels, she doesn't state whether Lavender is black or white; the casting directors chose the actresses to play her in the movies for any variety of possible reasons.

What J.K. Rowling did was make the Wizarding world as realistic as possible by combining fiction with reality. She created an entire fantasy world based on her imagination but integrated so many aspects of the world around her that it came to life for the reader. No one paid attention to the fact that non-white characters were minor characters. They were more interested in the story. As people reread the books as they get older,

Citing in the Disciplines

they notice the race issues that she so cleverly hid in them. She shows us how terrible racism can be in our own world by illustrating how disastrous it is in the Wizarding world.

Citing in the Disciplines

Works Cited

Adam. "Did You Know Harry Potter was Racist." *WordPress*, 21 April
      2013, http://xdind.com/did-you-know-harry-potter-was-racist/

Bertilsson, Andreas. "Freaks and Muggles: Intolerance and Prejudice
      in *Harry Potter and the Philosopher's Stone*." Kristianstad U.,
      2007, pp. 3-17.

"Rachel Rostad-'To JK Rowling, from Cho Chang' (CUPSI 2013 Finals)."
      YouTube, uploaded by Button Poetry, 13 April 2013, https://
      www.youtube.com/watch?v=iFPWwx96Kew.

Rowling, J.K. *Harry Potter and the Sorcerer's Stone*. Scholastic, 1998.

_____. *Harry Potter and the Chamber of Secrets*. Scholastic, 1999.

_____. *Harry Potter and the Prisoner of Azkaban*. Scholastic, 1999.

_____. *Harry Potter and the Order of the Phoenix*. Scholastic,
      2003.

_____. *Harry Potter and the Deathly Hallows*. New York:
      Scholastic, 2007.

Whited, Lana. "1492, 1942, 1992: The Theme of Race in the Harry Potter
      Series." *The Looking Glass: New Perspectives on Children's
      Literature*, vol. 10, no. 1, 2006, pp. 1-7.

SAMPLE PAPER IN APA STYLE: AN OP-ED
Courtney Baker
Written for Dr. Marcus Tribbett's Composition II class

• • • • • • • • •

Courtney Baker is an avid outdoors-person hailing from Yellville, AR. Courtney enjoys hunting, fishing, kayaking, and camping. She carries this enjoyment of nature into her major in Agricultural Business.

Courtney finds that arranging her thoughts is easier in writing than in speaking. She utilizes an outlining and peer-review process when writing for an assignment. Courtney says that once an outline is in place for a work, "putting it into essay or short-story form is a breeze." When asked specifically about her piece, "Coal Mining: From Providing to Destroying," she credits peer revision with assisting in finalizing the essay printed here.

Courtney urges her fellow students to have their work reviewed by others. Her initial skepticism of visiting a writing tutor was assuaged when she realized that the tutor helped her "see gaps" in her writing that she "never would have recognized" on her own.

Assignment: The Op-Ed

Opposite Editorials or Op-Eds are short, journalistic, argument-driven pieces commonly found in newspapers and online publications. Op-Eds can focus on almost anything: cultural, political, social, humanitarian, educational, or financial issues; particular people, places, or events; or even another Op-Ed. While informative, an Op-Ed's main purpose is to persuade the reader to see the issue, event, person, or place as the writer does. In fact, some Op-Eds go a step further and, in addition to adding to the readers' previous understanding of the issue, also ask for the readers to take action, such as writing a congresswoman a letter or boycotting a restaurant because of its discriminatory practices.

For this assignment, you will write an Op-Ed on a contemporary issue of interest to you. As you begin your paper, consider what sources and perspectives are missing from the current conversations and media coverage of this topic; what sources, information, and perspectives will add ethos to your argument; and what voice you, the writer, should adopt to best persuade your readers. Keep in mind that the tone and style of an Op-Ed should be dependent on its content, purpose, and audience. Many Op-Eds adopt informal, conversational tones and utilize colloquialisms.

Note: As you will see, Courtney's essay has been formatted into APA style. As is customary in APA style, Courtney has not included signal phrases throughout her piece where she has integrated sources. Instead, she has included only the in-text citation.

Citing in the Disciplines

Coal Mining: From Providing to Destroying
Courtney Baker
Arkansas State University
Coal Mining: From Providing to Destroying

Coal mining in the Appalachian Mountains of West Virginia seems as natural as the abundant forest that covers the land. For many years these hills have provided the United States with its primary source of electricity—coal. Recently, however, tides have changed in the coal mining industry, bringing a new method of mining that is leaving West Virginians in a heated debate. It is called Mountaintop Removal Valley-Fill Mining (MRVF). This process involves blowing the top off of a mountain using dynamite and then "stripping" the seams of coal that lay exposed after the blast (Geller, 2009). The efficiency of this act has been outweighed by its perceived stigma, and the controversy that surrounds it sees no end in sight. Ultimately, as is revealed in the informative documentary *Coal Country,* MRVF is the center point in an argument that is less about the method and more about money, beliefs, and long-standing ways of life (Geller, 2009).

One of the initial rationales for developing MRVF was its potential to save money. As opposed to underground mining, surface mining does not require near as many workers (Geller, 2009). Therefore, the mining companies are obligated to pay far fewer employees, which is where the companies see the bulk of their savings. Additionally, without the use of underground mining tunnels, there are far fewer safety precautions that must be met. Being able to extract coal without having to build safe tunneling for employees allows companies to cut safety costs and ship out coal even quicker than before. Thus, MRVF is less costly and more efficient, which leads directly to increased profit.

The question remains though, if MRVF is so cheap and efficient, why isn't it the universally preferred mining method? This is because while MRVF is profitable for the mining companies, it has not been profitable for the workers. This is illustrated through the mining district in West

Virginia, which is no longer seeing profit from its rich resources. The money being made from the region's coal is being monopolized strictly within the mining companies (Geller, 2009). Because of this, communities in the mining hills are quickly fading, many workers have lost their jobs, and many of the towns are now ghost towns with only a few faithful citizens. These once-thriving mining communities provide the majority of our country's electricity, yet the people that live there are now struggling to get by while the mining companies are making record profits.

Further opposition to MRVF comes from those who find that it conflicts with their values, such as conservationists. Conservationists are leading contenders in the fight against surface mining because it destroys so much of the Appalachian mountain range. When the miners remove the mountaintops, the mountains are gone forever. Proponents of MRVF, such as the mining companies who utilize this method, argue that they "reclaim" the mountain after they are done. This involves spreading the discarded rock back along the mining site to resurface the location as best they can (Geller, 2009). This may technically be true, but these reclamation sites are easily distinguished from the rest of the forest because they do not allow for comparable diverse vegetative growth. Environmental advocates are fighting for the preservation of the mountains and the forests that thrive on them. The miners and the mining companies, however, see it a little differently, believing that, as long as the mountain is there and the coal is inside, they have the right to harvest it and use it to their benefit.

Somewhere in the middle of this debate are the coal miners, many of who want to mine the way they always have, the way their fathers did, and the way their fathers' fathers did. They argue that mining has been a way of life for hundreds of years and that without coal mining, the communities present in places like Appalachia will be literally nonexistent.

In the end, MRVF is more efficient and less costly for the coal mining companies, but at what cost to the mining communities and the environment? The costs to coal miners, citizens of mining districts, and the environment are grave and many. By cutting jobs, and destroying and polluting the land, MRVF and the coal mining companies are not helping preserve coal mining heritage or the environment, they are destroying them, and, ultimately, only helping themselves.

COAL MINING: FROM PROVIDING TO DESTROYING   5

References

Geller, P. (Director & Producer). (2009). *Coal Country*. [Motion picture].

United States: Evening Star Productions.

SAMPLE ESSAY IN CHICAGO STYLE: RESEARCH PAPER

William Kazyak

Written for Dr. Marcus Tribbett's Composition II class

• • • • • • • • •

William Kazyak was born in Baltimore, MD, but considers his hometown to be Manila, AR. He is an Arkansas State University Piano Performance Major who enjoys playing the piano, listening to classical music and early pop/rock, likes the Beach Boys, building model airplanes, and learning about the military. He also enjoys playing sports and running.

Though Kazyak has not always enjoyed writing, he explains, "There have been plenty of times in which what I wanted to say seemed to simply flow out onto the paper. I enjoy being able to put my thoughts down in an orderly manner and being able to refer back to them later."

Kazak's advice to Composition I and II students? "Good, thoughtful writing takes time—it is not something that can be rushed." He further advises his peers: "Plan the work! Spread it out over time so you are not rushing at the end, and organize it thoughtfully, with smooth transitions from one idea to the next. Take advantage of spare time such as weekends or breaks to think through the assignment and what you want to say."

The Assignment: The Research Paper

Consider a topic about which you would like to learn more. This topic can be anything, as long as it is a topic appropriate for scholarly inquiry. Students in the past have chosen a historical event, a social or cultural issue, or a scientific theory. Unlike a Researched Argument Paper, which requires you to develop an argumentative thesis about which reasonable people might disagree and support that thesis, and that thesis alone, in the body of your paper, a Research Paper asks you to inform yourself and your audience more broadly about the topic.

For this assignment, you will read several primary and secondary sources on your topic. Then, you will share your newly found knowledge in the form of a research paper, integrating scholarly sources into your paper using summary, paraphrase, and quotation. You will need to choose an organization that supports your readers' likely expertise regarding the topic, recognizing that your readers, the A-State University community, are bright and know a lot about many things, but they don't know everything. To this end, you may need to provide background information, identify important concepts and people, and define key terms.

Note: *As you will see, William's essay has been formatted into Chicago style. As is customary in Chicago style, William has included footnotes and a bibliography.*

William Kazyak

Composition II

Professor Tribbett

March 29, 2014

Deception and Destruction: Operation Fortitude
and the Allied Aerial Support for Operation Overlord

"We're going in alone, and I don't think we're coming back" rang
the words of Wing Commander Josef "Pips" Priller to his wingman,
Sergeant Heinz Wodarczyk, on June 6, 1944 with the bleak prospect of
their mission. They were embarking on a mission to disrupt, as far as they
could, the massive Allied landings on the Normandy beaches. They would
be flying into an area infested with hostile aircraft and anti-aircraft guns
that would surely shoot them out of the sky before they had a chance to
mount an attack. However, Priller and his wingman did make one pass
on Sword Beach.[1] It was the only attack made by the German Luftwaffe
(air force) on that historic day.[2] The reasons for this have become clear
over the decades since D-Day. By June 6, 1944, the Allies had whittled
the Luftwaffe down to a mere shadow of its early war glory and gained
complete superiority in the skies over Europe.

Air superiority itself, however, did not ensure the success of Operation
Overlord. At this point, even without air superiority, the Germans
possessed the means for a successful counterattack that could dislodge
the allies and throw them back into the sea. The reasons for their lack of
appropriate reaction to the invasion stemmed primarily from the fact that
the Allies had deceived them concerning the date, location, and force of the

1 Wynn, *Prelude to Overlord*, 138.
2 McFarland, "Air Combat," 11.

invasion through a series of elaborate and ingenious ruses. Code named Operation Fortitude, these efforts, in conjunction with aerial dominance by the Allies, provided critical support to Operation Overlord.

Operation Fortitude was officially put into action on February 23, 1944; less than four months prior to the date of the Overlord landings.[3] Anthony Cave Brown, in his book *Bodyguard of Lies*, gives a very direct and comprehensive statement of the goals of Fortitude. Fortitude was designed to: 1) cause the Germans to make strategic errors by threatening Norway, 2) mislead them concerning the location and date of Overlord, and 3) cause them to make poor strategic decisions after the landings by threatening the Pas de Calais region of France.[4]

The first goal of Operation Fortitude was accomplished by one of its two distinct operations, Fortitude North. Norway was a valuable strategic asset for Germany because it was one of their primary naval bases.[5]

3 Hinsley, "Deception," 174.
4 Brown, *Bodyguard of Lies,* 460.
5 Penrose, *The D-Day Companion,* 61.

Germany had a total of twenty-seven divisions of soldiers stationed in Northwest Europe (including Norway) to guard against an attack there.[6] These soldiers, had they been allowed to be used to reinforce France, could have caused major problems for Overlord, so the Allies had to find a way to keep them in Northwest Europe. Fortunately, Adolf Hitler himself was obsessed with Norway as an asset and was determined to keep it at all costs.[7] This made it relatively easy for the planners of Fortitude North to figure out how to pin down German forces in Norway. In conjunction with the Soviets, the Allies devised a plan to assemble a fake army in Scotland, thereby threatening a two-front invasion. Brown relates the assembly of this army in great detail. In Scotland, the Allies utilized a number of ingenious methods to simulate the build-up of forces of what was supposed to be the British 4th Army Group. The primary method used was bogus radio traffic. A few skilled radio units could move around broadcasting messages to each other that sounded exactly like communications between different units of an army group. This was supplemented by calculated leaks to newspapers, radio, and other press about events supposedly going on involving units in the 4th army. Other methods included placing ships and dummy aircraft in plain view of German recon planes, as well as the purchase of £500,000 of Scandinavian securities by the British; actions that were interpreted by the Germans to mean that an invasion of Northwest Europe was imminent. But the icing on the cake came from agents of Britain's then-secret "XX-Committee," or Double Cross System. XX's agents "Mutt" and "Jeff" both played key roles in Fortitude North by feeding the Germans a mix of false and true information. One of their reports was that Soviet intelligence officer Klementi Budyenny had come to England to discuss the

6 Brown, *Bodyguard of Lies,* 460.
7 Ibid., 462.

joint invasion of Norway. In reality, Budyenny did come to England, but only to discuss the role the Russians were to play in Fortitude.[8]

Fortitude South was implemented in much the same way as Fortitude North, only it was more involved and played on more of the Germans' predispositions. In the first place, Fortitude South directly threatened an invasion in the Pas de Calais region of France.[9] This part of France was separated from England (specifically Dover) by a mere 25 miles of water.[10] This was the shortest distance between France and England, and the Germans knew this as well as the Allies. The Germans, for their part, built up their strength here, and even stationed the 15th Army, their best soldiers on the Western Front, at Calais.[11] The Allies, for their part, were determined to see to it that those defenses stayed in Calais and were not redeployed to Normandy; at least not until a significant and irreversible build up had occurred.[12] Here again, the Allies turned to bogus armies for this effort. They built-up FUSAG, the First U. S. Army Group, around the command of Lt. General George S. Patton, Jr., an American whom the Germans considered the best Allied commander and expected to lead the invasion.[13] The assembly of FUSAG utilized essentially the same methods as the assembly of 4th Army. Dummy ships, aircraft, tanks and installations as well as calculated press releases and skilled radio operators transmitting build-up communications all contributed to the FUSAG scam, and as with the 4th Army deception, XX's agents added further to the confusion. The agents code-named "Garbo" (who was the Germans'

---

8 Ibid., 464-468.
9 Hinsley, "Deception," 174.
10 Drez, *Voices of D-Day*, 19.
11 Brown, *Bodyguard of Lies*, 461.
12 Penrose, *The D-Day Companion,* 56.
13 Penrose, *The D-Day Companion,* 56. Ambrose, "Eisenhower," 267.

most trusted agent) and "Tricycle" played important parts in the scheme, primarily by feeding false information to the Germans.[14]

Fortitude South had one more key aspect: aerial deception. Prior to D-Day, the Allies implemented a strategy to disable as much of the German war effort as possible. This included coastal defenses, airfields, and rail targets.[15] However, if they bombed one area more heavily than the other, the Germans may have deduced the location of the invasion from that strategy. The Allies, therefore, proceeded to attack targets in Calais twice as hard as targets in Normandy in an extension of the effort to make the Germans look to Calais for the invasion.[16] A second role that aircraft played in Fortitude came in a revolutionary new area of warfare: electronic countermeasures. By D-Day, the Allies had developed radar-jamming devices like Window, Moonshine, and Filberts, and had discovered that when properly used in conjunction, they would paint a picture on radar screens of an invasion fleet headed in a certain direction. These methods were perfected and put into practice for D-Day.[17]

The Allies had obviously taken great pains to conceal their true intentions concerning Overlord; now the question was whether or not the Germans would take the bait. *The D-Day Companion*, edited by Jane Penrose, states that Fortitude did not cause the Germans to alter their battle plans; however, this statement is misleading on the surface.[18] According to Brown, the Germans actually reinforced their Norwegian garrisons.[19] Nevertheless, little response to Fortitude was observed prior to D-Day. It was only after the landings that the staggering success of this astronomical effort was felt. The Germans hesitated to

---

14 Brown, *Bodyguard of Lies*, 480-489.
15 Brown, *Bodyguard of Lies*, 521.
16 Penrose, *The D-Day Companion*, 62.
17 Brown, *Bodyguard of Lies*, 524-526.
18 Penrose, *The D-Day Companion,* 63.
19 Brown, *Bodyguard of Lies*, 472.

reinforce Normandy for as long as two weeks.[20] Thanks to reports from "Garbo" that Normandy was a fake and FUSAG still planned to invade Calais, the Germans not only failed to reinforce Normandy, but they recalled two Panzer divisions and an infantry division that were already en-route to Normandy and sent them to Calais.[21] The inflated order of battle that "Tricycle" had given the Germans prior to D-Day also came into play by conning the Germans into thinking that most of the Allies' forces were still in England waiting to pounce on Calais the minute they withdrew any forces from there.[22] Overall, Fortitude kept the Germans groping in the dark for the Allies' real intentions until the middle of July, and by that time Allied forces had built-up to the point where it would have been difficult at best to dislodge them.[23]

While this battle of wits was raging, another crucial battle was erupting in the skies over Europe as a prerequisite to D-Day. This was the battle for air superiority. Air superiority had been a major factor in another planned amphibious invasion earlier in the war: Operation Sea Lion, the German plan to invade England.[24] The Germans, however, had not been able to wrest control of the skies over Southern England and the English Channel from the British Royal Air Force, and now they were facing the same challenges that the RAF had met four years earlier. Both the Allies and the Germans knew how crucial air superiority was, and both fought tenaciously for it.

Dwight D. Eisenhower, the Supreme Allied Commander, had promised his troops prior to D-Day that, "if you see fighting aircraft over you, they will be ours."[25] This bold promise was not an empty one. Since

---

20 Budiansky, "The Art of the Double Cross," 44.
21 Ibid., 44.
22 Brown, *Bodyguard of Lies*, 487-499.
23 Penrose, *The D-Day Companion*, 64.
24 Galland, "The First and the Last," 10-16.
25 McFarland, "Air Combat," 12.

1943, Allied Bomber crews had been waging a costly war of attrition with the Germans in their attempts to knock out German industry.[26] The arrival of long-range fighter escorts (in particular the P-51 Mustang, which was superior to the German aircraft in nearly every aspect) changed the war entirely.[27] Now it was the Germans who were suffering catastrophic losses, in terms of both pilots and aircraft. At the beginning of 1944, the Germans had 2,395 fighter pilots available for combat, with about half of them actually ready to engage in battle. By the middle of the year, ninety-nine percent of these pilots had been lost.[28] Their aircraft strength had hardly fared better. By D-Day, only forty percent of their total available aircraft (on all fronts) were operable, and on top of that they had pulled the majority of their fighters back to Germany.[29] The German Third Air Force in France was left with around 100 fighters to stop an Allied onslaught of 6,000-7000 bombers and fighters.[30] Even when the Germans did order their fighters in Germany to head to France, P-51 patrols intercepted and shot down between thirty and fifty percent of them.[31] Those that escaped the dogfights often crashed before reaching their bases due to poor cross country training of the pilots.[32] Fourteen days after the start of the invasion, the German fighter reinforcements were no longer able to fight and were pulled back to Germany.[33]

While Allied long-range fighters systematically decimated the Luftwaffe, Allied bombers and fighter-bombers were waging an important tactical war to destroy the Germans' ability to reinforce Normandy. The primary aspect of this battle, known as the Transportation Plan, was aimed

---

26 Wynn, *Prelude to Overlord*, 14.
27 Penrose, *The D-Day Companion*, 118.
28 Ibid., 120-121.
29 Galland, *The First and the Last*, 211. Penrose, *The D-Day Companion*, 117).
30 Galland, *The First and the Last*, 213.
31 McFarland, "Air Combat," 11.
32 Galland, *The First and the Last*, 215.
33 Ibid., 219.

at obliterating the French Railway system. The Germans relied heavily on this system for movement of troops and especially armored vehicles, such as tanks.[34] Beginning in March, 1944, the Allies pulverized thirty-six rail yards with no less than 139 raids. After May 20, 1944, the juggernaut of the Allied air forces was unleashed against railway bridges and even individual trains. By D-Day, every bridge over the Seine River from Conflans to Rouen, a total of no less than thirty-five crossings, had been reduced to chunks of concrete and steel protruding from the water.[35]

The Transportation Plan effectively neutralized the Germans' ability to reinforce Normandy. The Allies had successfully disabled the Germans' quickest and most effective means of supply and reinforcement. Panzer divisions trying to get to Normandy, now forced to travel under their own power, took anywhere from five days to three weeks to arrive in the battle zone. Even then, their transit was turned into a nightmare as Allied fighter-bombers destroyed anything that moved (tanks were especially prime targets).[36]

On D-Day itself, the Allies made sure that the air over the fleet and the beaches were well covered. During the daytime, P-38 Lightning fighters guarded the shipping lanes between France and England, and when night arrived, the RAF took over the task with a force of night fighters. The beaches were covered by RAF Spitfire fighters down low and by USAAF P-47 Thunderbolt fighters up high. The Allies even added an extra insurance to the landings by sending P-51 Mustangs and more P-38s to form a kill zone further inland with the aim of stopping any German planes long before they got to the beaches. P-47s and RAF Typhoon fighter-bombers provided close support to the troops by hitting tanks

34 Ambrose, "Eisenhower," 270.
35 Wynn, *Prelude to an Overlord,* 104-106.
36 Penrose, *The D-Day Companion,* 123.

and other vehicles and by neutralizing threats when called upon by the ground forces. Only two Luftwaffe aircraft (the Fw-190 fighters flown by Priller and Wodarczyk) got through to the Allied landing zone; a stunning fulfillment of Eisenhower's promise.[37]

On July 31, 1944, the Allies broke out of Saint-Lô, France, making Overlord an official success.[38] This success, though, came about largely due to the cunning of Allied intelligence officers and the skill and bravery of Allied airmen. Operation Fortitude's stunning success in pinning down German forces elsewhere in Europe and in delaying orders to reinforce Normandy played a major role in buying the Allies the precious time they needed to consolidate their foothold in Europe, and Allied air power supplemented this by destroying both the Luftwaffe and the Germans' means of transportation. Looking back on Overlord, Eisenhower stated that "Without the overwhelming mastery of the air which we attained by that time, our assault on the Continent would have been a most hazardous, if not impossible undertaking," and Adolf Galland, the German Fighter Commander at the time of the invasion, echoes this statement in his book *The First and the Last*.[39] When Priller and Wodarczyk returned to their base after their bold attack on Sword beach, the best they could really do was sit back and look helplessly on as the Third Reich began to crumble under the massive Allied juggernaut; a juggernaut enabled and supported by a brilliant combination of deception and destruction.

---

37 Wynn, *Prelude to Overlord*, 137-138.
38 Galland, *The First and the Last*, 225.
39 Wynn, *Prelude to Overlord*, 26. Galland, *The First and the Last*, 225.

Citing in the Disciplines

Bibliography

Ambrose, Stephen E. "Eisenhower, the Intelligence Community, and the
D-Day Invasion." *The Wisconsin Magazine of History* 64, no. 4
(1981): 261-277.

Brown, Anthony Cave. *Bodyguard of Lies*. New York, NY: Harper and
Row, Publishers, Inc., 1975.

Budiansky, Stephen. "The Art of the Double Cross." *World War II* 24, no.1
(2009): 38-45.

Drez, Ronald J., ed. *Voices of D-Day*. Baton Rouge, LA: Louisiana State
University Press, 1994.

Galland, Adolf. *The First and the Last: The Rise and Fall of the German
Fighter Forces, 1938-1945,* 2nd ed. Translated by Mervyn Savill.
Cutchogue, NY: Buccaneer Books, 1954.

Hinsley, F. H. "Deception." *The D-Day Encyclopedia*. 1994.

McFarland, Stephen L. "Air Combat." *The D-Day Encyclopedia*. 1994.

Penrose, Jane, ed. *The D-Day Companion*. Oxford, United Kingdom:
Osprey Publishing, 2004.

Ryan, Cornelius. *The Longest Day: June 6, 1944*. New York, NY: Simon
and Schuster, 1959.Wynn, Humphrey and Susan Young. *Prelude
to Overlord: an account of the air   operations which preceded
and supported Operation Overlord, the Allied landings in
Normandy on D-Day, 6th of June 1944*. Novato, CA: Presidio
Press, 1984.

Sample Assignment Overviews

INTRODUCTION TO ASSIGNMENT OVERVIEWS

The Assignment Overview is a very important genre in the field and the practice of education. In the overview, or the assignment sheet, instructors need to address several stakeholders and audiences at once; first and foremost, though, is our students. The assignment sheet is primarily a way of communicating to you our goals and expectations. Additionally, we should at least be considering the learning outcomes that the department or curricular committee has set for the course, as well as determining, to some degree, how we will evaluate or assess how the students meet these outcomes. On yet another level, many instructors (and often many committees) will revisit assignment sheets from the prior year to assess what students responded to well, found clear, and enjoyed, versus what might need a little tweaking.

In A Note to Readers, we explained what drove us as a department to develop this new curriculum, how we determined our goals and outcomes for the course, and how these translated to each of the assignments. As you read through the overviews and assignments we provide here, read them critically to determine how each overview expresses our desires for the course, our expectations, and our goals for your learning. If the goal or outcome for the assignment seems unclear, engage in this conversation with your instructor or in your groups to try to clarify. Ask questions to help investigate further. Think about what skills the assignment might be asking you to develop, what these skills look like in relation to the learning outcomes of the assignment and the course, and maybe how the assignment might push you to do better research, form stronger arguments, or communicate in new genres or to new audiences.

A NOTE ON GROUP WORK

As you have realized by now, this course is highly collaborative and much of the work you will complete will occur in your group. This will require you to develop lots of different skills: organization, communication, time management, and perhaps anger management. We did not design this course with the intention of perpetuating the standard group work trope in which one or two students carry the group's weight. In fact, we hope we have set in place several safeguards against this pattern. Instead, what we hope to achieve is that each group member can identify their own strengths and weaknesses for the group, and labor can be divided as such. Some members may demonstrate leadership and organizational abilities that others may lack, and that's okay. Others will have a talent for proofreading, research, or content development. Use your strengths in the group, and work on developing your weaknesses. Most of all, though there may be frustrations as you work, remember that you are human, as are the members of your group. You might drop the ball, they might drop the ball, and someone somewhere will have to pick up some slack to some degree. So be patient, be considerate and compassionate, but also be wary: if someone establishes a pattern of not completing their work, or doing the absolute bare minimum, alert your instructor, but overall try to remain compassionate.

Sample Assignment Overviews

Unit I:
The Proposal

INTRODUCTION TO THE PROPOSAL

When designing the proposal, we recognized that composition courses are made up of students with diverse personal, professional, and educational backgrounds. While our responsibility as instructors is to provide each of you with the necessary tools to participate in academic discourses as you continue your university career, we also wanted to provide a space where you could explore your interests in, and impact on, modern public discourses.

Maybe you're concerned with current political ideologies or curious about the emerging effects of global climate change; perhaps you want to know more about the ways in which pop culture can be used to increase our understanding of academic pursuits. Whatever your passions, the proposal is a project that will allow you to discuss valuable topics, negotiate potentially differing opinions and approaches to problem-solving, and explore your discipline's participation in kairotic issues.

Purpose

The proposal is a genre used in several settings, both academic and professional. Perhaps the most recognizable are those from business fields and scientific research. Typically though, writers will outline the background of a selected problem, their methods of research, and their proposed solution to said problem. For Composition II, students will work in collaborative, interdisciplinary groups to create a variation of this prevalent genre. This unit will prepare students to write about modern civic, social, and academic debates by writing a proposal that identifies a debatable question they want to answer, why that issue is relevant, and who the stakeholders are in the debate. This assignment will aid students in the invention process by asking them to articulate the rhetorical situation they will respond to in the following units.

Audience

The intended audience for the proposal is the instructor but students will be asked to discuss their projects with their classmates.

Content and Requirements

Proposals will:

- Identify a debatable issue the group wants to research this semester;
- Articulate why the issue is important to a modern audience;
- Introduce the disciplinary focus each group member will take in units two and three; and
- Answer the following questions:
  - Why does this issue matter?
  - Who cares about it? Who might engage with your work?
  - What gives you the authority to say something about it?
  - How are you going to answer the big question?
  - What kind of answers do you anticipate?

Organization and Format

The proposal should:

- Be roughly 750 words;
- Be written collaboratively;
- Use standard MLA formatting; and
- Include a published bibliography on your topic.
  Strategies for Composing a Successful Proposal
- Discuss potential stakeholders invested in the debate.
- Locate and summarize previous research on the topic.
- Be open to the ideas of your group mates and willing to compromise.

Strategies for Composing a Successful Proposal

- Discuss potential stakeholders invested in the debate.
- Locate and summarize previous research on the topic.
- Be open to the ideas of your group mates and willing to compromise.

FROM PROBLEMS TO SOURCES

Wayne C. Booth, Gregory G. Colomb, Joseph M. Williams, Joseph Bizup, William T. Fitzgerald

· · · · · · · · ·

If you have not yet formulated a research question, you may have to spend time reading generally on your topic to find one. But if you have a question and at least one promising answer (the philosopher C. S. Peirce called it a *hypothesis on probation*), you can start looking for data to test it.

To do that efficiently, you need to have a plan. If you plunge into any and all sources on your topic, you risk losing yourself in an endless trail of books and articles. To be sure, aimless browsing can be fun, even productive. We indulge in it a lot. Many important discoveries have begun in a chance encounter with an unexpected idea. But if you have a deadline, you need more than luck to find good sources in time: you have to search systematically for those sources that will help you advance your research project or, just as usefully, challenge you to improve it. In this chapter, we discuss different ways you can use sources in your research, how you can find useful sources, and how you can winnow your sources to a manageable number. In the next chapter, we focus on how to use sources in your writing.

5.1 THREE KINDS OF SOURCES AND THEIR USES

Sources are conventionally categorized into three kinds: primary, secondary, and tertiary. Their boundaries are fuzzy, but knowing these categories can help you plan your research.

5.1.1 Primary Sources

Primary sources are "original" materials that provide you with the "raw data" or evidence you will use to develop, test, and ultimately justify your hypothesis or claim. What kinds of materials count as primary sources vary significantly by field. In history, primary sources are artifacts or documents that come directly from the period or event you are studying: letters, diaries, objects, maps, even clothing. In literature or philosophy, your main primary source is usually the text you are analyzing, and your data are the words on the page. In arts criticism, your primary source would be the work of art you are interpreting. In social sciences, such as sociology or political science, census or survey data would also count as primary sources. In the natural sciences, reports of original research are sometimes characterized as primary sources (although scientists themselves rarely use that term).

5.1.2 Secondary Sources

Secondary sources are books, articles, or reports that are based on primary sources and are intended for scholarly or professional audiences. The body of secondary sources in a field is sometimes called that field's "literature." The best secondary sources are books from reputable university presses and articles or reports that have been "peer-reviewed," meaning that they were vetted by experts in the field before they were published. Researchers read secondary sources to keep up with developments in their fields and, in this way, to stimulate their own thinking. The standard way of framing new research problems is to challenge or build on the conclusions or methods of others, as presented in secondary sources they have written. You can also borrow evidence from secondary sources to use in your own arguments, but you should do so only if you do not have access to the primary sources from which that evidence was originally taken. Otherwise you risk appearing careless or lazy.

5.1.3 Tertiary Sources

These are books and articles that synthesize and report on secondary sources for general readers, such as textbooks, articles in encyclopedias (including *Wikipedia*), and articles in mass-circulation publications like *Psychology Today*. In the early stages of research, you can use tertiary sources to get a feel for a topic. But if you are making a scholarly argument, you should rely on secondary sources, because these make up the "conversation" in which you are seeking to participate. If you cite tertiary sources in a scholarly argument, you will mark yourself as either a novice or an outsider, and many readers won't take you—or your argument—seriously.

This response may seem unfair, but it's not. Tertiary sources aren't necessarily wrong—many are in fact written by distinguished scholars—but they are limited. Because they are intended for broad audiences who are unfamiliar with the topics that they address, they can sometimes oversimplify the research on which they are based, and they are susceptible to becoming outdated. But if you keep these limitations in mind, tertiary sources can be valuable resources: they can inform you about topics that are new to you, and if they have bibliographies, they can sometimes lead you to valuable secondary sources.

5.1.4 Differentiating Primary, Secondary, and Tertiary Sources

Researchers haven't always divided their sources into these three categories. The distinction between primary and secondary sources originated with historians in the nineteenth century and then spread to other fields. The category of tertiary sources was added later. Although this scheme is now the standard way that students are taught to classify sources, it fits some disciplines better than others: it works very well for history, in which primary sources are materials directly connected to a historical event or moment, and for criticism, in which primary sources are the original works of art, music, or literature that you are interpreting. But it works less well for, say, philosophy, chemistry, or nursing.

It is also important to understand that the classifications of primary, secondary, and tertiary are not absolute but relative to a researcher's project. In most instances, an article in a scholarly journal would generally be considered a secondary source. But it would become a primary source if your research problem concerned its author or the field itself: if, for example, you are writing the author's biography or trying to figure out whether patriotic historians have distorted stories of the Alamo. Likewise, an encyclopedia article would usually be considered a tertiary source, but it would become a primary source if you were studying the way encyclopedias deal with gender issues. T. S. Eliot's essay "Hamlet and His Problems" would be a primary source if you were studying Eliot but a secondary source if you were studying Shakespeare. Change your focus and you change the classification of your sources.

If this is confusing, it need not be. Remember that these classifications are just a means to an end. The important thing, ultimately, is not what you *call* your sources but how well you *use* them to address your research problems, develop new ideas, and make interesting arguments. In the next chapter, we will talk more about how you can use sources in your writing.

5.2 NAVIGATING THE TWENTY-FIRST-CENTURY LIBRARY

Walk into a university library today and you might wonder, "Where are the *books*?" (Answer: they are still there, though many have been moved to off-site storage.) The card catalog has long since been replaced by electronic search engines, and print materials—books, journals, photographs, films, video and audio recordings—are increasingly being digitized. Today you don't even need to enter the library to use many of its resources. But whether you visit in person or through a website, the library is an indispensable tool for research.

Given the volume of data available on the Internet, you might think that libraries are no longer necessary—except, perhaps, for highly specialized research. We believe the opposite is true. Because *so much* information is now at our fingertips, libraries are more essential than ever when conducting research. Libraries not only let us access information but also ensure that our sources are reliable. Even if your public or academic library is comparatively small, it can serve as a *portal* to a much broader range of resources—research guides, reference works, and online databases—that extends the library's reach. Of course, to benefit from these resources, you must learn to navigate the twenty-first-century library.

5.2.1 Planning Your Library Search

Before you can use sources, you must first find and evaluate them. Some materials that will eventually serve as sources will be physically located in your library, but others are likely to be located elsewhere, whether online or at another library. To take advantage of what libraries have to offer, then, you must *plan* your search. Fortunately, this is where libraries—and librarians—are most useful.

Knowing where to begin your search can be overwhelming at first. It is tempting to simply search a few terms and see what comes up. We do this too, but we also know that the library offers more systematic and productive methods for discovering useful and credible sources. Use the library to learn more about your topic and about promising avenues for exploring your research question.

Ask a Librarian. Perhaps the best advice we can offer is to rely on the research expertise of librarians. Both general reference librarians and (in larger libraries) subject area specialists can help you refine your search parameters and direct you to the right tools for your specific research question. They can help you use the catalog to locate materials held by your library or by other libraries (and obtainable through interlibrary loan). These same librarians typically design research guides that identify reference works and online databases for specific fields.

And don't be shy. Librarians love to assist researchers of all levels and at all stages of the research process. They can help you formulate your research question and plan, develop search terms, and inventory your results to ensure you haven't overlooked something of value. The only embarrassing question is the one you *failed to ask* but should have. Of course, it pays to meet busy librarians halfway by preparing in advance. If you have a well-developed research question ready to share, your librarian will be able to give you better advice. You might describe your project using the three-step rubric from chapter 3:

1. I am working on educational policy in the 1980s
   2. to find out how school boards in the Midwest dealt with desegregation,
      3. because I want to understand regional differences in race relations.

Consult Reference Works. If you already know a lot about your topic, you probably also know how to find sources on it. But if you are new to a topic, resist the temptation to go straight to primary or secondary sources that strike you as relevant. This approach is unreliable and unpredictable and probably won't save you any time. A more successful strategy is to allow reference works to shape your search efforts. Complied by experts, both general reference works such as the *Encyclopaedia Britannica* and more specialized works such as the *Encyclopedia of Philosophy* will give you the lay of the land, so that later it will be easier to see how your sources fit within the bigger picture. In addition, reference works often include citations or bibliographies that can lead you to sources you might otherwise overlook.

Especially valuable at early stages of research are bibliographic works, many of which provide abstracts summarizing significant articles or books on a topic. Look, especially, for annotated bibliographies or annual literature reviews that sum up recent books or articles; these offer the most promising leads for your research.

Explore Online Databases. What sets libraries apart from the Internet are their subscriptions to indexes and databases. After books, these are arguably a library's most valuable assets, since they give researchers access to materials they could not obtain otherwise. Each library's subscriptions will differ, with major research libraries offering the most comprehensive access to specialized indexes and databases. However, every academic library and many public libraries offer a powerful set of online tools that greatly extend their actual collections. You will certainly want to make use of these general and specialized resources in your research. At least become familiar with the major databases to which your library subscribes, such as Academic Search Premier, MLA International Bibliography, or PubMed. Many academic databases either provide abstracts or direct you to articles that include abstracts. Looking at these can help you decide if an article itself is worth reading carefully. Some databases allow you to access full-text articles and even books. But be aware: If your library does not subscribe to a particular journal included in a database, you might be asked to pay a fee to access a full-text article. Before doing so, *always* speak with a librarian about other means of access.

5.2.2 Finding Specific Sources

Having identified a range of search strategies and resources, you are now in a position to look for specific sources in and beyond the library. Of course, this process is not strictly linear. A single source can lead to others and return you to catalogs and databases you have already visited, only this time with new search terms. Novice researchers often rely too heavily on only a few terms or on terms that prove to be too broad—or narrow— to call up relevant sources. Successful researches know they have to be flexible: searches typically involve trial and error to discover those terms that will yield the most relevant sources.

Search Your Library Catalog. In your research, you will probably need to use your library's catalog in two complementary ways: keyword searching and browsing. When you have examined some sources to identify a list of *keywords* associated with your topic, you are ready to use these terms to search the catalog. In most libraries, you must choose the category (books, articles, journals, etc.) you wish to use for your search.

If your sources include books, you can use Library of Congress subject headings, found either on the back of their title page or on their "details" page in the online catalog, to search for related materials. On the back of this book's title page are the terms

1. Research—Methodology. 2. Technical writing.

If you search an online catalog for those terms, you will find all the books on those subjects in that library. A book may be cross-listed under multiple subject headings. In that case, take a quick look at the titles listed under those headings as well. You may find useful sources you would have missed otherwise. You can also *browse* the catalog for books with similar *call numbers*. Once you identify a book that seems on target, use its call number to find others shelved along with it. Look for the browse link in your book's catalog entry. This list will be less focused than a keyword list, but it may also contain unexpected gems. So don't restrict yourself to books nearest your target. Invest the time to browse widely.

The problem with any online search is that it may produce an overwhelming number of titles. The University of Chicago library has more than three hundred books on Napoleon and thousands with the word *environment* in their titles. If your search turns up too many sources, narrow it down. Today's online catalogs let you limit searches in many ways: by date of publication, language, subject, resource type (books, articles, databases, etc.), and possibly others depending on the catalog. If you can't decide how to narrow your search, start with the date of publication. Restrict it to those sources published in the last fifteen years; if that still turns up too many, cut to the last ten years.

After you search the Library of Congress or a large university catalog, you may discover that your own library holds only a fraction of what you found, but that it can borrow most of what you need. For books too new to be in a library catalog but crucial to your research, find an online bookseller. Those books might turn up on your library's new acquisitions shelf, and you can always recommend books to your library for acquisition. But if you need those books quickly, you'll probably have to buy them.

On the other hand, if you find nothing, your topic may be too narrow or too far off the beaten track to yield quick results. But you could also be on to an important question that nobody else has thought about, at least not for a while. For example, "friendship" was once an important topic for philosophers, but it was then ignored by major encyclopedias for centuries. Recently, though, it has reemerged as a topic of serious research. Chances are you'll make something of a neglected topic only through your own hard thinking. In the long run, that research might make you famous, but it probably won't work for a paper due in a few weeks.

Prowl the Stacks. Doing research online is faster than on foot, but if you never go into the stacks of your library (assuming you're allowed to), you may miss crucial sources that you'll find only there. More important, you'll miss the benefits of serendipity—a chance encounter with a valuable source that occurs only when a title happens to catch your eye. (All of us have found important sources in this way.)

If you can get into the stacks, find the shelf with books on your topic, then scan the titles on that shelf, then on the ones above, below, and on either side, especially for books with new bindings published by university presses. Then turn around and skim titles behind you; you never know. When you spot a promising title, skim its table of contents and index for keywords related to your question and answer. Then skim its bibliography for titles that look relevant. You can do all that faster with a book in your hand than you can online. Be suspicious of a book with no index or bibliography. (See 5.4 for more on systematic skimming.)

You can check tables of contents for most journals online, but browsing among shelved journals can be more productive. Once you identify promising journals online or in bibliographies, find them on the shelf. Skim the bound volumes for the last ten years (most have an annual table of contents in front). Then take a quick look at journals shelved nearby. You'll be surprised how often you find a relevant article that you would have missed online.

Follow Bibliographic Trails. Most sources will give you trailheads for bibliographical searches. When you find a book that seems useful, skim its bibliography or works cited. Its index will list the authors cited most often (generally, the more citations, the most important an author is). Journal articles usually begin with a review of previous research, all cited. By following this bibliographic trail, you can navigate the most difficult research territory, because one source always leads to others, which lead to others, which lead to . . .

Use Citation Indexing. Many online catalogs and databases let you look up *other* sources that cite one that you already know. This technique, called citation indexing, is like following a bibliographic trail, forward or backward. Instead of searching for sources that a given source cites, *backward* citation, you can search for sources that cite a given source, or *forward* citation. A source's credibility can thus be gauged both by the sources it cites and by the sources that cite it. The more a given source is later cited, the greater its reputation and its impact factor.

To do this kind of research, researchers used to have to consult printed citation indexes, a process that could take hours or even days. But today's online catalogs and databases make it easy. By following bibliographic trails and using citation indexing in tandem, you can build up a rich network of sources to support your own research.

5.3 LOCATING SOURCES ON THE INTERNET

You probably already know how to search the publicly available Internet: type a few words into the text box of a public search engine like Google, and pages of links—delivered as URLs, or uniform resource locators—arrive on your screen. We use this technique all the time, to find movie times, restaurant reviews, stock prices, news items, and so on. Its ubiquity in our everyday lives is reflected in our language. We've turned the name of a company into a verb: in everyday parlance, to "Google" something is to search for it.

Your practical experience with such everyday research might lead you to regard the Internet as comprehensive and reliable. (You use it to price a smartphone or pair of jeans, so why not for your academic or professional research?) But that would be a mistake. Again, remember that your library's catalogs and databases will allow you to access a great deal of information that you cannot get through a search engine. When using the Internet for research, maintain a healthy skepticism: most of what we retrieve using Google or some other search engine is perfectly reliable, but not everything is. In contrast to your library's catalogs and databases, the Internet is essentially unmonitored. There is no one to vouch for the credibility of materials posted to, and sent from, countless websites. And finally, keep in mind that companies offering free search engines make their money by acquiring data about you through your online behavior and by selling advertising, and that webmasters routinely modify their sites to make them appear higher in search results. These practices are not necessarily nefarious, but you should remember that search engine companies and websites themselves have an interest in where you go and what you see online.

But if you keep these limitations in mind, using the Internet can be a valuable component of your research plan. Here are some ways in which we use the Internet in our own research:

- To get our bearings with respect to a new topic—regarding everything we learn at this stage as provisional

- To explore potential keywords to use in a more systematic search

- To remind ourselves of dates or facts—again remembering to check these against more reliable sources

- To locate the authors of sources whom we might wish to contact: profiles of many scholars and researchers are available on college and university websites

- To get a "ballpark" sense of what we are likely to find through a search of specialized databases by a quick search using Google Scholar

Publicly available general tertiary sources such as *Wikipedia* and specialized ones such as the Victorian Web are often quite reliable. But you should still view them skeptically. In general, don't use the Internet to find secondary sources, as these depend for their credibility on the checks inherent in the academic publishing system, especially that of peer review. You can, however, use the Internet freely as a primary source. For example, if you study how soap opera story lines respond to their fans' reactions, fan blogs would be fine primary sources. (We discuss evaluating sources in the next section.)

Respecting Authors' Rights. Sites such as Project Gutenberg and Google Books can provide reliable online copies of older texts no longer in copyright. But postings of more recent texts (in the United States, those published in 1923 or later) may violate the author's copyright. Careful readers dislike seeing unauthorized copies cited not only because that breaks the law but also because such text are often inaccurately reproduced. So unless a recent text is posted with the author's clear permission (as in a database), use its print rather than its e-version.

5.4 EVALUATING SOURCES FOR RELEVANCE AND RELIABILITY

When you start looking for sources, you'll find more than you can use, so you must quickly evaluate their usefulness. To do so use two criteria: relevance and reliability.

5.4.1 Evaluating Sources for Relevance

If your source is a book, do this:

- Skim its index for your keywords, then skim the pages on which those words occur.
- Skim the first and last paragraphs in chapters that use a lot of your keywords.
- Skim prologues, introductions, summary chapters, and so on.
- Skim the last chapter, especially the first and last two or three pages.
- If the source is a collection of articles, skim the editor's introduction.
- Check the bibliography for the titles relevant to your topic.

If your source is an e-book, you should still follow these steps, but you can also search the whole text for your keywords.

If your source is an article, do this:

- Read the abstract, if it has one.
- Skim the introduction and conclusion; or if they are not marked off by headings, skim the first six or seven paragraphs and the last four or five.
- Skim for section headings, and read the first and last paragraphs of those sections.
- Check the bibliography for titles relevant to your topic.

If your source is online, do this:

- If it looks like a printed article, follow the steps for a journal article, and also search on your keywords.

- Skim sections labeled "introduction," "overview," "summary," or the like. If there are none, look for a link labeled "About the Site" or something similar.

- If the site has a link labeled "Site Map" or "Index," check it for your keywords and skim the referenced pages.

- If the site has a "search" resource, type in your keywords.

This kind of speedy reading can guide your own writing and revision. If you do not structure your paper so your readers can skim it quickly and see the outlines of your argument, your paper has a problem, an issue we discuss in chapters 12 and 13.

5.4.2 Evaluating Sources for Reliability

You can't judge a source until you read it, but there are signs of its reliability:

1. **Is the source published or posted online by a reputable press?** Most university presses are reliable, especially if you recognize the name of the university. Some commercial presses, which are presses not associated with a university, are reliable in some fields, such as Norton in literature, Ablex in sciences, or West in law. Be skeptical of a commercial book that makes sensational claims, even if its author has a PhD after his name. Be especially careful about sources on hotly contested social issues such as stem-cell research, gun control, and global warming. Many books and articles are published by individuals or organizations driven by ideology. Libraries often include them for the sake of coverage, but don't assume they are reliable.

2. **Was the book or article peer-reviewed?** Most reputable presses and journals ask experts to review a book or article before it is published; this is called peer review. Essay collections published by university presses are often but not always peer-reviewed; sometimes they are reviewed only by the named editor or editors. Few commercial magazines use peer review. If a publication hasn't been peer-reviewed, be suspicious.

3. **Is the author a reputable scholar?** This is hard to answer if you are new to a field. Most publications cite an author's academic credentials; you can find more with a search engine. Most established

scholars are reliable, but be cautious if the topic is a contested social issue such as gun control or abortion. Even reputable scholars can have axes to grind, especially if their research is financially supported by a special interest group. Go online to check out anyone an author thanks for support, including foundations that support her work.

4. **If the source is available only online, is it sponsored by a reputable organization?** A website is only as reliable as its sponsor. You can usually trust one that is sponsored and maintained by a reputable organization. But if the site has not been updated recently, it may have been abandoned and may no longer be endorsed by its sponsor. Some sites supported by individuals are reliable; most are not. Do a web search for the name of the sponsor to find out more about it.

5. **Is the source current?** You must use up-to-date sources, but what counts as current depends on the field. In computer science, a journal article can be out-of-date in months; in the social sciences, ten years pushes the limit. Publications have a longer shelf life in the humanities: literary or art criticism, for example, can remain relevant for decades and even centuries. In general, a source that sets out a major position or theory that other researchers accept will stay current longer than those that respond to or develop it. Assume that most textbooks are *not* current. If you are unsure whether a source will be considered current, take your lead from the practice of established researchers in the field. Look at the dates of articles in the works cited lists of a few recent books or articles in the field: a good rule of thumb is that you can cite works as old as the older ones in that list (but to be safe, perhaps not as old as the oldest). Try to find a standard edition of primary works such as novels, plays, letters, and so on: it is usually not the most recent. Be sure that you can consult the most recent edition of a secondary or tertiary source: researchers often change their views, even rejecting ones they espoused in earlier editions.

6. **If the source is a book, does it have notes and a bibliography?** If not, be suspicious, because you have no way to follow up on anything that the source claims.

7. **If the source is a website, does it include bibliographical data?** You cannot judge the reliability of a site that does not indicate who sponsors and maintains it, who wrote what's posted there, and when it was posted or last updated.

8. **If the source is a website, does it approach its topic judiciously?** Your readers are unlikely to trust a site that engages in heated advocacy, attacks those who disagree, makes wild claims, uses abusive language, or makes errors of spelling, punctuation, and grammar.

The following criteria are particularly important for advanced students:

9. **If the source is a book, has it been well reviewed?** Many fields have indexes to published reviews that tell you how others evaluate a source (see our "Appendix: Bibliographic Resources").
10. **Has the source been frequently cited by others?** You can roughly estimate how influential a source is by how often others cite it. Citation indexing makes this easy to do (see 5.2.2) If you find that a source is cited repeatedly by other scholars, you can infer that experts in the field regard it as reliable and significant. Such sources are said to have a high "impact factor." You should keep an eye out for such sources and use them to orient yourself in your field of research.

Whom Can You Trust?

The highly respected *Journal of the American Medical Association* appointed a committee to review articles published by reputable journals for reliability. Even though those papers had been approved by experts in the field, the reviewers reported that "statistical and methodological errors were common" ("When Peer Review Produces Unsound Science," *New York Times,* June 11, 2002, p. D6). In the face of such revelations, some just dismiss what scientists publish: if the reviewers of scientific articles can't guarantee reliable data, what is a mere layperson to do? You do what we all do—the best you can: read critically, and when you report data, do so as accurately as you can.

Error is bad, but dishonesty is worse. One of Booth's students got a summer job with a drug company and was assigned to go through stacks of doctor's answers to questionnaires and shred certain ones until nine out of ten of those left endorsed the company's product. These bogus data were then used to "prove" that the product worked. The student quit in disgust and was, no doubt, replaced by someone less ethical.

These indicators do not guarantee reliability. Reviewers sometimes recommend that a reputable press publish something weakly argued or with thin data because other aspects of its argument are too important to miss—we have each done so. So, don't assume that you can read uncritically just because a report is written by a reputable researcher and published by a reputable press.

5.5 LOOKING BEYOND PREDICTABLE SOURCES

For a class paper, you'll probably use the sources typical in your field. But if you are doing an advanced project, an MA thesis, or a PhD dissertation, search beyond them. If, for example, your project were on the economic effects of agricultural changes in late sixteenth-century England, you might read Elizabethan plays involving country characters, look at wood prints of agricultural life, find commentary by religious figures on rural social behavior. Conversely, if you were working on visual representations of daily life in London, you might research the economic history of the time and place. When you look beyond the standard *kinds* of references relevant to your question, you enrich not only your analysis but your range of intellectual reference and your ability to synthesize diverse kinds of data, a crucial competence of an inquiring mind. Don't ignore a work on your topic that is not mentioned in the bibliographies of your most relevant sources—you will get credit for originality if you turn up a good source that others have ignored.

When They Beat You to the Punch

Don't panic if you find a source that seems to pose and solve precisely your problem: "Transforming the Alamo Legend: History in the Service of Politics." At that moment you might think, *I'm dead. Nothing new to say.* (It happened to Williams when he was writing his doctoral dissertation and to Colomb just before his first book came out.) You may be right, but probably not. If the source does in fact settle your exact question, you have to formulate a new one. But the question your source asked is probably not as close to yours as your first feared. And you may find that you can do the source one better: if the author failed to get things entirely right, you have an unwitting ally in formulating your problem.

5.6 USING PEOPLE TO FURTHER YOUR RESEARCH

One of the paradoxes of twenty-first-century research is that even as new technologies allow us to access an unprecedented wealth of materials with unprecedented ease, research has also become more personal. So as you undertake your project, don't forget about the human element.

Most obviously, people can be sources of primary data, collected through observation, surveys, or interviews. Be creative when using people for primary research: don't ignore people in local business, government, or civic organizations. For example, if you were researching school desegregation in your town, you might go beyond the documents to ask the local school district whether anyone there has memories to share. We can't explain the complexities of interviewing (there are many guides to that process), but remember that the more you plan by determining *exactly* what you want to know, the more efficiently you will get what you need. You don't need to script an interview around a set list of questions—in fact, that can be a bad idea if it makes the interviewee freeze up. But prepare so that you don't question your source aimlessly. You can always reread a book for what you missed, but you can't keep going back to people because you didn't prepare well enough to get what you needed the first time. And always remember that when conducting primary research that involves people, you must adhere to rigorous ethical standards (see the Quick Tip at the end of this chapter).

People can also lead you to good secondary sources or serve as such sources themselves. We noted earlier that the body of secondary sources on a topic constitutes the scholarly "conversation" about it. That was a metaphor. But you can and should have real conversations about your research as well. Above we encouraged you to discuss your research with one kind of expert: your reference librarian. Your librarian is an expert on the processes of library research. You can also benefit from talking directly with experts on your topic. Ask them about the important open questions in the field. Ask them what they think of your project or provisional thesis. Ask them to suggest secondary sources for you to read. This kind of personal guidance can be invaluable to a novice researcher, and many experts will be happy to talk with you (or at least engage in a little e-mail correspondence).

All of us have made these kinds of queries with great success in our own research, and all of us have responded to them in turn, by helping those who have contacted us. One of us once invited an eminent scholar to talk about his research process to a group of first-year college students. He began his talk by saying, "I don't really have a research process; I just ask my smart friends what I should read." This scholar was being at least a bit tongue in cheek, but we could all do worse than to rely on such smart friends, at least to get us started.

QUICK TIP: The Ethics of Using People as Sources of Data

In recent years we have become increasingly aware that research using people may inadvertently harm them—not just physically but by embarrassing them, violating their privacy, and so on. So every college or university now has a committee that reviews all research directly or indirectly involving people, whether done by students or professional researchers. These committees go by different names—Human Subjects Committee, Institutional Review Board, Ethics Research Board, and so on—but they all aim to ensure that researchers follow the maxim that should govern research as it does medicine: *Do no harm.* Consult with that committee if you use people as sources of data—whether by interviewing, surveying, perhaps even just observing them. Jumping through these hoops may feel like bureaucratic make-work, but if you don't, you could harm those who help you and may even damage your institution.

FROM TOPICS TO QUESTIONS

Wayne C. Booth, Gregory G. Colomb, Joseph M. Williams, Joseph Bizup,
William T. Fitzgerald

. . . .

If you are new to research, the freedom to pick your own topic can seem daunting. Where do you begin? How do you tell a good topic from a bad one? Inexperienced researchers typically wonder, *Will I find enough information on this topic to write about it?* To their surprise they often compile too much information, much of it not very useful. They do so because their topic lacks focus. Without that focus, any evidence you assemble risks appearing to your readers as little more than a mound of random facts. As you begin a research project, you will want to distinguish a topic from a subject. A subject is a broad area of knowledge (e.g., climate change), while a topic is a specific interest within that area (e.g., the effect of climate change on migratory birds). However, finding a topic is not simply a matter of narrowing your subject. A topic is an approach to a subject, one that asks a *question* whose answer solves a *problem* that your readers care about.

In all research communities, some questions are "in the air," widely debated and researched, such as whether traits like shyness or an attraction to risk are learned or genetically inherited. But other questions may intrigue only the researcher: *Why do cats rub their faces against us? Why does a coffee spill dry up in the shape of a ring?* That's how a lot of research begins—not with a big question that attracts everyone in a field, but with a mental itch about a small question that only a single researcher wants to scratch. If you feel that itch, start scratching. But at some point, you must decide whether the answer to your question solves a problem significant to some community of researchers or even to a public whose lives your research could change.

Now, that word *problem* is itself a problem. Commonly, a problem means trouble, but among researchers it has a meaning so special that we devote the next chapter to it. But before you can frame your research problem, you have to find a topic that might lead to one. So we'll start there, with finding a topic.

Question or Problem?

You may have noticed that we've been using the words *question* and *problem* almost interchangeably. But they are not quite the same. Some questions raise problems; others do not. A question raises a problem if not answering it keeps us from knowing something more important than its answer. For example, if we cannot answer the question *Are there ultimate particles?*, we cannot know something even more important: the nature of physical existence. On the other hand, a question does not raise a problem if not answering it has no apparent consequences. For example, *Was Abraham Lincoln's right thumb longer than his nose?* We cannot think of what we would gain by knowing. At least at the moment.

3.1 FROM AN INTEREST TO A TOPIC

Most of us have more than enough interests, but beginners often find it hard to locate among theirs a topic focused enough to support a substantial research project. They may also believe they lack the expertise for the project. However, a research topic is an interest stated specifically enough for you to imagine *becoming* a local expert on it. That doesn't mean you already know a lot about it or that you'll have to know more about it than others, including your teacher. You just want to know a lot more about it than you do now.

If you can work on any topic, we offer only a cliché: start with what most interests you. Nothing contributes to the quality of your work more than your commitment to it. But also ask yourself: *What interests me about this topic? What would interest others?*

3.1.1 Finding a Topic in a Writing Course

Start by listing as many interests as you can that you'd like to explore. Don't limit yourself to what you think might interest a teacher or make you look like a serious student. Let your ideas flow. Prime the pump by asking friends, classmates, even your teacher about topics that interest them. If no good topics come to mind, consult the Quick Tip at the end of this chapter.

Once you have a list of topics, choose the one or two that interest you most and explore their research potential. Do this:

- In the library, look up your topic in a general guide such as *CQ Researcher* and skim the subheadings. In an online database such as Academic Search Premier, you can explore your topic through subject terms. If you have a more narrow focus, you can do the same with specialized guides such as *Women's Studies International*. While some libraries will have copies of general and specialized guides on the shelf, most now subscribe to their online equivalents, but not all of them let you skim subject headings.

- On the Internet, Google your topic, but don't surf indiscriminately. Look first for websites that are roughly like sources you would find in a library, such as online encyclopedias. Read the entry on your general topic, and then copy the list of references at the end for a closer look. Use *Wikipedia* to find ideas and sources, but always confirm what you find there in a reliable source. Few experienced researchers trust *Wikipedia,* so *under no circumstances cite it as a source of evidence* (unless your topic is *Wikipedia* itself).

- Remember, at this point you are exploring a topic to spur your thinking and to see if that topic is viable. With that in mind, you can also find ideas in blogs, which discuss almost every contentious issue. Since most issues are usually too big for a research paper, look for posts that take a position on narrow aspects of larger issues. If you disagree with a view, investigate it.

3.1.2 Finding a Topic for a First Research Project in a Particular Field

Start by listing topics relevant to your particular class *and* that interest you, then narrow them to one or two promising ones. If the topic is general, such as *religious masks,* you'll have to do some random reading to narrow it. But read with a plan:

- Skim encyclopedia entries in your library or online. Start with standard ones such as the *Encyclopaedia Britannica.* Then consult specialized ones such as the *Encyclopedia of Religion* or the *Stanford Encyclopedia of Philosophy.*

- Skim headings in specialized indexes such as the *Philosopher's Index, Psychological Abstracts,* or *Women's Studies Abstracts.* Use subheadings for ideas of how others have narrowed your topic.

- Google your topic, but not indiscriminately. Use Google Scholar, a search engine that focuses on scholarly journals and books. Skim the articles it turns up, especially their lists of sources.

When you know the general outline of your topic and how others have narrowed theirs, try to narrow yours. If you can't, browse through journals and websites until your topic becomes more clearly defined. That takes time, so start early.

3.1.3 Finding a Topic for an Advanced Project

Most advanced students already have interests in topics relevant to their field. Often topics find them as they become immersed in a field. If that is not yet the case, focus on what interests you, but remember that you must eventually show why it should also interest others.

- Find what interests other researchers. Look online for recurring issues and debates in the archives of professional discussion lists relevant to your interests. Search online and in journals like the *Chronicle of Higher Education* for conference announcements, conference programs, calls for papers, anything that reflects what others find interesting.

- Skim the latest issues of journals in your field, not just for articles, but also for conference announcements, calls for papers, and reviews. Skim recent articles in your library's online databases in your field (e.g., the MLA International Bibliography).

- Investigate the resources that your library is particularly rich in. If, for example, it (or a library nearby) holds a collection of rare papers on an interesting topic, you have found not only a topic but a way into it. Many unexpected finds await discovery in your library's archives.

3.2 FROM A BROAD TOPIC TO A FOCUSED ONE

The most useful way to think about a topic is as a starting place for your research. (The word "topic" comes from *topos,* which is Greek for "place.") From this starting place, you can head off in a particular direction and this narrow an overly broad topic into a productively focused one. At this point, your biggest risk is settling on a topic so broad that it could be a subheading in a library catalog: *spaceflight; Shakespeare's problem plays; natural law.* A topic is probably too broad if you can state it in four or five words:

Free will in Tolstoy

The history of commercial aviation

A topic so broad can intimidate you with the task of finding, much less reading, even a fraction of the sources available. So narrow it down:

Free will in Tolstoy	→	The conflict of free will and inevitability in Tolstoy's description of three battles in *War and Peace*
The history of commercial aviation	→	The contribution of the military in developing the DC-3 in the early years of commercial aviation

We narrowed those topics by adding words and phrases, but of a special kind: *conflict, description, contribution,* and *developing.* Those nouns are derived from verbs expressing actions or relationships: *to conflict, to describe, to contribute,* and *to develop.* Lacking such "action" words, your topic is a static thing.

Note what happens when we restate static topics as full sentences. Topics (1) and (2) change almost not at all:

(1) Free will in Tolstoy_{topic} → There is free will in Tolstoy's novels._{claim}

(2) The history of commercial aviation_{topic} → Commercial aviation has a history._{claim}

In reality, (1) and (2) are not topics at all because they do not lead anywhere. But when (3) and (4) are revised into full sentences, they are closer to claims that a reader might find interesting.

(3) The *conflict* of free will and inevitability in Tolstoy's *description* of three battles in *War and Peace*_{topic} → In *War and Peace*, Tolstoy *describes* three battles in which free will and inevitability *conflict.*_{claim}

(4) The *contribution* of the military in *developing* the DC-3 in the early years of commercial aviation_{topic} → In the early years of commercial aviation, the military *contributed* to the way the DC-3 *developed.*_{claim}

Such claims may at first seem thin, but you'll make them richer as you work through your project. And that's the point: these topics are actually paths to pursue when devising your project.

Caution: Don't narrow your topic so much that you can't find information on it. Too much information is available on *the history of commercial aviation* but too little (at least for beginning researchers) on *the decision to lengthen the wingtips on the DC-3 prototype for military use as a cargo carrier.*

3.3 FROM A FOCUSED TOPIC TO QUESTIONS

Once they have a focused topic, many new researchers make a beginner's mistake: they immediately start plowing through all the sources they can find on the topic, taking notes on everything they read. With a promising topic such as *the political origins of legends about the Battle of the Alamo,* they mound up endless facts connected with the battle: what led up to it, histories of the Texas Revolution, the floor plan of the mission, even biographies of generals Santa Anna and Sam Houston. They accumulate notes, summaries, descriptions of differences and similarities, ways in which the stories conflict with one another and with what historians think really happened, and so on. Then they dump it all into a paper that concludes, *Thus we see many differences and similarities between . . .*

Many high school teachers would reward such a paper with a good grade, because it shows that the writer can focus on a topic, find information on it, and assemble that information into a report, no small achievement—for a first project. But in *any* college course, such a report falls short if it is seen as just a pastiche of vaguely related facts. If a writer asks no specific *question* worth asking, he can offer no specific *answer* worth supporting. And without an answer to support, he cannot *select* from all the data he could find on a topic just those relevant to his answer. To be sure, those fascinated by Elvis Presley movie posters or the first generation of video games will read *anything* new about them, no matter how trivial. Serious researchers, however, do not document information for its own sake, but to support the answer to a question that they (and they hope their readers) think is worth asking.

So the best way to begin working on your focused topic is not to find all the information you can on it, but to formulate questions that direct you to just that information you need to answer them.

Start with the standard journalistic questions: *who, what, when,* and *where,* but focus on *how* and *why.* To engage your best critical thinking, systematically ask questions about your topic's history, composition, and categories. Then ask any other question you can think of or find in your sources. Record all the questions, but don't stop to answer them even when one or two grab your attention. This inventory of possible questions will help to direct your search activities and enable you to make sense of information you find. (Don't worry about keeping these categories straight; their only purpose is to stimulate questions and organize your answers.) Let's take up the example of masks mentioned earlier.

3.3.1 Ask about the History of Your Topic

- How does it fit into a **larger developmental context**? Why did your topic come into being? *What came before masks? How were masks invented? Why? What might come after masks?*

- What is its own **internal history**? How and why has the topic itself changed through time? *How have Native American masks changed? Why? How have Halloween masks changed? How has the role of masks in society changed? How has the booming market for kachina* masks influenced traditional design? Why have masks helped make Halloween the biggest American holiday after Christmas?

3.3.2 Ask about Its Structure and Composition

- How does your topic fit into the **context of a larger structure or function as part of a larger system**? *How do masks reflect the values of different societies and cultures? What roles do masks play in Hopi dances? In scary movies? In masquerade parties? How are masks used other than for disguise?*

- How do its parts **fit together as a system**? *What parts of a mask are most significant in Hopi ceremonies? Why? Why do some masks cover only the eyes? Why do few masks cover just the bottom half of the face? How do their colors play a role in their function?*

3.3.3 Ask How Your Topic Is Categorized

- How can your topic be **grouped into kinds**? *What are the different kinds of masks? Of Halloween masks? Of African masks? How are they categorized by appearance? By use? By geography or society? What are the different qualities of masks?*

- How does your topic **compare to and contrast with** others like it? *How do Native Americans ceremonial masks differ from those in Japan? How do Halloween masks compare with Mardi Gras masks?*

3.3.4 Turn Positive Questions into Negative Ones

- *Why have masks* not *become a part of other holidays, like Presidents' Day or Memorial Day? How do Native American masks* not *differ from those in Africa? What parts of masks are typically* not *significant in religious ceremonies?*

3.3.5 Ask *What If?* and Other Speculative Questions

- How would things be different if your topic never existed, disappeared, or were put into a new context? *What if no one ever wore masks except for safety? What if everyone wore masks in public? What if it were customary to wear masks on blind dates? In marriage ceremonies? At funerals? Why are masks common in African religions but not in Western ones? Why don't hunters in camouflage wear masks? How are masks and cosmetic surgery alike?*

3.3.6 Ask Questions Suggested by Your Sources

You won't be able to do this until you've done some reading on your topic. Ask questions that **build on agreement**:

- If a source makes a claim you think is persuasive, ask questions that might extend its reach. *Elias shows that masked balls became popular in eighteenth-century London in response to anxieties about social mobility. Did the same anxieties cause similar developments in Venice?*

- Ask questions that might support the same claim with new evidence. *Elias supports his claim about masked balls with published sources. Is it also supported by letters and diaries?*

- Ask questions analogous to those that sources have asked about similar topics. *Smith analyzes costumes from an economic point of view. What would an economic analysis of masks turn up?*

Now ask questions that reflect **disagreement**:

- *Martinez claims that carnival masks uniquely allow wearers to escape social norms. But could there be a larger pattern of all masks creating a sense of alternative forms of social or sprirual life?*

If you are an experienced researcher, look for questions that other researchers ask but don't answer. Many journal articles end with a paragraph or two about open questions, ideas for more research, and so on. You might not be able to do all the research they suggest, but you might carve out a piece of it. You can also look for Internet discussions on your topic, then "lurk," just reading the exchanges to understand the kinds of questions those on the list debate. Record questions that spark your interest. You can also post questions to the list if they are specific and narrowly focused.

3.3.7 Evaluate Your Questions

After asking all the questions you can think of, evaluate them, because not all questions are equally good. Look for questions whose answers might make you (and, ideally, your readers) think about your topic in a new way Avoid questions like these:

- Their answers are settled fact that you could just look up. *Do the Inuit use masks in their wedding ceremonies?* Questions that ask *how* and *why* invite deeper thinking than *who, what, when,* or *where,* and deeper thinking leads to more interesting answers.

- Their answers would be merely speculative. *Would church services be as well attended if the congregation all wore masks?* If you can't imagine finding hard data that might settle the question, it's a question you can't settle.

- Their answers are dead ends. *How many black cats slept in the Alamo the night before the battle?* It is hard to see how an answer would help us think about any larger issue worth understanding better, so it's a question that's probably not worth asking.

You might, however, be wrong about that. Some questions that seemed trivial, even silly, have answers more significant than expected. One researcher wondered why a coffee spill dries up in the form of a ring and discovered things about the properties of fluids that others in his field thought important—and that paint manufactures found valuable. So who knows where a question about cats in the Alamo might take you? You can't know until you get there.

Once you have a few promising questions, try to combine them into larger ones. For example, many questions about the Alamo story ask about the interests of the storytellers and their effects on their stories: *How have politicians used the story? How have the storytellers' motives changed? Whose purposes does each story serve?* These can be combined into a single question:

> *How and why have users of the Alamo story given the event a mythic quality?*

A question like this gives direction to your research (and helps avoid the gathering of endless information). And it begins to imagine readers who will judge whether your question is significant.

3.4 THE MOST SIGNIFICANT QUESTION: *SO WHAT?*

Even if you are an experienced researcher, you might not be able to take the next step until you are well into your project, and if you are a beginner, you may find it frustrating. Even so, once you have a question that holds your interest, you must pose a tougher one about it: *So what?* Beyond your own interest in its answer, why would others think it a question worth asking? You might not be able to answer that *So what?* question early on, but it's one you have to start thinking about, because it forces you to look beyond your own interests to consider how your work might strike others.

Think of it like this: What will be lost if you *don't* answer your question? How will *not* answering it keep us from understanding something else better than we do? Start by asking *So what?* at first of yourself:

> So what if I don't know or understand how butterflies know where to go in the winter, or how fifteenth-century musicians tuned their instruments, or why the Alamo story has become a myth? So what if I can't answer my question? What do we lose?

Your answer might be *Nothing. I just want to know.* Good enough to start, but not to finish, because eventually your readers will ask as well, and they will want an answer beyond *Just curious.* Answering *So what?* vexes all researchers, beginners and experienced alike, because when you have only a question, it's hard to predict whether others will think its answer is significant. But you must work toward that answer throughout your project. You can do that in three steps.

3.4.1 Step 1: Name Your Topic

If you are beginning a project with only a topic and maybe the glimmerings of a good question or two, start by naming your project:

> *I am trying to learn about / working on / studying*
> _____.

Fill in the blank with your topic, using some of those nouns derived from verbs:

> *I am studying the causes of the disappearance of large North American mammals . . .*

> *I am working on Lincoln's beliefs about predestination and their influence on his reasoning . . .*

3.4.2 Step 2: Add an Indirect Question

Add an indirect question that indicates what you do not know or understand about your topic:

1. I am studying / working on _____
   2. **because I want to find out who / what / when / where / whether / why / how _____.**

1. I am studying the causes of the disappearance of large North American mammals
   2. **because I want to find out whether they were hunted to extinction . . .**

1. I am working on Lincoln's beliefs about predestination and its influence on his reasoning
   2. **because I want to find out how his belief in destiny influenced his understanding of the causes of the Civil War . . .**

When you add that *because I want you to find out how/why/whether* clause, you state why *you* are pursuing your topic: to answer a question important to you.

If you are a new researcher and get this far, congratulate yourself, because you have moved beyond the aimless collection of data. But now, if you can, take one step more. It's one that advanced researchers know they must take, because they know their work will be judged not by its significance to them but by its significance to others in their field. They must have an answer to *So what?*

3.4.3 Step 3: Answer *So What?* by Motivating Your Question

This step tells you whether your question might interest not just you but others. To do that, add a second indirect question that explains why you asked your first question. Introduce this second implied question with *in order to help my reader understand how, why, or whether:*

1. I am studying the causes of the disappearance of large North American mammals
   2. because I want to find out whether the earliest peoples hunted them to extinction,
      3. **in order to help my reader understand whether native peoples lived in harmony with nature or helped destroy it.**

1. I am working on Lincoln's beliefs about predestination and their influence on his reasoning
   2. because I want to find out how his belief in destiny and God's will influenced his understanding of the causes of the Civil War,
      3. **in order to help my reader understand how his religious beliefs may have influenced his military decisions.**

It is the indirect question in step 3 that you hope will seize your readers' interest. If it touches on issues important to your field, even indirectly, then your readers should care about its answer.

Some advanced researchers begin with questions that others in their field already care about: *Why did the giant sloth and woolly mammoth disappear from North America? Or: Is risk taking genetically based?* But many researchers, including at times the five of us, find that they can't flesh out the last step in that three-part sentence until they finish a first draft. So you make no mistake *beginning* your research without a good answer to that third question—*Why does this matter?*—but you face a problem when you *finish* your research without having thought through those three steps at all. And if you are doing advanced research, you *must* take that step, because answering that last question is your ticket into the conversation of your community of researchers.

Regularly test your progress by asking a roommate, relative, or friend to force you to flesh out those three steps. Even if you can't take them all confidently, you'll know where you are and where you still have to go. To summarize: Your aim is to explain

1. what you are writing about—*I am working on the topic of* . . .
2. what you don't know about it—*because I want to find out* . . .
3. why you want your reader to know and care about *it—in order to help my reader understand better* . . .

In the following chapters, we return to those three steps and their implied questions, because they are crucial not just for finding questions but for framing the research problem that you want your readers to value.

Quick Tip: Finding Topics

If you are a beginner, start with our suggestions about exploring the Internet and skimming bibliographical guides (see 3.1). If you still draw a blank, try these steps.

For General Interest Topics

- What special interest do you have—sailing, chess, finches, old comic books? The less common, the better. Investigate something about it you don't know: its origins, its technology, how it is practiced in another culture, and so on.
- Where would you like to travel? Surf the Internet, finding out all you can about your destination. What particular aspect surprises you or makes you want to know more?

- Wander through a museum with exhibitions that appeal to you—artworks, dinosaurs, old cars. If you can't browse in person, browse a "virtual museum" on the Internet. Stop when something catches your interest. What more do you want to know about it?

- Wander through a shopping mall or store, asking yourself, *How do they make that?* Or, *I wonder who thought up that product?*

- Leaf through a Sunday newspaper, especially its features sections. Skim reviews of books or movies, in newspapers or on the Internet.

- Browse a large magazine rack. Look for trade magazines or those that cater to specialized interests. Investigate whatever catches your interest.

- Tune into talk radio or interview programs on TV until you hear a claim that you disagree with. Or find something to disagree with on the websites connected with well-known talk shows. See whether you can make a case to refute it.

- Use an Internet search engine to find websites related to your topic. These include blogs maintained by individuals and organizations. You'll get hundreds of hits, but look only at the ones that surprise you.

- Is there a common belief that you suspect is simplistic or just wrong? A common practice that you find pointless or irritating? Do research to make a case against it.

- What courses will you take in the future? What research would help you prepare for them?

For Topics Focused on a Particular Field

If you have experience in your field, review 3.1.2–3.

- Browse through a textbook of a course that is one level beyond yours or a course that you know you will have to take. Look especially hard at the study questions.

- Attend a lecture for an advanced class in your field, and listen for something you disagree with, don't understand, or want to know more about.

- Ask your instructor about the most contested issues in your field.

- Find an Internet discussion list in your field. Browse its archives, looking for matters of controversy or uncertainty.

- Surf the websites of departments at major universities, including class sites. Also check websites of museums, national associations, and government agencies, if they seem relevant.

GETTING STARTED ON THE PROPOSAL

Before you start researching, you need to choose a topic that all members of your group can agree on. Begin your project by brainstorming subjects. Spend at least five minutes listing all the elements of campus life that you would like to see changed or improved in some way. If you have time left over, list a few things you know you would not be interested in pursuing. Then, trade lists with the other members of your group and discuss what you each listed. You'll likely have at least one or two interests in common. You can use these common passions as the starting point for your research.

Unit II:
The Annotated Bibliography

INTRODUCTION TO THE ANNOTATED BIBLIOGRAPHY

The Annotated Bibliography unit asks you to move forward from the collaborative efforts of your group proposal and begin taking a focused, individual approach to one aspect of your group's research question. You will be asked to step into the role of academic researcher by collecting sources through your selected disciplinary lens. Scholarly and professional organizations sometimes publish annotated bibliographies with the goal of helping researchers decide what sources are worth reading in more detail. Your bibliography should serve this purpose for your group members, but also will help you keep track of the research you conduct in preparation for your next assignment, which will put these and other sources in conversation with one another.

Though your instructor will provide you with some necessary tools, such as library visits, an introduction to databases, and a discussion of pertinent literature, this project will be primarily self-directed. It will be your responsibility to discover the citation conventions of your field to ensure both ethical attribution of ideas and that your audience will recognize the ways in which you are attempting to communicate with them. The annotated bibliography should be more than just a list of sources and their summaries, though. This process may uncover potential flaws in your original research questions, causing you to take your project in a direction you had not originally planned. Try to enjoy this discovery phase of the research and remember that this, like writing, is a process that can sometimes require a reimagining of your goals.

Purpose

The annotated bibliography is a document used by professional and scholarly organizations alike to organize sources that relate to a common theme, connecting those sources to each other, your argument as a whole, and the larger conversation in which they are participating. Each entry should focus on a single source, evaluating and exposing the strength of that source in terms of its clarity, appropriateness of expression, authority of the author, and its rhetorical relevance to your work. We chose this genre because, as scholars ourselves, we recognize that gathering sources can be one of the most deceptively difficult tasks of the writing process. This will help you decide how your discipline responds to a certain topic and establishes the foundation for the next project, the Literature Review.

Audience

Typically, the audience for an annotated bibliography would be other scholars researching the same topic or theme. For this course, your audience will be your instructor, your groupmates, and potentially the other members of your class.

Content and Requirements

The annotated bibliography should contain:

- A one-paragraph, reflective introduction that introduces the theme of your work as well as your initial research question. This should situate your reader in the broader context of your intentions but may also provide you with space to address any limitations in the sources you have gathered.

- Three 200- to 500-word entries that each:
  - Contain a full citation of the source;
  - Introduce the author, their genre, and methods;
  - Summarize the central purpose of the source;
  - Evaluate the article's methods, progression of information, and conclusions; and
  - Compare the source with the others you include.

Organization and Format

- List full citation information for each source.
  - Maintain the citation style that is most common for your discipline.
- Arrange these citations in alphabetical order.
- Below each citation, include a one- to two-paragraph, evaluative annotation.

Outcomes Addressed in this Unit

- *Engage with larger ongoing civic, social, and academic conversations.*
- *Find, evaluate, and synthesize disciplinary and professional sources by integrating that research into their written work appropriately using summary, paraphrase, and direct quotation.*

Unit II: The Annotated Bibliography

- *Understand the significance of intellectual property, academic honesty, and the rhetorical and disciplinary purposes of citation styles with an emphasis on MLA.*

Strategies

- Focus on a narrowly defined and arguable topic or research question within the scope of your group's chosen topic.

- Conduct background research on the authors and publications from which you are selecting sources.

- Familiarize yourself with the citation style or styles common among other researchers in your field and document your sources accordingly.

- Summarize each source accurately, making sure to mention only the most important information in the text. There is no need include small details that will not affect the overall message of the text.

HOW TO READ A SCIENTIFIC PAPER

Adam Ruben

. . . .

Nothing makes you feel stupid quite like reading a scientific journal article.

I remember my first experience with these ultra-congested and aggressively bland manuscripts so dense that scientists are sometimes caught eating them to stay regular. I was in college taking a seminar course in which we had to read and discuss a new paper each week. And something just wasn't working for me.

Every week I would sit with the article, read every single sentence, and then discover that I hadn't learned a single thing. I'd attend class armed with exactly one piece of knowledge: I knew I had read the paper. The instructor would ask a question; I'd have no idea what she was asking. She'd ask a simpler question—still no idea. *But I'd read the damn paper!*

It reminded me of kindergarten, when I would feel proud after reading a book above my grade level. But if you had asked me a simple question about the book's contents—What kind of animal is Wilbur? How did Encyclopedia Brown know that Bugs Meany wasn't really birdwatching?—I couldn't have answered it.

A few weeks into the seminar, I decided enough was enough. I wasn't going to read another paper without understanding it. So I took that week's journal article to the library. Not just the regular library, but the obscure little biology library, one of those dusty academic hidey-holes only populated by the most wretched forms of life, which are, of course, insects and postdocs.

I placed the paper on a large empty desk. I eliminated all other distractions. To avoid interruptions from friends encouraging alcohol consumption, as friends do in college, I sat in an obscure anteroom with no foot traffic. To avoid interruptions from cellphone calls, I made sure it was 1999.

Most importantly, if I didn't understand a word in a sentence, I forbade myself from proceeding to the next sentence until I looked it up in a textbook and then reread the sentence until it made sense.

I specifically remember this happening with the word "exogenous." Somehow I had always glossed over this word, as though it was probably unimportant to its sentence. Wrong.

It took me more than 2 hours to read a three-page paper. But this time, I actually understood it.

And I thought, "Wow. I *get* it. I really *get* it."

And I thought, "Oh crap. I'm going to have to do this again, aren't I?" **Every week I would sit with the article, read every single sentence, and then discover that I hadn't learned a single thing.**

If you're at the beginning of your career in science, you may be struggling with the same problem. It may help you to familiarize yourself with the 10 Stages of Reading a Scientific Paper:

1. **Optimism.** "This can't be too difficult," you tell yourself with a smile—in the same way you tell yourself, "It's not damaging to drink eight cups of coffee a day" or "There are plenty of tenure-track jobs." After all, you've been reading *words* for decades. And that's all a scientific paper is, right? Words?

2. **Fear.** This is the stage when you realize, "Uh … I don't think all of these are words." So you slow down a little. Sound out the syllables, parse the jargon, look up the acronyms, and review your work several times. Congratulations: You have now read the title.

3. **Regret.** You begin to realize that you should have budgeted much more time for this whole undertaking. Why, oh why, did you think you could read the article in a single bus ride? If only you had more time. If only you had one of those buzzer buttons from workplaces in the 1960s, and you could just press it and say, "Phoebe, cancel my January." If only there was a compact version of the same article, something on the order of 250 or fewer words, printed in bold at the beginning of the paper...

4. **Corner-cutting.** Why, what's this? An abstract, all for me? Blessed be the editors of scientific journals who knew that no article is comprehensible, so they asked their writers to provide, à la *Spaceballs*, "the short, short version." Okay. Let's do this.

5. **Bafflement.** What the hell? Was that abstract supposed to explain something? Why was the average sentence 40 words long? Why were there so many acronyms? Why did the authors use the word "characterize" five times?

6. **Distraction.** What if there was, like, a smartphone for ducks? How would that work? What would they use it for? And what was that Paul Simon lyric, the one from "You Can Call Me Al," that's been in your head all day? How would your life change if you owned a bread maker? You'd have to buy yeast. Is yeast expensive? You could make your own bread every few days, but then it might go stale. It's not the same as store-bought bread; it's just not. Oh, right! "Don't want to

end up a cartoon in a cartoon graveyard." Is Paul Simon still alive? You should check Wikipedia. Sometimes you confuse him with Paul McCartney or Paul Shaffer. Shame about David Bowie. Can you put coffee in a humidifier?

7. **Realization that 15 minutes have gone by and you haven't progressed to the next sentence.**

8. **Determination.** All righty. Really gonna read this time. Really gonna do it. Yup, yuppers, yup-a-roo, readin' words is what you do. Let's just point those pupils at the dried ink on the page, and …

9. **Rage.** HOW COULD ANY HUMAN BRAIN PRODUCE SUCH SENTENCES?

10. **Genuine contemplation of a career in the humanities.** Academic papers written on nonscientific subjects are easy to understand, right? Right?

What a strange document a scientific journal article is. We work on them for months or even years. We write them in a highly specialized vernacular that even most other scientists don't share. We place them behind a paywall and charge something ridiculous, like $34.95, for the privilege of reading them. We so readily accept their inaccessibility that we have to start "journal clubs" in the hopes that our friends might understand them and summarize them for us.

Can you imagine if mainstream magazine articles were like science papers? Picture a *Time* cover story with 48 authors. Or a piece in *The Economist* that required, after every object described, a parenthetical listing of the company that produced the object and the city where that company is based. Or a *People* editorial about Jimmy Kimmel that could only be published following a rigorous review process by experts in the field of Jimmy Kimmel.

Do you know what you'd call a magazine article that required intellectual scrutiny and uninterrupted neural commitment to figure out what it's even trying to say? You'd call it a badly written article.

So for those new to reading journals, welcome. Good luck. And we're sorry. We're *trying* to write articles comprehensibly, but sometimes our subdiscipline is so hyperspecific that we need a million acronyms. And sometimes we're attempting to sound like good scientists by copying the tone of every article we've read. And sometimes we're just writing badly.

Quackberry. That's what you'd call the smartphone for ducks.

HOW TO (SERIOUSLY) READ A SCIENTIFIC PAPER
Elisabeth Pain

· · · · · · · · ·

Adam Ruben's tongue-in-cheek column about the common difficulties and frustrations of reading a scientific paper broadly resonated among *Science* Careers readers. Many of you have come to us asking for more (and more serious) advice on how to make sense of the scientific literature, so we've asked a dozen scientists at different career stages and in a broad range of fields to tell us how they do it. Although it is clear that reading scientific papers becomes easier with experience, the stumbling blocks are real, and it is up to each scientist to identify and apply the techniques that work best for them. The responses have been edited for clarity and brevity.

How do you approach reading a paper?

I start by reading the abstract. Then, I skim the introduction and flip through the article to look at the figures. I try to identify the most prominent one or two figures, and I really make sure I understand what's going on in them. Then, I read the conclusion/summary. Only when I have done that will I go back into the technical details to clarify any questions I might have.

- ***Jesse Shanahan***, master's candidate in astronomy at Wesleyan University in Middletown, Connecticut

I first get a general idea by reading the abstract and conclusions. The conclusions help me understand if the goal summarized in the abstract has been reached, and if the described work can be of interest for my own study. I also always look at plots/figures, as they help me get a first impression of a paper. Then I usually read the entire article from beginning to end, going through the sections in the order they appear so that I can follow the flow of work that the authors want to communicate.

If you want to make it a productive exercise, you need to have a clear idea of which kind of information you need to get in the first place, and then focus on that aspect. It could be to compare your results with the ones presented by the authors, put your own analysis into context, or extend it using the newly published data. Citation lists can help you decide why the paper may be most relevant to you by giving you a first impression of how colleagues that do similar research as you do may have used the paper.

- ***Cecilia Tubiana***, scientist at the Max Planck Institute for Solar System Research in Göttingen, Germany

If I'm aiming to just get the main points, I'll read the abstract, hop to the figures, and scan the discussion for important points. I think the figures are the most important part of the paper, because the abstract and body of the paper can be manipulated and shaped to tell a compelling story. Then anything I'm unclear about, I head to the methodology.

If I want to delve deeper into the paper, I typically read it in its entirety and then also read a few of the previous papers from that group or other articles on the same topic. If there is a reference after a statement that I find particularly interesting or controversial, I also look it up. Should I need more detail, I access any provided data repositories or supplemental information.

Then, if the authors' research is similar to my own, I see if their relevant data match our findings or if there are any inconsistencies. If there are, I think about what could be causing them. Additionally, I think about what would happen in our model if we used the same methods as they did and what we could learn from that. Sometimes, it is also important to pay attention to why the authors decided to conduct an experiment in a certain way. Did the authors use an obscure test instead of a routine assay, and why would they do this?

- *Jeremy C. Borniger*, doctoral candidate in neuroscience at Ohio State University, Columbus

I always start with title and abstract. That tells me whether or not it's an article I'm interested in and whether I'll actually be able to understand it—both scientifically and linguistically. I then read the introduction so that I can understand the question being framed, and jump right to the figures and tables so I can get a feel for the data. I then read the discussion to get an idea of how the paper fits into the general body of knowledge.

I pay attention to acknowledgement of limitations and proper inference of data. Some people stretch their claims more than others, and that can be a red flag for me. I also put on my epidemiologist hat so that I can try to make sure the study design is adequate to actually test the hypotheses being examined.

As I go deeper into the argument framing, figures, and discussion, I also think about which pieces are exciting and new, which ones are biologically or logically relevant, and which ones are most supported by the literature. I also consider which pieces fit with my pre-existing hypotheses and research questions.

- *Kevin Boehnke*, doctoral candidate in environmental health sciences at the University of Michigan, Ann Arbor

My reading strategy depends on the paper. Sometimes I start by skimming through to see how much might be relevant. If it is directly applicable to my current topic, I'll read the paper closely, apart from the introduction that is probably already familiar. But I always try to figure out if there are particular places or figures that I need to pay close attention to, and then I go and read the related information in the results and discussion.

I also check if there are references that I may be interested in. Sometimes I am curious to see who in the field has—or more likely has not—been referenced, to see whether the authors are choosing to ignore certain aspects of the research. I often find that the supplementary figures actually offer the most curious and interesting results, especially if the results relate to parts of the field that the authors did not reference or if they are unclear or unhelpful to their interpretation of the overall story.

- ***Gary McDowell***, postdoctoral fellow in developmental biology at Tufts University in Medford, Massachusetts, and visiting scholar at Boston College

When reading papers, it helps me to have a writing task so that I am being an active reader instead of letting my eyes glaze over mountains of text only to forget everything I just read. So for example, when I read for background information, I will save informative sentences from each article about a specific topic in a Word document. I'll write comments along the way about new ideas I got or questions I need to explore further. Then, in the future, I'll only need to read this document instead of re-reading all the individual papers.

Likewise, when I want to figure out how to conduct a particular experiment, I create a handy table in Excel summarizing how a variety of research teams went about doing a particular experiment.

- ***Lina A. Colucci***, doctoral candidate at the Harvard-MIT Health Sciences and Technology program

I usually start with the abstract, which gives me a brief snapshot of what the study is all about. Then I read the entire article, leaving the methods to the end unless I can't make sense of the results or I'm unfamiliar with the experiments.

The results and methods sections allow you to pull apart a paper to ensure it stands up to scientific rigor. Always think about the type of experiments performed, and whether these are the most appropriate to address the question proposed. Ensure that the authors have included relevant and sufficient numbers of controls. Often, conclusions can also be based on a limited number of samples, which limits their significance.

I like to print out the paper and highlight the most relevant information, so on a quick rescan I can be reminded of the major points. Most relevant points would be things that change your thinking about your research topic or give you new ideas and directions.

- ***Lachlan Gray***, deputy head of the HIV Neuropathogenesis Lab at the Burnet Institute and adjunct research fellow in the Department of Infectious Disease at Monash University in Melbourne, Australia

What I choose to read is based on relation to my research areas and things that are generating lots of interest and discussion because they are driving the way we do psychology, or science more widely, in new directions. Most often, what I am trying to get out of the papers is issues of methodology, experimental design, and statistical analysis. And so for me, the most important section is first what the authors did (methods) and second what they found (results).

It can also be interesting to understand why the authors thought they were doing the study (introduction) and what they think the results mean (discussion). When it is an area that I know a lot about, I don't usually care much about these sections because they often reflect the authors' theoretical predilections and one of many ways to think about the method and results. But when it is an area that I know very little about, I read these closely because then I learn a lot about the assumptions and explanatory approaches in that area of research.

- ***Brian Nosek***, professor in the Department of Psychology at the University of Virginia and executive director of the Center for Open Science in Charlottesville

First I read very fast: The point of the first reading is simply to see whether the paper is interesting for me. If it is I read it a second time, slower and with more attention to detail.

If the paper is vital to my research—and if it is theoretical—I would reinvent the paper. In such cases, I only take the starting point and then work out everything else on my own, not looking into the paper. Sometimes this is a painfully slow process. Sometimes I get angry about the authors not writing clearly enough, omitting essential points and dwelling on superfluous nonsense. Sometimes I am electrified by a paper.

- ***Ulf Leonhardt***, professor of physics at the Weizmann Institute of Science in Rehovot, Israel

I nearly always read the abstract first and only continue on to the paper if the abstract indicates that the paper will be of value to me. Then, if the topic of the paper is one I know well, I generally skim the introduction, reading its last paragraph to make sure I know the specific question being addressed in the paper. Then I look at the figures and tables, either read or skim the results, and lastly skim or read the discussion.

If the topic is not one I know well, I usually read the introduction much more carefully so that the study is placed into context for me. Then I skim the figures and tables and read the results.

- *Charles W. Fox*, professor in the Department of Entomology at the University of Kentucky in Lexington

It is important to realize that shortcuts have to be taken when reading papers so that there is time left to get our other work done, including writing, conducting research, attending meetings, teaching, and grading papers. Starting as a Ph.D. student, I have been reading the conclusions and methods of academic journal articles and chapters rather than entire books.

- *Rima Wilkes*, professor in the Department of Sociology at the University of British Columbia, Vancouver

As editor-in-chief of *Science*, I have to read and comprehend papers outside of my field all the time. Generally, I start with the corresponding editors' summaries, which are meant for someone like me: a science generalist who is interested in everything but dives deeply only into one field. Next, I check to see if someone wrote a News article on the paper. Third, I check to see if there is a Perspective by another scientist. The main goal of a Perspective is to broaden the message of the paper, but often the authors do a great job of extracting the essence of the article for non-specialists at the same time.

Then I tackle the abstract, which has been written to broadly communicate to the readership of the journal. Finally, I move on to the paper itself, reading, in order, the intro, conclusions, scanning the figures, and then reading the paper through.

- *Marcia K. McNutt*, Editor-in-Chief, *Science* journals

What do you do when there is something you don't understand?

I like to read online so that I can easily cut and paste words I don't know into a browser to check what they mean.

- McNutt

If it's only a few things in the article, I'll make a note to look them up later. If I am really struggling to proceed through the paper, I try to look up a review article or a textbook chapter to give me the necessary background to proceed, which I generally find much more efficient.

There are a lot of acronyms and jargon that can be subfield-specific, so I usually don't wade through the details unless it's for my own research. But I always try to take my time to really understand the methods being used.

- Shanahan

I will typically pause immediately to look up things I don't understand. The rest of the reading may not make sense if I don't understand a key phrase or jargon. This can backfire a bit, though, as I often go down never-ending rabbit holes after looking something up (What is X? Oh, X influences Y. ... So what's Y? etc...). This can be sort of fun as you learn how everything is connected, but if you're crunched for time this can pull your attention away from the task at hand.

Sometimes, all the jargon in a paper can cloud the whole point of the experiments in the first place. In such cases, it helps to ask yourself, "What question were the authors trying to answer?" Then you can determine whether they succeeded or failed.

- Borniger

It depends on how much the non-understandable bits prevent me from following the main ideas. I usually do not try to understand all the details in all the sections the first time I read a paper. If non-understandable parts appear important for my research, I try to ask colleagues or even contact the lead author directly. Going back to the original references to get all the background information is the last resort, because time can be limited and collaborations and personal contacts can be much more efficient in solving specific problems.

- Tubiana

Sometimes, you can just read through a paper and any terms you're not familiar with will become clearer by the end. If it is very heavy going, then stopping and seeking additional information is usually the way to go. I do a quick Google search on the topic, theme, method, jargon, etc. If it is a very dense article, sometimes it will require a few read-throughs before it all starts to make sense.

- Gray

The question I ask myself is, "Do I need to understand what that means in order to get what I need from this paper?" I now read articles in research areas well outside of my expertise, and I often don't need more than superficial knowledge of the substantive content. If I can't do anything with the paper unless I don't understand that depth, then I do more background research.

- Nosek

Lately, I have had to read a number of papers outside my area of expertise with a lot of unfamiliar jargon. In some cases, I am able to directly extract the information I need from the results or figures and tables. In other cases, I use Google searches to define terms and concepts in the paper or read the cited references to better understand the points being made. Occasionally, papers are so incomprehensible (to me, at least) that I don't bother reading them.

- Fox

Do you ever feel overwhelmed reading papers, and how do you deal with that?

All the time. If the paper is relevant to a problem I am trying to solve, you can be sure that there are key things in the paper that I do not understand. That confusion is not a threat; it is an opportunity. I am **ignorant**; I need to become less ignorant. This paper may help me.

Simultaneously, some papers are written terribly and are not worth the effort. Someone else has surely written about the concepts more clearly so that I can keep my confusion focused on understanding substance rather than poor grammar.

- Nosek

I especially get overwhelmed if it's not in my subfield, if it's long, and if it's full of technical jargon. When this happens, I break it down into chunks and will read it over the course of a few days, if possible. For really difficult papers, it also helps to sit down and work through it with a colleague.

- Shanahan

Yes, many times. This is why I developed my own reading strategies, by talking to other scientists and by trial and error. I also have thrown up my hands in frustration and tossed the offending papers away, never to read them again.

- Boehnke

Yes, and in these cases you have to realize that some papers are the result of years of work by dozens of scientists. Expecting to digest and understand everything in it in one afternoon is a far-fetched idea.
- Borniger

I have often felt overwhelmed! But certain sections might not need as deep an understanding as others. You also need to know your own limits: Are there some parts of the paper that you would like to emulate but are not part of your expertise and might become "accessible" through collaborations?
- Tubiana

If I feel the paper is very important to what I'm doing, I'll leave it a while and go back to it again a couple of times. But if it's too overwhelming, then I have to leave it aside, unless someone among the colleagues I have contacted has been able to interpret it.
- McDowell

Do you have any other tips you'd like to share?

If there is a seminal paper I want to thoroughly understand, I find some way to give a journal club-style presentation about it. Speaking about a particular paper and answering questions is the best way for me to learn the material.

Also, get a good reference manager. Mendeley helps me do my research, read literature, and write papers.
- Colucci

At the beginning, new academic readers find it slow because they have no frame of reference for what they are reading. But there are **ways** to use reading as a system of creating a mental library, and after a few years, it becomes easy to slot papers onto your mental shelves. Then you can quickly skim a paper to know its contribution.
- Wilkes

Be patient. Don't be afraid or ashamed to use Wikipedia or other, more lay-audience sources like blog posts to get a feel for your topic. Ask many, many questions. If you can't get a clear understanding of the paper, talk with people in your circle. If you are still confused and it's really important to understand the concepts, email the authors.
- Boehnke

Unit II: The Annotated Bibliography

Don't hesitate to talk to more experienced scientists. You will be doing THEM a favor by having them explain to you in terms you understand what a complex paper means. All scientists need more experience translating complex concepts into common terms.

- McNutt

If at all possible, read often. Try to keep a bibliography file with a summary of the article, any important points, even a figure or two, along with citation information. Pay attention to different ways of structuring an article, and pay attention to different styles of writing. This will help you develop a style that is effective and also unique.

- Shanahan

HOW TO READ A SCIENTIFIC ARTICLE
Mary Purugganan, Ph.D. & Jan Hewitt, Ph.D.

• • • • • • • • •

Reading a scientific article is a complex task. The *worst* way to approach this task is to treat it like the reading of a textbook—reading from title to literature cited, digesting every word along the way without any reflection or criticism. Rather, you should begin by skimming the article to identify its structure and features. As you read, look for the author's main points. Generate questions before, during, and after reading. Draw inferences based on your own experiences and knowledge. And to really improve understanding and recall, take notes as you read. This handout discusses each of these strategies in more detail.

1. Skim the article and identify its structure.

Most journals use a conventional IMRD structure: An abstract followed by Introduction, Methods, Results, and Discussion. Each of these sections normally contains easily recognized conventional features, and if you read with an anticipation of these features, you will read an article more quickly and comprehend more.

Features of Abstracts

Abstracts usually contain four kinds of information:

• purpose or rationale of study (why they did it)

• methodology (how they did it)

• results (what they found)

• conclusion (what it means)

Most scientists read the abstract first. Others—especially experts in the field—skip right from the title to the visuals because the visuals, in many cases, tell the reader what kinds of experiments were done and what results were obtained. You should probably begin reading a paper by reading the abstract carefully and noting the four kinds of information outlined above. Then move first to the visuals and then to the rest of the paper.

Features of Introductions

Introductions serve two purposes: creating readers' interest in the subject and providing them with enough information to understand the article. Generally, introductions accomplish this by leading readers from broad information (what is *known* about the topic) to more specific information (what is *not known*) to a focal point (what *question* the authors asked and answered). Thus, authors describe previous work that led to current understanding of the topic (the broad) and then situate their work (the specific) within the field.

Features of Methods

The Methods section tells the reader what experiments were done to answer the question stated in the Introduction. Methods are often difficult to read, especially for graduate students, because of technical language and a level of detail sufficient for another trained scientist to repeat the experiments. However, you can more fully understand the design of the experiments and evaluate their validity by reading the Methods section carefully.

Features of Results and Discussion

The Results section contains results—statements of what was found, and reference to the data shown in visuals (figures and tables). Normally, authors do not include information that would need to be referenced, such as comparison to others' results. Instead, that material is placed in the Discussion—placing the work in context of the broader field. The Discussion also functions to provide a clear answer to the question posed in the Introduction and to explain how the results support that conclusion.

Atypical Structure

Some articles you read will deviate from the conventional content of IMRD sections. For instance, Letters to *Nature* appear to begin with an abstract, followed by the body of the article. Upon reading, however, you will see that the "abstract" is a summary of the work filled with extensive introduction (for the purpose of catching the attention of a wide audience), and the next paragraph begins a description of the experiments.

Therefore, when you begin to read an article for the first time, skim the article to analyze the document as a whole. Are the sections labeled with headings that identify the structure? If not, note what the structure is. Decide which sections contain the material most essential to your understanding of the article. Then decide the order in which you will read the sections.

2. Distinguish main points.

Because articles contain so much information, it may be difficult to distinguish the *main points* of an article from the *subordinate points*. Fortunately, there are many indicators of the author's main points:

Document level

- Title
- Abstract
- Keywords
- visuals (especially figure and table titles)
- first sentence or the last 1-2 sentences of the Introduction

Paragraph level: words or phrases to look for

- *surprising*
- *unexpected*
- *in contrast with previous work*
- *has seldom been addressed*
- *we hypothesize that*
- *we propose*
- *we introduce*
- *we develop*
- *the data suggest*

3. Generate questions and be aware of your understanding.

Reading is an active task. Before and during your reading, ask yourself these questions:

- Who are these authors? What journal is this? Might I question the credibility of the work?
- Have I taken the time to understand all the terminology?
- Have I gone back to read an article or review that would help me understand this work better?
- Am I spending too much time reading the less important parts of this article?
- Is there someone I can talk to about confusing parts of this article?

After reading, ask yourself these questions:

- What specific problem does this research address? Why is it important?

- Is the method used a good one? The best one?

- What are the specific findings? Am I able to summarize them in one or two sentences?

- Are the findings supported by persuasive evidence?

- Is there an alternative interpretation of the data that the author did not address?

- How are the findings unique/new/unusual or supportive of other work in the field?

- How do these results relate to the work I'm interested in? To other work I've read about?

- What are some of the specific applications of the ideas presented here? What are some further experiments that would answer remaining questions?

4. Draw inferences.

Not everything that you learn from an article is stated explicitly. As you read, rely on your prior knowledge and world experience, as well as the background provided in the article, to draw inferences from the material. Research has shown that readers who actively draw inferences are better able to understand and recall information.

As an example, in the box below is an excerpt from the Introduction of an article in the journal *Biochemistry (Ballestar et al., 2000)*. The comments in italics are questions and inferences that might be drawn by a student reader.

Rett Syndrome is a childhood neurodevelopmental disorder and one of the most common causes of mental retardation in females *Comment: Hmmm...must be related to a gene on the X-chromosome*, with an incidence of 1 in 10000-15000. *Comment: How common is that? Not too likely to happen to me, but there must be several such children born in Houston every year.* Rett syndrome patients are characterized by a period of normal growth and development (6-18 months) followed by regression with loss of speech and purposeful hand use. *Comment: What happens? Something must be triggered or activated at late infancy.* Patients also

---

develop seizures, autism, and ataxia. After initial regression, the condition stabilizes and patients survive into adulthood. Studies of familial cases provided evidence that Rett is caused by X-linked dominant mutations in a gene subject to X-chromosome inactivation. Recently, a number of mutations in the gene encoding the methyl-CpG binding transcriptional repressor MeCP2 have been associated with Rett Syndrome. *Comment: MeCP2 mutations probably cause Rett Syndrome. This must be an important master-regulator to affect so many processes in the brain. I wonder what they know about it...*

5. Take notes as you read.

Effective readers take notes—it improves recall and comprehension. You may think you'll remember everything you read in researching class assignments, professional papers, proposals, or your thesis, but details will slip away. Develop a template for recording notes on articles you read, or adapt the template below for use. As you accumulate a large collection of articles, this template will help you distinguish articles and quickly locate the correct reference for your own writing. The time spent filling out the form will save you hours of rereading when you write a Background, Related Work, or a Literature Review section.

Template for Taking Notes on Research Articles:
Easy access for later use

Complete citation. Author(s), Date of publication, Title (book or article), publisher, Journal, Volume #, Issue #, pages. How you use this information will vary by journal Style Sheet requirements, class requirements, or thesis advisor/departmental requirements. Put everything down initially so you'll have what you later need. If you import the information, be certain it is complete. Check key journals in your field for Style requirements; use the Web to access detailed examples of Chicago or APA styles. You can also find examples in a recent edition of a writer's handbook such as Diana Hacker's *The Bedford Handbook*. Always be consistent within a document!

If electronic source: URL (may be required by your advisor or professional journal); DOI (digital object identifier) if available or name of database or document number; date retrieved. PUT QUOTATION MARKS

AROUND ANY IMPORTED BLOCK OF TEXT so that you won't later think it is your wording. Indicate the DATE ACCESSED.

Key Words (Be precise, not general):

Specific subject:

Authors' Hypothesis or Claim (What do they say they are presenting that is NEW?):

Method(s):

Result(s):

Evidence:

Summary of key points: Use quotation marks around any exact wording.

Context and relationships: How does this article relate to YOUR work and to other research? What ISSUES are raised by the authors?   What is your stand on them? (Needed for a lit review):

Important Figures and/or Tables (Import or give brief description; page number):

Cited References to follow up on (Cite those obviously related to your topic AND any papers frequently cited by others because those works may well prove to be important as you develop your own work):

Your evaluative comments on the work: For example, does the paper clearly identify its contribution to the field? Is the method used an appropriate one? Do the results match the claim? Is the evidence sufficient and convincing? What flaws do you see in the paper? What strengths? How can this paper be helpful to your own research and/or writing?

References

Ballestar, E., Yusufzai, T.M., and Wolffe, A.P. (2000) Effects of Rett Syndrome Mutations of the Methyl-CpG Binding Domain of the Transcriptional Repressor MeCP2 on Selectivity for Association with Methylated DNA. *Biochemistry* 31, 7100-7106.

Burnett, R. (2001) *Technical Communication*. 5th ed. San Antonio: Harcourt College Publishers.

Zeiger, M. (2000) *Essentials of Writing Biomedical Research Papers*. 2nd Ed. St. Louis: McGraw-Hill. Supported by the Cain Project for Engineering and Professional Communication Rice University, 2004

Unit II: The Annotated Bibliography

GETTING STARTED WRITING PROMPT

It may be surprising to hear that, in order to complete this work well, writing will need to be one of your final steps. In the beginning, you should focus your attention on *preparing to write* by collecting reliable sources and taking detailed notes over them. This seems simple; you may envision yourself browsing the internet, skimming a few sources, and writing a paragraph or two about what you read, but this is only superficially true. Since the Annotated Bibliography requires a unique dedication to ethicacy and organization within your research process, you should consider practicing rhetorical reading.

Because each individual is different, and different situations might require different strategies, we don't feel that it is wise for us to prescribe reading strategies as a formula or to suggest that one strategy is better than the other. However, as you begin to collect and sift through the mounds of research that likely already exists about your topic, you may find working through each of the following questions useful in determining which sources are most relevant for the work you want to create.

- Who is the author/editor/creator of this source? What credibility do they bring with them to the text? What credibility to do they build within the text's content?

- How is the text organized, and why do you think that is? In other words, in what order is the information presented, and what does that tell you about the discipline in a broader sense?

- What information does the text focus on, and what information is missing? (If the text discusses limitations of the study, you might look more closely to see what they cover and what still goes undiscussed).

- What words are repeated throughout the text? What words are new to you? What familiar words take on new meanings in this disciplinary context?

- What claims does the author make explicitly versus what claims seem to be implicit?

- To whom is this text directed? Who might be a secondary audience? What markers led you to this conclusion?

- What bibliographic information does the author include for his references? What relation do these texts have to the text at hand?

Remember, academic databases are tricky animals that can morph as often as the texts and genres found within them; as you search, you will need to remain adaptable to new rhetorical environments, genres, purposes, and discourse conventions.

Unit III: The Persuasive Literature Review

INTRODUCTION TO THE LITERATURE REVIEW

The literature review serves a very specific purpose in academic writing, though it does not always take the same form in each discipline. Broadly, the literature review looks at specific questions in a specific discipline and provides a broad overview of how the discipline has responded to the question. Some disciplines prefer that the literature review remain objective in tone, while others perceive it as an inherently persuasive genre. The purpose and audience of the literature review will change depending on the rhetorical situation, but many of the characteristics will remain the same.

As you progress throughout your academic career you will probably be asked to read, and to write, at least a few more literature reviews, and you will notice slightly nuanced differences in each assignment or each lit review you pore over. Paying attention to these slight differences can help you best grasp the expectations of your instructor and, more broadly, the discipline you are entering; after all, they provide scholars with an overview and a history of the conversations the discipline has engaged with and, often just as importantly, those it has not engaged with. Knowing this can help you situate your own scholarship, and maybe even make a contribution to your field!

Purpose

The literature review section follows the annotated bibliography for a reason. Both the annotated bibliography and the literature review are legitimate academic genres in their own right, but when we design our courses we look to scaffold assignments—that is, to build later assignments off those which precede them. Therefore, while the annotated bibliography asks you to develop many skills, such as analysis, summary, and writing to make your points as concise as possible, the literature review asks you to expand these skills and engage in further critical thinking. This assignment should help you begin to think about how research begins to tell a story of disciplinary engagement with a topic and how to best organize and present this material to suit your purpose and your audience's needs.

Audience

The intended audience (outside of your instructor) is your group members, who will need to see the way your discipline, overall, has responded to your chosen topic.

Content and Requirements

The literature review will:

- Provide an overview of the scholarship your discipline has undertaken on your chosen topic;
- Persuade your audience that this contribution fits with your chosen research question;
- Follow a clear organizational pattern; and
- Address any shortcomings or gaps in the literature.

Organization and Format

The literature review should:

- Be about 1,400 words in length;
- Contain at least five and no more than seven sources, of which at least three should be scholarly and the rest should be reliable; and
- Be formatted in the style guide of the author's chosen discipline.

Strategies for Composing a Successful Literature Review

- Find agreements and points of departure among your sources.
- Look for gaps in the literature; what is not covered is as important as what is covered.
- Be aware of the importance of continuously making your connections clear to the reader.

THE IMPORTANCE OF GLOBAL JOURNALISM

Karis Evans

Literature Review: Written for Airek Beauchamp's Composition II class

• • • • • • • • •

Karis is a sophomore majoring in Multimedia Journalism and minoring in Political Science. She worked diligently on her essay, as she found the topic not only interesting but also germane to her future career.

Minor state elections in the United States may never appear to be important on the national radar. However, while examining the crises outside the borders, every issue has the potential to be internationally significant. Due to globalization, countries hold one another accountable economically and politically. Journalists covering stories on the global spectrum have several aspects to consider in what issues are to be included for citizen speculation, such as relevance and close connections to the countries being discussed. Furthermore, they need to focus more on what is happening globally to properly inform the public since the events could be closer to home than the general population may realize.

Global journalism is a very broad subject, and it's imperative to understand what it encompasses. Peter Berglez presented research on international journalism and how the style contrasts to domestic journalism used within countries. However, one definition isn't possible to pin down due to the constantly changing state of globalization. Berglez wrote, ". . . global journalism ought to be the kind of journalistic practice which 'makes it into an everyday routine to investigate how people and their actions, practices, problems, life conditions etc. in different parts of the world are interrelated'" (Berglez 846). Reporting on the global scale includes seeking out connections between different cultures and people, because the audience would then be able to understand the social background and what may have attributed to the event or disaster. Using the global outlook would allow journalists to seek commonalities so they could provide information on pandemic threats, transnational processes, and unrestricted economic flow (Berglez 847). Journalism is always examining relations between people and practices, and the same practices are used on the global scale.

The media, however, may highlight one focus or country over others in the examination of global news. Brandon Gorman and Charles Seguin dive into the subject of certain foreign leaders in media coverage, and what makes some countries more important than others. They approach the subject from two different viewpoints: realist and liberal. From realist traditions, the world thrives from the logic of self-help and survival, and liberal views would see the world as cooperative and interdependent (Gorman, Seguin 776). The two scholars work to identify the reasons some countries get more air time over others. Applying the realist view, "The most powerful countries are the most important in the international system, and events that can potentially alter the global balance of power, such as wars are central features" (Gorman, Seguin 777). This perspective would reveal that the only news-worthy stories on the global spectrum would be those that have greater possibility of affecting the home country. However, with the liberal view, "[S]tates that are prominent within international organizations are thus seen as the most influential in the international system, and processes that increase connectivity among states, such as trade, are central features" (Gorman, Seguin 777). As a result of this stance, the media coverage of partners will interconnect the countries from their economic ties. With either perspective, global news coverage has the tendency to neglect countries that don't play major firsthand roles in the betterment of the United States, economically or politically.

From the changing technological world, the way citizens get their news has broadened to the use of the internet. George Lazaroiu wrote about the expansion of journalistic styles due to the new medium. He wrote, ". . . although online journalism is still dominated by breaking news coverage, new genres are emerging that differentiate it more and more from old journalism" (Lazaroiu 165). Traditional news sources such as BBC, CNN, and the *New York Times* are prime examples of informants that use the internet to post their breaking news stories. However, bias is a recurring issue for media when looking at global news, so the new genres could be used as an advantage to remain equal in reporting news from different countries. Lazaroiu wrote on the issue, stating, "Media skew has serious ramifications for people's understanding of and perceptions of a hazard situation or disastrous event. Internet media may compensate for the basing influence of capital concentration in the print and broadcast journalism" (Lazaroiu 166). The alternative news sources would be able to write on an event and not worry about viewership numbers as print and broadcast media does. In Gorman's writing, the issue of focusing on main contributors to the US was discussed, and part of the reason is that citizens will pay attention to news of countries they recognize. When they don't show interest in certain international stories, print and broadcast media don't give those pieces as much air time as breaking news stories. The

Internet gives the opportunity to dive into those global events to provide in depth features through that medium.

Globalization plays a major role in the world today, including media and news coverage. Simon Cottle studied how distant disasters feel close to home due to globalization. As a result of efforts to connect with other countries, every fundamental problem is globally oriented and invigorated (Cottle 78). Every natural disaster, rebellion, or political conflict would always hold the possibility of retaliation from both allies and enemies. For example, natural disasters or conflicts surrounding a region could lead to the advancement of war aims from opponents (Cottle 80). Cottle further examines the effects of globalization on journalism techniques, and the lack of coverage on international disasters. He wrote, ". . . [networks] have yet to recognize global crises more theoretically as critical drivers in ongoing processes of globalization . . ." (80). He reveals through several references to scholars, that journalists must look at global crises from a new perspective to fully be able to cover the global stories efficiently for their audience.

Further research reveals how the audience reacts to the news of distant disasters and human suffering. Maria Kyriakidou studied how media coverage of distant suffering is perceived by the audience. The study was carried out by having focus groups read news articles through different mediums and recording their reactions to the stories. Before revealing the results of the study, she first identifies that mediation is the key concept in understanding the inclusion of international media in the news. She wrote of the practices of producers providing social, economic, and political context to the images used, and that such practices "cannot be taken for granted on the basis of the global dissemination of media cultural products" (Kyriakidou 486). This practice was significant in the focus groups in order for the participants to fully comprehend the disasters discussed. Cosmopolitanism was discussed as respondents made connections with the suffering as "empathy towards the victims, as an awareness of a global community of viewers, and finally, as a responsibility for the alleviation of the suffering" (Kyriakidou 487). As the participants were made aware of how much others were suffering, their first instinct is to help instead of turning a blind eye since they aren't close in proximity to the issue.

The research presented gives several different aspects of globalization and covering global news. One major underlying theme throughout the scholarly articles is that news on the global scale is significant for all people to be aware of. The media offers a number of news sources for people to take advantage of, but it's their choice to acknowledge the world around them. Not only are citizens supposed to know what is happening in their town, county, or state, but they should look beyond their country's borders to examine the interdependence of the global system.

Work Cited

Berglez, Peter. "What Is Global Journalism?." *Journalism Studies* 9.6 (2008): 845-858. *Communication & Mass Media Complete.* Web. 11 Mar. 2016.

Cottle, Simon. "Taking Global Crises in the News Seriously: Notes from the Dark Side of Globalization."*Global Media & Communication* 7.2 (2011): 77-95. *Communication & Mass Media Complete.* Web. 11 Mar. 2016.

Gorman, Brandon, and Charles Seguin. "Reporting The International System: Attention To Foreign Leaders In The US News Media, 1950-2008." *Social Forces* 2 (2015): 775. *Opposing Viewpoints in Context.* Web. 11 Mar. 2016.

Kyriakidou, Maria. "Imagining Ourselves Beyond The Nation? Exploring Cosmopolitanism In Relation To Media Coverage Of Distant Suffering." *Studies In Ethnicity & Nationalism* 9.3 (2009): 481. Publisher Provided Full Text Searching File. Web. 11 Mar. 2016.

Lāzāroiu, George. "Global Journalism And The Heterogeneity Of Internet Communication." Annals Of Spiru Haret University, *Journalism Studies* 10.(2009): 165-170. *Communication & Mass Media Complete.* Web. 11 Mar. 2016.

"THE GREAT DEBATE"

Austin May

Literature Review: Written for Airek Beauchamp's Composition II class

• • • • • • • •

Austin is a Junior Finance and Accounting major from Little Rock, Arkansas. As might be evident by his essay, in his first year he was an Engineering major and his Literature Review reflects on the nature of writing for that specific discipline. He has enjoyed all of his time spent at Arkansas State University and hopes to share more great experiences with his peers during his remaining few semesters. He plans to graduate in May of 2018 and pursue a career in banking specializing in personal wealth management. As a student, Austin challenges everyone to take pride in their work since the results can and mostly will be a direct reflection of the student.

When writing, Austin takes time to look into his work from many different perspectives and likes to get insight from others whom review his work. He feels that the writing center has helped him take different approaches at writing papers and feels he is more efficient at closing the gap between what the writer is trying to say and what the reader is pulling from the text. He feels that knowledge is the greatest tool we have and everyone should view education as a useful and necessary means to growing oneself.

When considering professions and how they affect people, we may initially think about occupations in medicine and business. Fewer, however, give thought to the field of engineering and how directly it impacts people's lives. Every day, billions of commuters travel across bridges but how many recognize the thought, planning, and effort put into each detail of the work of art? Given the important function of this art however, as well as the potential for disaster should it fail, some are concerned about the current qualifications—or lack thereof—required for students to become engineers.

Over the years, the requirements to be an engineer have completely shifted. Up until about the 1950s, anyone with an above average ability to solve problems and ingenuity could easily prove themselves worthy of building structures. Back then "engineers" were simply farmers trying to solve problems on their own land, cheaply but efficiently building bridges, structures, and other devices used for farming. Calling that kind of person an engineer today is laughable, now we have to earn the title through strenuous and time-consuming classes just for a bachelor's degree in any field of engineering. And as our understanding of science and physics increases, many people believe the requisite qualifications to become an engineer should increase, as well.

Is four years of college enough to prepare a person for the responsibility of millions of commuters lives? To become a civil engineer specializing in structures, all that is needed is a bachelor's degree and a professional engineering license. To acquire a PE license, one must pass an eight-hour test which "comprises engineering-specific skills [including how to] identify, formulate, and solve technical/engineering problems, . . . use appropriate/modern tools, . . . and apply knowledge of mathematics, science, engineering" (Blom 9).

This strikes an argument amongst those unfamiliar with engineering and licenses. Here Blom did well on hitting the key points of what the test consist of, although he did not go into further detail about what exact subjects and types of questions lie within the test. If revised, Blom would likely need to further support the statements by telling the reader the laundry list of steps just to qualify to take the test, as well as more deeply investigate the test itself. This is where the argument begins. Most think that since bachelor's degrees are one of the most acquired degrees by college students, engineers with bachelor's degrees fall short of the proper knowledge and training needed to design and construct a structure meant to support heavy vehicles and lives of the drivers operating them.

We must also consider whether qualifications are examined thoroughly by the institutions responsible for finding and hiring engineers to build structures. "In one study of 149 firms hiring scientists and engineers fresh from college, it was found that for 80% of the firms, the personality factor was of primary importance. It was more important than the individual's course of training, work experience, and college grades" (French 270). Here the author, French, uses research from a study done to prove a point being made in his article. French adds a statistic found during a study to help attract the reader's attention and also give his side of the argument more concrete support. French argues from the opposite side of the fence but gives the readers something that sounds more credible. Thinking this way gives the writer, the ability to add an even more solid foundation of text to the articles read and gives him/her the advantage to sway people's minds in the direction of the argument.

Of course, we should take into account the course work, time, money and natural problem-solving abilities engineers have. These may speak volumes themselves and could easily persuade some readers that even basic engineers are actually over qualified. This article does an excellent job of arguing how well rounded an engineer with "just" a bachelor's degree really is by stating that to receive a BSCE one must complete the program which has the aspiration to train the students to become critical, conscious and committed engineering scientists in a spirit of liberal examination from a non-dogmatic and pluralistic point of view towards society and the chosen engineering specialization field, with emphasis on the sustainability of the solutions, ethics and awareness of the implications to the environment (Van Biesen 221).

Here, Van Biesen uses extremely impressive diction which not only makes himself sound more intelligent, but also shows how educated he is in the field. Biesen talks about two points of view (non-dogmatic and Pluralistic) when approaching the path of not only gaining a bachelor's degree in civil engineering but also further applying the degree in the working world. He then goes on to point out that gaining a bachelor's degree will also teach the engineer the importance of "ethics and awareness" when working with different environments.

Biesen did a fine job breaking down the attributes an engineer will gain and explaining the whole process of engineer qualifications. He used in-depth research and incredible diction, but also told the readers the mental attributes and morals that are gained with just a four-year degree. The writer also shows strong bias towards the appreciation and commitment of basic level engineers which helps support the argument presented in the piece.

Looking at it from the other side means exploring the minds of those who think engineers are under qualified in their fields of expertise. A prime example is the collapse of the Hoan Bridge many years ago due to "the geometric arrangement of the lateral bracing connection into the web of the girders that created a highly constrained condition and prevented yielding of the girder web when overloaded" (Hesse 1). Hesse then follows with "This paper describes the failure and its causes and suggests engineering lessons to be learned. The unique details of the failure offer the opportunity to promote critical thinking and problem solving at levels appropriate to undergraduate students" (Hesse 1). Hesse shows readers that he has a deep level of understanding about the function of bridges by stating specific parts and how they work. He then goes on to further his argument by stating that "undergraduates" can promote their skills as engineers, which in a way manipulates readers into thinking that undergraduate students are responsible for the collapse of the bridge solely due to being under qualified. The writer can be seen using accurate descriptions of what actually happened to further his credibility on the subject. Hesse then makes his argument clear by stating who can learn from the mistakes made.

I believe that engineers should stand out as one of, if not the most, ethical people in the workforce showing that not only do they take pride in their work but also apply themselves when learning as well. It is stated very clearly in the Engineering preamble "Engineers must perform under a standard of professional behavior that requires adherence to the highest principles of ethical conduct" emphasizing that being an ethical worker and thinker is the backbone of the engineering world (Burgess 1). Implicit in this statement are the extremely challenging four years of school work to acquire a bachelor's degree as well as the preparation needed to take and pass the Professional Engineering exam. It is safe to say that engineers are easily well qualified to hold the responsibility of building a structure that will hold and support human lives.

Engineering is, and always will be, a changing process due to the steady inflow of new research and the many ways the world is constantly changing. This is not a bad thing though. Since engineering is always evolving, this means that the modern-day engineer has a very small chance of making mistakes that an engineer even fifteen years ago could make. When it comes to structural engineering, the methods and plans of building bridges have come an astonishingly long way from our ancient, first attempts. The minimum requirement of today's structural engineer isn't even imaginable to an engineer of the 1950's. This is mostly due to the thousands of changes and laws set in place with only one purpose; keeping the public safe.

As an engineering student myself, I can personally attest to the qualifications of a four-year degree. Though only in the second semester of my Freshman year, I have already taken mathematics and science courses that some will not take until junior or senior year. Success lies within the student's ability to work and learn. If one has good work ethic and is responsible, then that person will one day be a very good engineer. If one does not have good work ethic and is not very responsible, the engineering program will more than likely weed that person out. Reason is, engineering classes are all building classes meaning that to go on to higher level courses, one must actually learn and master the prerequisites. This means that unless one is a modern-day Einstein, there is no way possible that one can slide through the cracks to obtain a four-year degree in any type of engineering.

Passing the Professional Engineering exam is another feat which most cannot conquer. This exam is eight hours long and covers almost every key subject involved in engineering. To be precise, only about twenty percent of all graduated students actually hold a Professional Engineering license; only the most qualified engineers only holding a bachelor's degree are the ones that we rely on to build the structures and bridges that support our everyday transportation and livelihoods. Most do not even realize that a prerequisite to taking the Professional Engineering exam is another eight hours exam called the Fundamentals of Engineering Exam which typically has a passing rate of less than 80%. From this point the statistics continue to spiral downward leaving us at a final percentage of about 20% who actually receive their PE license.

The guidelines and requirements in the modern era of engineering prove reliable when promoting public safety and welfare. Not only do the laws set in place never fail, they continue to grow safer as newer technology is created and used. Modern engineers have proved themselves worthy holding the lowest failure rate ever recorded in history. Structural engineering has become a much-mastered art form due to the many safe and consistently employed methods existing in the new century. It is easy to see that "Engineers are uniquely suited to contribute to the solution rather than the problem" (Burgess 1404). Showing us all that engineering and the writing that is associated with it is a beautiful and necessary art that lets us sustain life through the use of science.

Works Cited

Blom, Andreas and Hiroshi Saeki. "Employability and Skill Sets of Newly Graduated Engineers in India: A Study." *IUP Journal of Soft Skills,* vol. 6, no. 4, Dec. 2012, pp. 7-50. EBSCOhost, ezproxy. library.astate.edu/login?url=http://search.ebscohost.com/login. aspx?direct=true&db=bsh&AN=85170845&site=ehost-live.

Burgess, Richard1, et al. "Engineering Ethics: Looking Back, Looking Forward." *Science & Engineering Ethics,* vol. 19, no. 3, Sept. 2013, pp. 1395-1404. EBSCOhost, doi:10.1007/s11948-012-9374-7.

French, Earl B. "The Organization Scientist: Myth or Reality." *Academy of Management Journal,* vol. 10, no. 3, Sept. 1967, pp. 269-273. EBSCOhost, doi:10.2307/255285.

Hesse, Alex A., et al. "Approach-Span Failure of the Hoan Bridge as a Case Study for Engineering Students and Practicing Engineers." *Journal of Performance of Constructed Facilities,* vol. 28, no. 2, Number 2/April 2014, pp. 341-348. EBSCOhost, ezproxy.library. astate.edu/login?url=http://search.ebscohost.com/login.aspx?direct=true&db=eoah&AN=32405556&site=ehost-live.

Van Biesen, Leo Pierre, et al. "Engineering Skills Education: The Bachelor of Engineering Programme of the 'Vrije Universiteit Brussel' as a Case Study." *European Journal of Engineering Education,* vol. 34, no. 3, June 2009, pp. 217-228. EBSCOhost, doi:10.1080/03043790902721496.

GETTING STARTED ON THE LITERATURE REVIEW

As you consider what the transition from annotated bibliography to literature review will look like, spend about five minutes listing common themes and any gaps in the information. Spend another five putting the sources in chronological order, paying attention to any significant changes over time. These two brief sketches can provide an outline of the two most common organizational patterns for a literature review: thematic and chronological. Fill these outlines in with the research you develop throughout the assignment, and once you begin drafting you will be able to see what each iteration of your literature review should look like as a fleshed-out draft.

Unit IV: Colloquium Presentations and Reflection

INTRODUCTION TO THE COLLOQUIUM
Leslie Reed

· · · · · · · · ·

Celebrations mark important milestones in our lives by recognizing our hard work and celebrating our accomplishments. While you are familiar with traditional celebrations, such as birthdays and graduations, have you celebrated work produced in one semester? You may have participated in a science fair or an end-of-term presentation, or this might be your first opportunity. Yes, we will celebrate our work in Composition II at the A-State Composition Colloquium. Not only will we take time enjoy the semester's work, we will share the knowledge gained from your collaborative endeavor with the A-State community.

When we designed the colloquium, we designed it with an eye on several outcomes, but mainly we wanted to disrupt many of the traditional ways we think of what it means to have your work made public and what speaking about your work in public looks and sounds like. There is definitely a place for standard speeches and oral reports, but we didn't feel like this was that place. We wanted to continue our focus on genre, audience, purpose, and to highlight what revision looks like in a new and very transformative way—but we also wanted to hand the reins to the students.

You might be a bit nervous about presenting your work, but you will find that by the end of the semester, being informed about your issue makes it easier to talk with others, as you will have a valuable contribution to make. Students also find it helpful to know that projects are presented in a large room side-by-side. The audience will come to your table to see your project and talk with you personally as opposed to you being on a stage speaking to a large audience. As you talk with visitors about your work, we hope that you will find that you are enjoying celebrating the success of your project.

Purpose

Beyond the excitement of presenting and celebrating, knowing that the colloquium is part of the curriculum changes the drafting process in subtle but important ways. Having an audience outside of the classroom causes you think differently about your work; the goal of "getting a good grade" is no longer the only consideration when you know that an audience from across the university will be viewing your work.

In addition to changes in drafting processes, preparing and presenting at the colloquium creates an opportunity to practice other important skills. Collaborating with others, organizing and developing a project, designing a presentation, presenting to an audience, and all of the other aspects of this project are skills that you will find meaningful throughout your academic and professional lives.

Audience

The audiences for this assignment stretch across the academic and public, and each audience will have at least a slightly different understanding of the purpose of the assignment. Public stakeholders in your project will be looking largely for practicality and ease of communication. Members of the academic community might look more closely at your research and formatting. It might be daunting to think of these audiences all viewing your work, but keep in mind that you communicate across genres and to different purposes all the time.

Content and Requirements

The requirements for your presentation will vary by instructor, intended audience, and the genres and platforms you choose to create within. The one constant that we can prescribe is that presentations should engage your audience in your research.

Strategies for Composing a Successful Colloquium Presentation

- Observe and consider different forms of digital and public genres.
- Think about the affordances and limitations of each.
  - How does each offer unique and effective characteristics?
  - What factors ultimately limit functionality or effectiveness?
- Draft out your desired audiences and impacts.
  - What genres are best suited to each of these?

GETTING STARTED ON THE
COLLOQUIUM PRESENTATION

Starting this project will probably initially seem daunting, but as long as there is clear and open communication between the members of your group, it should be a matter of continuing conversation, experimentation, and revision. Be honest with your group members about your availability. Spend some time getting to know each other's strengths and weaknesses.

Probably the most important thing to know as you begin this project is that you should remain open to new ideas and new approaches. Spend as much time as you can experimenting and thinking through the rhetorical situations, specifically the audiences you will be addressing, as you consider your options.

WHAT AMERICANS LACK IN SCIENTIFIC KNOWLEDGE
Gabrielle Rannals
Argument in an Infographic: Written in Elizabeth Chamberlain's
Composition I class

· · · · · · · · ·

Gabrielle Rannals was born in Jonesboro, AR, and raised in Paragould, AR. She lives on a farm with her two dogs that she adores. Even though she resides almost an hour from the A-State campus, she commutes and arrives hours before her classes start. She says, "being ahead of my tasks and consistently being prepared is a huge part of my motivation and success with my academics." She believes it is important to stay true to yourself and to do the best in everything you do. She loves her family and she encourages others to creatively express themselves.

The Assignment: Argument in an Infographic

You may have heard that everything around you is a form of argument, but it is unlikely that you have ever tried to create one outside the familiar medium of the printed word. However, traditional textual arguments are only one of many ways authors can present their positions to their audiences. Using charts, graphs and other images to display information, known as infographics, can also be effective means to convey desired messages.

By reading data with a critical eye and arranging it carefully, you can use scientific research to persuade your audience, perhaps even when the same group could not be easily swayed through the use of words alone. To this end, you will use rhetorical strategies to practice the art of visual argumentation. Your infographic must present data from a research report in variety of charts and graphs. The title of your infographic should make a clear point that is supported with subheadings (which make subclaims), and you should demonstrate your point through the evidence in your graphs. Be sure to represent ten or more data points both literally and abstractly in those graphs, making sure they are arranged in an interesting way. Finally, cite the name of the research group responsible for the report you used to create your infographic along with a URL to the actual report you used.

Regarding citations, Gabrielle's instructor for the class, Elizabeth Chamberlain, notes that: This infographic is the only piece in this book without citations in MLA, APA, or Chicago style. When you compose in a genre outside the bounds of traditional academic essays, you'll look for models to understand how it works: How it begins. How it ends. How it looks. How it's organized. But you should also consider how its composers treat sources. Do they cite in the body of the piece, or only at the end? Do they include links? Titles? Names of creators? Do they follow any standard citation format, or does it vary?

Most infographics cite sources, as Gabrielle Rannals has done, in a footnote at the bottom of the image. This infographic draws from just one source—but when an infographic has multiple sources, composers will sometimes distinguish among them in the body with symbols corresponding to footnotes (e.g., * vs † vs +).

If your composition instructor assigns a digital composition (such as an infographic, a video, or an audio essay), you'll discuss how to cite appropriately in that genre. Though citation styles differ from genre to genre and field to field, they all have the same goal: To give credit where credit is due.

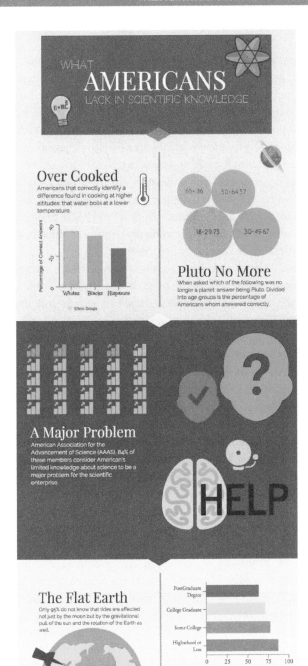

THE REFLECTIVE PORTFOLIO

The final assignment for this course is a reflective portfolio. This project can, and should, take different forms for different writers, but the single commonality is that you will compile all of your major projects from this course—the proposal, the annotated bibliography, the literature review, and the colloquium presentation—and place them together into one text. Depending upon your instructor's directives, you may choose from a variety of textual mediums in which to combine your work. You may want to digitize your texts by creating an interactive website, or maybe you will take a classical approach by arranging everything into a single document with a cover page. However you choose to display your completed work is only the first portion of this project, though. We must focus our attention on that first word: "reflective."

At its most simple definition, to reflect means to look at something again and contemplate it in an intentionally thoughtful manner. In the context of this course, you will look at the work you have compiled for your portfolio, and the process you went through to complete them, and write about that experience. This kind of writing about writing is an important aspect of the composition process because it provides an opportunity for scholars to observe the progression of their skills through an objective lens. This meta-cognitive action requires the writer-scholar to pause after the completion of a major project, or set of projects, to take stock of what she has accomplished, what she has learned, and what she can still improve upon. Reflective writing gives scholars a unique opportunity to recognize a making of knowledge. It is not the doing of the original work that teaches us all we need to know, but when we write about our writing, we can begin to identify themes and patterns within our process that can help us improve in the future. It can also reveal to us strengths that we may not have known we possessed.

You have covered a vast terrain of intellectual ground this semester; you have been introduced to some of the origins of rhetorical theory, the various forms of academic research, and to the process of writing itself. You have experimented with genre conventions, engaged in civic, social, and academic conversations. You've even conducted academic research through a focused, disciplinary lens. It is likely that all of these concepts have not always been easy for you. You may not have understood how to use an academic database (most freshmen don't), or perhaps you were uncomfortable with group work. Maybe you have never had to recognize and confront your own preconceived notions on a topic in a meaningful way. Or, maybe you are just really terrible at keeping a deadline. Whatever your imperfection may be, take time now to review and recognize those aspects of your writer-self that may have changed or that still need to change in order to be the scholar you hope to become. You should also focus on the wins here as well. What are you really proud of from your work in this course? Are there skills or concepts learned here that you applied to other courses?

QUESTIONS TO CONSIDER

- How did the assignments you completed help you understand rhetorical concepts such as purpose, audience, genre and tone?
- How did you feel about engaging in lager civic, social and academic conversations at the start of the semester compared to now?
- How have the research elements of the course prepared you to participate in academic conversations in the future?
- Consider your writing process: how has it changed since the start of the course, what do you do differently, are there any skills or practices you will continue to work on?

Sample
Student Portfolios

INTRODUCTION

Having provided you with examples of assignment sheets, and a peek into the pedagogical drives that informed our composition of the assignments, it is time for you to see student writing in action. Each of the essays in this chapter was provided by actual students in Composition II classes on the Arkansas State campus. Along with each assignment, we have asked the author to provide a brief bio and writing advice for future students (you!). We have structured this chapter to reflect the same order in which we presented the sample assignment sheets in the previous chapter: beginning with assignments that familiarize students with the discourses and conventions of their chosen field, followed by assignments that guide students in developing scholarly research, and concluding with the assignments that ask students to develop sound academic arguments in their chosen disciplines.

Reviewing the work of fellow Comp II students may provide you with a more concrete sense of how to navigate writing in Composition II. Analyze these examples with an eye for the writer's strengths within the project—ways in which the project functions effectively within the genre conventions of the assignment—as well as the aspects you would address or incorporate differently because they less persuasive and in need of further development or revision. While you won't replicate the work of these students, you can learn from their texts, building upon, "stealing," and transforming the elements of the projects to inform your own work within the course. In plainer terms, read these examples for what works well and what you might change within your own projects.

Harris2

K'yonna Harris

Tabatha Simpson Farrow

Composition II

27 April 2019

Reflection

Over the course of this semester, I have progressed in many aspects of my writing and comprehension ability. After studying the origins of rhetorical theory, different forms of academic writing, and the different forms when it comes to the process of writing I can confidently say that I have developed a strong connection with the work over this semester and these tools have impacted my writing greatly. Even learning from classmates after having social, civic, and academic conversations have influenced the way I interpret and respond to other research. Now when it comes to my specific assignments they helped me understand rhetorical concepts greatly. Starting on the purpose I had a really hard time at the beginning of the semester finding the determined focus. It would sometimes come off very unorganized and not as thought out as it could be. There were even moments where explaining it would be difficult because I didn't understand my main focus/purpose. But, many of these assignments had questions that required a lot of thinking and time dedicated to sitting down and wondering how to approach an assignment as a whole. Once I got over that hump of having a set idea and knowing what I want to write about it became easier and easier as time passed this semester. Onto the audience and genre, I learned how to appeal to me and to an audience who may not have the same common interest or opinion as me. Being able to write out the problems and not being completely biased

Harris1

K'yonna Harris

Composition II

Over the course of this year, we have completed three different essays focusing on different aspects and ways of writing. First, there is the reflection discussing the changes and improvement that has been happening over the course of this semester. Next, there is the group proposal which required working together with assigned teammates, the annotated bibliography which used scholarly sources and included our takeaways from said sources, the literature review which used scholarly sources, and lastly the final project of the semester.

to a topic is something that was very hard in the beginning. I typically write for myself and I don't challenge myself with sources that disagree with my set opinion, but realizing that presenting in front of people and talking in classes helped me understand that not everyone will agree, so you have to note that in your writing and be somewhat natural. Engaging in larger civic, social, and academic conversations was not as hard at the beginning of the semester compared to now. I didn't have any relationships with these students, so I really didn't have the pressure to say what was 'right' but I had more room to express myself without the fear of judgment. As the semester progressed I began to worry about what to say because I built these relationships with everyone and I started to get scared I would embarrass myself. For me, it is a lot easier to talk when I am around people I don't know because if embarrassment arises my ethos is not as threatened as much if it was the other way around. When it comes to research elements they have helped me for the conversations to be had in the future. One of the main things I have learned is when doing research don't do an injustice to yourself by only looking at things that agree with your stance on anything. Being objective and looking at the faults is important. You have to look at the faults in order to provide a solution because there is a problem in any stance you take on a topic, but putting it in the conversation makes you look as if you did deep research and not anything surface level. Beyond that, it taught me how to look in depth of the sources and who wrote what. It helps you get credible information which is vital to these kinds of conversations. It makes you look more credible because you didn't take something off the internet and just believed it was true or correct. Thinking about the writing process as a whole and what has changed is that I've started using the rough draft method instead of just writing something in its final form. This helps me a lot to see many mistakes but also see how I

want to organize certain topics in my essay as a whole. As well as when I free write I gain more insight on my topic that a be incorporated into my final paper. Doing so really working in my favor when it came to our literature review and giving myself time to just be messy and not think other elements other than the content itself gave me more to add. As far as what I need to work on I will continue to work on my confidence when it comes to speaking in public or my peers because regardless of any field there will be a time that I need to express my opinion and I need to be proud and less fragile of scared. Another thing is my grammar skills in my writing. I have always had a problem with grammar and it is something I am not confident in what so ever. But, learning grammar skills comes with more writing paper so there is an improvement. Even though I need help in areas there is always room to grow and get better.

Harris6

BIG BOY

Tabatha Simpson-Farrow

Composition II

9 February 2019

Education System and Why it Sucks

Who is the smartest country? Most Americans will swear up and down it's America but the truth is... it's not. The United States was ranked 14th in the world based on Reading, 26th in Math, and 17th in Science. The United States has one of the largest Economies in the world so why does our Education system suck? Is it lack of funding? Low wages for teachers? Or are we segregated into groups based on academic performance, therefore, hindering some students from growing by being surrounded by the more academically inclined? We will analyze these questions based on our group's specific disciplines to get a better understanding of how closely related yet so different we as a society of college students are.

The education system in the south is not letting students reach their potential. When you compare to other regions or private schools in the same area it seems to be lacking academically. Private schools tend to have better test scores because they are not under supervision while public institutions are typically being told what to teach. Some sources revealed that many schools are become segregated by academic performance. Also by looking at other curriculums around the world, you see a difference with how things are constructed. For example, China

Harris5

Thoughts on Group Proposal

Now what it comes to the Group Proposal I thought it was a great assignment for us to learn more and get comfortable with our classmates. Having to work fast with a new group of people along with the fact of finding a happy medium with everyone who was in my group was a tough challenge. Taking it was a challenge to make sure I was doing everything in the groups favor instead of my own. Working with other people can be a weakness of mine, so being able to pull through and work at my teammate's pace and figure out what is best for the group helped me with my collaborating skills and be more open to others opinion and still feel confident in my way of doing things. Overall it was a good experience to meet new people and learn how to work with others quickly.

Harris7

starts teaching their students formal education at the age of two along with that China is improving their education with curriculum reform. With our low-quality curriculums, it results in low scoring. Sakeholders could be teachers who are involved in the public school system as well as the children who are limited by the lack of curriculum provided.

Since Cole is an engineering major he will discuss the building and infrastructures of many schools and compare how they are doing academically. If there is a possibility that overcrowding and unkept school buildings are a cause to schools in the south not reaching their potential, there could be a solution to that. Maybe building larger facilities is a way of fixing this problem. He could use sources that talk about how where you are depending on how a building looks could affect your ability to work smarter and better. Adam being an education major he can take the approach of a teacher and what lacks in that department as well as a government official and how their curriculum is lacking. Adam can look into sources that talks about what goes on inside the school. So, teachers and how their pay equals their efforts, students and how separation in the classroom hurts certain kids academic ability, and the government and how their curriculum is not beneficial. K'yonna is a multimedia journalism major and she will discuss how many student journalists are fading out. Public schools are hindering journalism programs. When you treat journalism as an unimportant area of learning it results in fewer students participating in programs. Children have to be able to get their point across with minimal words and journalism classes are a great tool to have. Along with that, many people are moving out of the south to pursue better education because the opportunities offered here after school and education for writers do not compare to places up north.

Harris8

Our audience understands the education system is weak but, there are more reasons for this happening other than what's going on inside the school. There is no quick fix and our audience doesn't understand. What we may lose is the ability to learn. This is a system that we walk into at the age of five. We have to be here by law so it has to provide the tools to be able to make it in this world. Our future kids will be going to the same institutions and they need to be enlightened with the same education as students in private schools as well as up North.

Our problem at hand is that the public education system is letting down the kid mainly of the south. Public schools don't compare academically to institutions up north or even private schools that are located in the south. When it comes to solving the problem there can be mainly solutions the pertain to fixing school building exterior and interior, having the government change the curriculum to benefit more students with various ways of learning, and even look at possible classes that can benefit kids with other educational hobbies. But, before we can reach a conclusion we need to know how much room we have to make changes to school buildings, government control curriculum, etc.

Annotated Bibliography: Why the Education System Sucks

K'yonna Harris

Composition II

Tabatha Simpson-Farrow

February 2019

Thoughts on Annotated Bibliography

This being the first major assignment of the semester that was done by ourselves I wanted to make a good impression. Using JSTOR to find the required sources needed I was able to find different sources that helped me explain the importance of journalism as well as some of the problems that arise in journalism classes. This second major project helped me greatly with finding a credible source as well as looking deeper into the sources I was looking at. It taught me that I can't always just trust what is out there and I have to do a little more work to make sure the people involved in my source are credible. Overall I can say about this assignment is yea it was challenging to find sources for my section of the project, but once I found those sources it was no longer such a hard challenge.

Reflective Introduction

When it comes what I expected I really didn't have any expectations. I was really scared that I would be hopelessly searching through the library database to only find sources that would either only talk about journalism or public education, but not both. I found academic articles that made a point to talk about journalism in education whether that be in high school, college, or even after school. These sources help answer the research question because it discusses how close English and journalism is and how how they both have what students would find beneficial that they tend to lack, how journalism is changing and that means the way we teach it needs to change as well, and how journalism is being offered to students with problems that haven't been fixed. These sources have me looking at public schools, but journalism as well and how it can be updated so that public schools can see that it is beneficial to the curriculum which is a different approach I did not think about before. Questions I have left are; even if journalism can prove to be beneficial, will the government still think it should be added to the curriculum, and how much time or development would it take for the government to like the idea of adding journalism?.

Annotated Bibliography: Why the Education System Sucks

Griffin, P. (1949). The Correlation of English and Journalism. *The English Journal*, 38(4), 189-194. doi:10.2307/809690

Philip F. Griffin, an associate professor from the University of California, Berkeley claims that teachers of composition, journalism, and teacher trainers all have a task that is almost identical to each other. His end goal is to make children aware of the usefulness of language, requirements of form and tone, the purpose of communication, etc. The problem at hand is that journalism has gained new methods of teaching and teachers should be aware of the challenges that are arising because of the updated curriculum. There are many students who come to college or in the working being completely inexperienced not able to use language effectively for simple purposes. These negative results are happening because of these four reasons. Informal language is now becoming less complex and reliant when it comes to the standards of usage. It is not backing away from the truth, but it still was not subscribing to the structural demands to language. Secondly, we rely on devices and patterns. No statement is any clearer because it has or does not have subordinate statements. Griffin explains that we try to answer the five W's in one sentence just makes it long and unreadable to the point that the main point will be

Sample Student Portfolios

Harris13

looked over. Relying on order just leads us to digression. We are taught that A plus B equals C and we don't want to explore beyond that. Thirdly we fail our students when we make them believe that facts can speak for themselves. Teaching them that not all sources are credible or equally reliable we help them not fall for false statements created in media. There is a big difference between fact and truth. Lastly, high schoolers lack experience reading literature from the past. Some of us are completely unaware of the values of literature because they don't know where they originated from. With the correlation with English and journalism, you can tackle these four major problems that children are having out of high school and college even. Griffin wants students to have a respect for language and knowledge about past literature so that going forward they can when they write or speak there is moral and intellectual integrity. This is an important time for us to be able to speak and write honestly and with clarity, but there is a way to do it that is not boring, confusing, or basic.

Pavlik, J (2001). New Media and Journalism Education: Preparing the Next Generation. In *Journalism and New Media*(pp 193-208). NEW YORK: Columbia University Press. Retrieved from http://www.jstor.org/stable/10.7312/pavl11482.18

American author John V. Pavlik believes with the way media, itself is changing it also changes how journalist and communications professors do their job efficiently. Even as teachers and scholars they want to keep up with the world around them to work with a media surrounded generation. If you think about it the way we communicate with students is completely different when it comes to emails, assignments, etc. Teachers

Harris14

and professors are even incorporating technology in the way they teach so the content of their lectures is enriching to the students. Multimedia and journalism content is already a complex concept to grasp, so by using tools that this generation understands it is easier for the student to understand and helps the teacher move on quickly. Many schools now are adding courses on new media.

With the world evolving and engulfing themselves with technology that means that the way we get information out into the world is changing as well. Pavlik being an author on the impact technology has on journalism and media he thinks the way we teach and work in the journalism field needs to be updated. When it comes to editing in print, online, or video there is a new way of doing things, and to keep the students well up to date you have to change the curriculum. But, even with new technology changing modern media and journalism, there are some things that don't change. Becoming a fact checkers and making sure what you put in the world is true, using reliable sources that have a credible author behind it, asking tough questions even if it is uncomfortable, and having high ethical standards are all elements in journalism that should not ever disappear. It's the way we are going about teaching these timeless methods that are still useful to a new generation of children in the journalism and communication field who are also engulfed in modern media. The end goal is to move with the times because yes the delivery may be different, but truth and facts will always be permanent want journalism. In conclusion, children are being left behind because with news-times comes new changes and with the education system not keeping up with the world it leaves high school kids behind others who moves with the times of technology.

Thoughts on Literature Review

The Literature Review was definitely one of the most challenging assignments for me. Being that it was something I have never done before it was hard for me to figure out the direction I was going in when it was assigned. Another issue I had was the time crunch I had because I had to think a lot about how I wanted to write it, and when that was over I had only a short amount of time to actually write it. I was actually scared since it was a writing style I've never done before and I wasn't sure if it was going to be the 'right' way of writing the draft for this assignment. Once I was told to just do it how I felt it should be done I became a lot more comfortable and it produced a better final paper.

Pollard, J. (1939). Journalism and the College. *The Journal of Higher Education, 10*(7), 356-362. doi:10.2307/1974447

According to a professor of journalism at Ohio State University, Dr. Pollard, many educators doubt that journalism really has no proper place in the curriculum, you have some that somewhat see a need for it, and then you have those who feel that it is so deeply connected to English that it is necessary. But, regardless of your standpoint, there are some problems that need to be fixed. The former director of the school of journalism sees one problem is that the course offering are becoming slim to none and now with these rapid journalism offerings in the real world there is a disconnect in college students are becoming knowledgeable. Next, they need more trained teachers in all phases of journalism. Along with that, there are more problems such as the rapidly changing conditions of journalism, the need for sympathetic help and supervision over undergraduate publications and newspapers, etc. the requirements of a person working in this field is asking for much than what it used to and that means there needs to be changing to journalism in general. Without knowing the changes that need to be made then changes can't happen.

Literature Review: Why the Education System Sucks

K'yonna Harris

Composition II

Tabatha Simpson-Farrow

March 2019

It appears that journalism has lost interest among the people in charge of the curriculum of public schools. Many representatives feel that it is outdated and not as important or not important at all to public school students to keep it as a requirement. All in all the journalism department is losing value, but it is proven to be important to students in high school all across the nation and beyond to the real world of work. With it being valuable in its lessons that you cannot teach anywhere else journalism is beneficial regardless of the popular belief that it is useless, disregarded by students in school, and only used by people involved in newspaper and other journalism fields. By taking away journalism you're putting the future writers, creators, and overall students in jeopardy of missing out on some important and helpful material. With the various online news reports, articles, and blogs there is a plethora of information, some that are happening closer to you than you would believe.

Regarding public schools located in the southern region of this nation; Little Rock, Arkansas last summer in 2018 experienced a major change in public schools (Glisovic, 2018). From June in 2018 and onward public school will no longer be required to offer journalism classes. Some felt that it was a way to give up unnecessary mandates while the lawmakers in favor of keeping journalism as a requirement believe that it is not necessary, but indeed the exact opposite is true.; teaching students skills that are not just beneficial to a journalist, but to anyone. Representative Greg Leding in district 86 says that the people against keeping journalism as a requirement are the people who have hostility to the press and what it has now become, but in this era, good journalism is more important than ever. Leding also states that he doesn't understand why as a state we would want to reduce our role in telling our stories that shape the history of this nation. Rep Greg Leding has even gone as far as to say that the people who are for making journalism classes not a requirement are the same people who have something against the press, the media, and news and how people are portrayed altogether which is a sad situation. Yes, this a sad loss for students who want to pursue journalism in their middle/high school career. They have been stripped away from that opportunity and will possibly be denied to pursue their wants because of the school they are attending. Now, Senate Bart Hester disagrees with Leding saying that it is less than other required courses and should not be looked at as one. This has been in place since Bill Clinton appointed his wife, Hillary Clinton to overlook the decisions with these mandates being done. That was in 1983, so it is time to take a new look and change some things. It is still allowed in public school, the only problem is that it is no longer required and does not have to be offered by every public school. Even though journalism was removed as a requirement, interest in the field has grown. Arkansas Press Association sees it as a sad day for students, schools, and journalism. This is hindering students especially those who attend schools who don't provide journalism even as an elective. Having this put in place allows students who believe the idea that this course doesn't carry quality content will allow them to miss out on something important and that will help them once they are in college and beyond. Taking away the opportunity to learn more is never the way to go when it comes to education and what we can provide to our students. This being so personally close to these communities it shows that this is already in effect and this change is coming fast. With the change already occurring it is shown how people are willing for this change to happen. Before this manifests its way across the nation journalism classes and courses have to show that they are beneficial to everyone and not just newspaper writers and reporter junkies.

Sasha Jones (2019) conducted several surveys to see if journalism was still in demand by teachers in schools as well as the student's ability to perform certain tasks that could be used in the real world. Across 45 states, as well as different media and journalism educators we have insight straight from the classroom as well as the teachers who can see how the students are taking these skills and applying them. 28% of educators say that there has been a slight increase in enrollment as well as 29% believing that more students are enrolling in new outlets provided by their schools, such as newspapers and yearbooks. Now, why is there an increase of want by students even after public schools have debunked it to an elective and not a requirement? The Executive Director of the National Scholastic Press Association, Laura Widmer says that political climate has a lot to do with it. We are in a Trump-era presidency and with all the attacks on media, people are interested in how to tell what is real and what is fake. Widmer even goes as far as saying that, "this is this generation's Watergate." Watergate was the kick start to students involving themselves in major journalism. Once Nixon was president, this era is doing the same thing to our new generation of young teens. Educators have also been able to rate their student's ability to use journalism skills and put them into real-world use. Many of these students are good at communicating information accurately, communicating in an objective manner, verifying information, telling the difference between opinion and fact, and efficiently communicating information. These surveys prove to show that students want to learn this material and find it interesting enough to not just do it for the benefits but to even pursue this beyond secondary education. We can infer that many students don't have these abilities discussed in the surveys which seem to be helpful in the classroom as well as life. It is important to be able to tell the difference between fact and opinion, accurately communicate, and be objective in any workplace no matter whatever field a student is in. Now, seeing that there is an increase in this field of work, the next question is what do we have to do to make it even better? In such time that more and more students are being involved in journalism what can be done to update it and show that it is important just as the next core class? Private schools have their own personal designed curriculum that allows the school to make decisions that best suits the students there. If journalism is not a requirement at a private institution it is certainly offered by the school just like other electives, so it is least provided to the student who wants to learn more about journalism and what it offers. The public school system is making the decision that also best fits their students, but by not allowing the students to have a range of choices, they are hampering them from exploring their inner potential and seek something new, innovative, and promising.

The dean of the University of North Carolina at Chapel Hill, Jean Folkerts states that people who take courses in the realm of journalism will have better chances of being picked in the job searching section of our lives. With that much of an advantage, journalism courses need to make sure they are constantly with the times of technology and media shifting. With merging classes together and creating new ones that provide understanding concepts that your core classes cannot teach you is a start to proving how beneficial journalism truly is to students. How we teach in general has changed so much being in the digital revolution, and how we report or write has changed drastically as well. In order to keep this want for journalism, you have to keep changing it to fit your audience (Folkerts, 2019). The end goal is to add depth to newer students' education and at the least, we need to make sure students think and work across a wide range of things to gain skills that are needed. Progressing and working towards a professional lifestyle and making our students think in mutual ways will get them there. With the world evolving and

engulfing themselves with technology that means that the way we get information out into the world is changing as well. American author John V. Pavlik believes with the way media itself is changing; it also changes how journalist and communications professors do their job efficiently. Being an author on the impact technology has on journalism and media he thinks the way we teach and work in the journalism field needs to be updated. When it comes to editing in print, online, or video there is a new way of doing things, and to keep the students well up to date you have to change the curriculum. But, even with new technology changing modern media and journalism, there are some things that don't change. Becoming a fact checker and making sure what you put in the world is true, using reliable sources, asking tough questions even if it is uncomfortable, and having high ethical standards are all elements in journalism that should not ever disappear. It's the way we are going about teaching these timeless methods that are still useful to a new generation of children in the journalism and communication field who are also engulfed in modern media (Pavlik, 2001). The end goal is to move with the times because while the delivery may be different, the truth and facts will always be a permanent need for journalism. In conclusion, children are being left behind because with new times come with new changes and with the education system not keeping up with the world it leaves high school kids behind others who move with the times of technology.

Dr. James Pollard, professor of journalism at Ohio State University says many educators doubt that journalism really has no proper place in the curriculum, you have some that somewhat see a need for it, and then you have those who feel that it is so deeply connected to English that it is necessary. But, regardless of your standpoint, there are some problems that need to be fixed. The former director of the school of journalism sees one problem is that the course offers are

Harris23

becoming slim to none and now with these rapid journalism offerings in the real world there is a disconnect in college students becoming knowledgeable. Next, they need more trained teachers in all phases of journalism (Pollard,1939). Along with that, there are more problems, such as the rapidly changing conditions of journalism, the need for sympathetic help, and supervision over undergraduate publications and newspapers. The requirements of a person working in this field are asking for more than what it used to and that means there need to be changes to journalism in general. Without knowing the changes that need to be made then changes can't happen.

With the era we are in today, journalism has been proven to be beneficial to the people who want and need information. With young adults being so involved in the political climate and having an urge to seek truth, learning the aspects of journalism helps many students gain knowledge. There are many problems with journalism classes, and they need to be updated with new technology in order to get the point across faster. When this occurs more people will feel that it is less outdated and will want to invest in journalism. Once we start with the issues concerning journalism hopefully the people in charge will want to invest in this opportunity to help and empower our students.

Harris24

Work Cited

Folkerts, J. (n.d.). Credibility Resides at the Core of Teaching Journalism. Retrieved March 19, 2019, from

https://niemanreports.org/articles/credibility-resides-at-the-core-of-teaching-journalism/

Glisovic, M. (2018, June 15). Arkansas public schools no longer required to offer journalism classes. Retrieved March 11, 2019, from

https://katv.com/news/local/arkansas-public-schools-no-longer-required-to-offer-journalism-classes

Jones, S. (2019, February 20). Student Journalism Classes Going Strong, Poll Finds. Retrieved March 11, 2019, from

Pavlik, J. (2001). New Media and Journalism Education: Preparing the Next Generation. In *Journalism and New Media*(pp. 193-208). NEW YORK: Columbia University Press. Retrieved from http://www.jstor.org/stable/10.7312/pavl11482.18

Pollard, J. (1939). Journalism and the College. *The Journal of Higher Education. 10*(7), 356-362. doi:10.2307/1974447

Harris25

Thought on Final Project

The last project being so different than the rest I had such a fun time with it. Since it was mainly just explaining all the information I've gathered over the course of the semester I felt confident in this last section. I used a blog because I felt that no one else would be doing one, but also because it was to prove that journalism can be updated and work with technology for the betterment of students in secondary education as well as college students. Using the blog I made it and styled it how I wanted to. It gave me a lot of freedom and space to make it appealing to the eye as well as have the information displayed it a new way that was different from anyone at the event. Overall the project was different than anything we did this semester which made it interesting. I felt like I was doing something different and that made it cool for me.

Harris26

Use the above QR code to view K'yonna Harris's final project.

If you do not have a QR code scanner already downloaded on your smartphone or tablet, search "QR code scanner" in the app store to download a QR scanner to your device.

Wofford 1

Final Portfolio

Sydney Wofford

ENG 1013

Tabatha Simpson-Farrow

30 April 2019

This portfolio contains a reflection, group proposal, annotated bibliography, literature review, and a final project all covering the the topic of plastic pollution.

Wofford 2

Sydney Wofford

Tabatha Simpson-Farrow

ENG 1013

30 April 2019

Reflection

Though I have learned that reflection can take many different forms at any time, I have always believed that the end of the year (or semester) is a great time for classic reflection. This semester, I have really learned a lot about myself in general – anywhere from my bad habits to my writing abilities. This composition II class has challenged me in more ways than I could have imagined, and that is not always a bad thing. Each unit had a different effect on me in a variety of ways, and my own topic that I emphasized on throughout the semester actually taught me a lot that I didn't know. It is always important to look back and reflect on what has happened so that you can learn how to incorporate that information into your life moving forward.

I have always been one to follow the rules, and I like for there to be structure to everything. Creativity is fun, but I enjoy the grammar and punctuation that goes along with writing. In my mind, I have always thought that writing essays was a strong point of mine because these elements have always made sense to me. Before the start of the semester, becoming an english teacher even became the top job of choice when I was still trying to figure out my future because I believed that I could help others understand writing the same way I did. It was not until this past semester that I realized that sentence length and colons had almost nothing to do with good writing. We all come from different backgrounds, so just because academic writing does not come easy to everyone, doesn't mean that what they are saying isn't

Wofford 4

not a waste of time. It did challenge me in many ways, but what is the point of going to college if

you don't plan on learning anything?

Wofford 3

important. It finally made sense to me why kids who didn't seem to be on the same scale of

writing as I was still made better grades than me.

Even though academic writing is not the most important part of the process, I do feel like

I have learned a lot about it that helped me grow as a writer. I had never even heard of a

literature review or an annotated bibliography before, and the research process has already come

in handy for other classes. Scanning and skimming make a lot more sense to me now. I struggled

a lot this semester with the content of my writing and making everything flow, and this honestly

made my personal struggle with depression worse. I always try to put out my best work, and

when my audience doesn't exactly agree with that, I take it personally. I push myself a little too

hard at times. Constructive criticism and revision is something I have always struggled with.

Looking back now though, I have realized that every individual has a different idea of what

"good writing" actually is. Moving forward, I am going to attempt to change my perspective

when it comes to people reading my work.

I feel as though this course had more of a personal effect on me than it was supposed to.

Yes, we learned about different genres and engaged with larger audiences as you might expect a

regular english class to do, but in class, we had many discussions that opened my mind to

different ideas, regardless of whether or not I agreed. All together I would say that I have learned

some really vital lessons. The most important thing that I have learned is that you are always

growing and changing as a person and as a writer. Sure, there are things that I wish I would have

approached differently, but all you can do is learn from it and move on. I am glad that the

semester is over in all honesty, but I mean that in the best way possible. This class definitely was

The Group Proposal

When it came to writing the group proposal, I struggled quite a bit with deciding on a topic. I did not personally like the idea of not getting to choose who I was in a group with, but it turned out to be one of the best group projects I have been apart of. At first, I thought I would be doing the whole thing by myself. My groupmate proved me wrong and we equally collaborated on this proposal. Even though it was off to a rocky start, working on this together turned out to be the start of a good group project. It was easy to break it down into different sections and then put it all together.

Sydney Wofford

Annemarie Widby

Tabatha Simpson-Farrow

ENG 1013

7 February 2019

The Truth About Plastic Pollution

"Reduce, reuse, recycle." It's a phrase that we all know and has been drilled into our minds as one of the best things we can do for our planet. But when you recycle your plastic bottles, do you know where they really go or what they're actually being used for? You might find the answers to these questions to be quite shocking. The students at A-State need to be better informed as to what actually happens in the recycling process and why we need to do more than the bare minimum. There are multiple possibilities to make Arkansas State University a green campus.

Recycling and plastic pollution is a field that many people have touched on to the point where you may get a few eyerolls upon mentioning it. People seem to naturally assume that everyone in the world recycles and knows that plastic waste is bad for our planet, and those that don't are living under a rock. People also have an assumption that just recycling our plastic waste will fix everything. In this topic, we would like to explore the consequences of plastic waste and recycling that exists in our environment today by answering questions like, "where does it actually go?" and, "who or what does it affect?" Every living thing on this earth is considered a stakeholder including animals, students, and employees here at A-State. Helen

Wofford 7

McCoy is in charge of A-State's recycling system as well as the sustainability office and administration here on campus.

By purchasing single-use plastic, we are creating a demand for it. Ecologycenter.org states that most plastics aren't recyclable, unlike glass, fibers, and metals. Sciencemag.org presents the issue that "about 4 million to 12 million metric tons of plastic washed offshore in 2010 alone, or about 1.5% to 4.5% of the world's total plastic production—enough to cover every foot of coastline on the planet. That's just the beginning of the problems, the team says, as scientists still don't know where more than 99% of ocean plastic debris ends up—and what impact it's having on marine life and the human food supply." These are some scary statistics that should not be ignored because it affects every single person in the world. Even though ASU is in a landlocked state, our waste still makes its way into rivers and streams. This not only affects the oceans, it affects local water supply.

As a Communications major, Sydney will approach the topic of recycling on campus by educating her audience through the use of social media. Using this platform is a form of Mass Communications. She expects to use videos and websites as her sources. Sydney will look into the use of screens constantly presenting the information that is vital for people to know at the water filtering stations that are already in place to draw attention to them. She will introduce new ways of informing the students on campus about the harmful effects of plastic. Annemarie, a nursing major, will do research in her field to find answers about how much plastic waste hospitals and the program at A-State generate and see if we can find an answer to reduce such numbers. We will also look into where the recycled materials are going and how we can change that. We will consider the effects that plastic has on the food chain and the human body.

Wofford 8

In conclusion, we would like to bring attention to recycling and plastic waste as a whole and see how effective or ineffective it actually is. We will bring light to where plastic waste goes and look into what ways we can change it and encourage our campus to do the same. Plastic is a problem that should not and cannot be ignored. If we don't cover this topic, we may never learn the consequences of our actions when it comes to plastic. It will just fall into the back of our minds until it is too late to fix. The effects of plastic need to be advertised in a more effective way, and recycling simply is not the answer to all of our problems. Arkansas State University needs to do more to enforce the idea of saving the planet and encourage their students to do the same!

Wofford 10

Annotated Bibliography: Plastic Pollution Education on College Campuses

Sydney Wofford

ENG 1013

Tabatha Simpson-Farrow

3 March 2019

Wofford 9

The Annotated Bibliography

I had never really had experience with researching peer reviewed academic articles before. I actually really hated the process, but I've already had to do it for other classes. I'm thankful that I learned how to do it. It is not my proudest work due to the fact that I really had to stretch it to make the connections, but I do believe I put a lot of effort into it. It did make it a lot easier whenever I broke up each part and focused on each portion at a different time. I was able to experience writing in APA format for the first time, so that was interesting.

Wofford 11

Plastic Pollution Education on College Campuses

Topic: Plastic Pollution on Campus

Thesis: Students at Arkansas State University would benefit from being better informed over the topic of plastic pollution and become more involved with the solutions because it is hard to make change if you do not understand everything that is going on.

Reflective Introduction:

In this research, I expected to find articles that were more focused on if plastic pollution was a problem or not. This differs with what I actually found because most of the articles were focused on policy and potential solutions since the topic is already recognized as a global issue. The research process was difficult when it came to being specific with campuses, so I had to broaden my search and make new connections. These sources help answer my group's research question because they all recognize the importance of education in regards to solving the issue of plastic pollution. The articles I reviewed help approach my perspective on the solution because I believe that communicating facts to students at Arkansas State University will lead to more awareness and better efforts when it comes to doing their part in fixing the issue presented. It is very crucial that everyone understands the severity of the problem at hand so that we can work together and come up with a solution to save the planet. The questions I am still left with about

Wofford 12

the topic is what would be the most effective way to relay the message and how do I draw the attention of the students.

Annotated Bibliography:

Kitagawa, L., Pomba, E., & Davis, T. (2018). Plastic Pollution to Solution. *Science and Children, 55*(7), 38-45. Retrieved from https://ezproxy.library.astate.edu/login?url=http://search.ebscohost.com/login.aspx?direct=true&db=eric&AN=EJ1172596&site=eds-live&scope=site

Tina Davis, Elizabeth Pomba, and Laura Kitagawa are all second grade teachers (as well as the authors of this article) who created a cross-curricular Project Based Learning (PBL) unit for the children. The intended audience would be other teachers in a general sense. The unit they covered was recycling. They informed the children about the effects of plastic pollution and then had their students develop a fun way to recycle. The students decided on decoration their own recycling bins. The outcome was that the project had a lasting impact on the school and the community as the kids continued to recycle. The only limitation to the text that comes to mind would be the fact that it is a recent article, so you don't really know how long the kids will be impacted about the subject.

Wofford 13

This research is important because it shows how students are impacted by getting involved and are encouraged by faculty. Everyone needs to work together as a team in order to see a difference. We would take a different approach than the way it worked with the second graders, but it still works together. This article differs from the others because it shows the process of educating students rather than just presenting facts and statistics.

Kronrod, A., Grinstein, A., & Wathieu, L. (2012). Go Green!! Should Environmental Messages Be So Assertive?? *Journal of Marketing, 76*(1), 95–102.

https://doi.org/10.1509/jm.10.0416

The authors, Kronrod, Grinstein, and Wathieu, are all marketing professors. In this piece, the authors claim that assertive environmental messages should not be so assertive if the audience is not already informed about the topic or they won't listen. Their studies include video clips, slogan comparisons, and percentages of clicks on ad links. They have authority to speak on this because of their marketing background. The intended audience would be environmental agencies, which are a specialized audience.

This article is important because it backs up my point in both of my other sources about how audiences need to be informed or they will not listen. The main limitations in the article would be their assumption that people who aren't majoring in environmental

Wofford 14

studies care less about the issue. The information provided is useful because it gives insight on how Arkansas State should approach plastic pollution on campus. In comparison to the other articles, this piece takes an approach that is based on how the audience is affected rather than the process of educating or only stating facts.

Xanthos, D., & Walker, T. R. (2017). Review: International policies to reduce plastic marine pollution from single-use plastics (plastic bags and microbeads): A review. *Marine Pollution Bulletin, 118*, 17–26.

https://doi-org.ezproxy.library.astate.edu/10.1016/j.marpolbul.2017.02.048

Authors Xanthos and Walker present plastic pollution as a global issue by providing an in depth review of international policies that attempt to reduce the use of single use plastics and microbeads. They found that many countries still don't have the necessary policies in place to contribute to fixing the issue. They recommend continuing or implementing educational campaigns about plastic in order to see lasting results.

Both of the authors of this piece are involved with the School for Resource and Environmental Studies at Dalhousie University, Halifax, NS, Canada, giving them authority. The politicians who cover policy on plastic bans are the specialized intended audience. This work is important in regards to my research because it shows how many places aren't actually doing anything about the issue of plastic pollution because people

Wofford 15

aren't informed on the issue. A limitation to this text is the fact that it isn't actually

arguing anything, it is just stating facts. This article flows with the other sources

mentioned because it covers the education of people when it comes to plastic pollution as

a main factor in the issue, though it mainly only presents facts while the others focus

more on the experiments and results.

Wofford 16

The Literature Review

The part that I enjoyed the most about the literature review was that we didn't have to

only use the academic journals, while the part that I struggled the most with is my sentence

transitions. Again, I wrote each portion individually. They ended up working well by themselves,

but getting them to flow was a challenge. I didn't really feel as though I easily grasped the idea

of what a literature review is supposed to be. I over thought this unit way too much and ended up

not enjoying the writing process.

Wofford 17

Plastic Pollution Education Literature Review

Sydney Wofford

ENG 1013

Tabatha Simpson-Farrow

19 April 2019

Wofford 18

As you walk onto the campus of Arkansas State University, you can see that they have multiple recycle bins and water filtration stations placed around. These are often considered suggestions rather than common everyday items to most students because they do not understand what is happening to the planet they live on. The severity of the global issue of plastic pollution just doesn't seem to matter to many humans, but it definitely should. It is important to educate students about plastic pollution because if they do not fully understand the effects that plastic has on all aspects of the environment, they are less likely to implement change in their daily lifestyles to solve the issue at hand.

It is easy to see that many of the environmentally friendly and recycling options get ignored or looked over. Even if students are recycling (which is better than doing nothing at all considering we have to start somewhere), it is crucial that they understand that recycling is not the solution to the problem. Plastic is not something that should be treated as disposable and abundant. Amanda Keetley, the founder of Less Plastic LTD, has a huge goal, which is "to raise awareness of the growing issue of plastic pollution and the practical steps we can all take to tackle ocean plastic" (Keetley, 2015). Keetley (2015) states, "We are addicted to the convenience of single-use plastic." This is the honest truth when it comes to the way people take advantage of everything. People love having easy choices and tasks. In one article on her website, she goes into depth about the negative effects of plastic and proposes nine reasons to refuse single-use plastic. The reasons are that it is "made from fossil fuels, [it leaves a] huge carbon footprint, will still be here in hundreds of years, only a tiny percentage is recycled, leaches toxins into food and drink, causes hormone disruption and cancers, pollutes our oceans, kills marine animals and birds, and enters our food chain" (Keetley, 2015). The main idea of the article is how by purchasing single-use plastic, we are creating a demand for it (Keetley, 2015). This goes to show how recycling isn't the cure. It also shows that there are many more portions of the earth affected, and that it is not just the ocean. People need to be more conscious about the decisions they make in order to save the planet.

While understanding the reasons why plastics are bad is a huge part of the education process, it is important to emphasize that recycling does not solve the problem like most people assume. Often times people won't listen or care about the negative effects plastic has because they think they are already doing their part by recycling. The Ecology Center, a nonprofit organization that focuses on bettering the health and the treatment of the environment by residents, illustrates facts about how most plastics are not recyclable, unlike the way glass, fibers, and metals are (Ecocolycenter.org, n.d.). Even when plastics are recycled, they are rarely reformed into new products. Many people don't know that most products aren't actually recyclable, despite the label that appears on the item. Only eight percent of plastic in the United States actually gets recycled, and most of it actually end up in landfills, which then leads to a

variety of other problems (The Problems With Plastics, n.d.). This is why citizens need to be educated on the different labels and the process recyclables go through. Glass and metals are always a better option if they are available. It might not seem like that big of a deal to some people, but it is hard to care about something if you do not fully understand it.

Supposing that people do understand the issue regarding plastics, they still often fail to make the necessary life changes because the don't realize how easy it can be. Humans naturally like the easy route, so it is important that they are educated on the small ways they can contribute to saving the planet. There are so many simple ways to cut back on the amount of plastic a person uses daily. Most of the time people do not even realize just how much plastic we use! Reef Relief, an organization that focuses on informing the public and persuading policy makers about the importance of coral reefs, published an article called "51 Ways to reduce plastic use or completely eliminate it!" Some of the options that would be good for students to consider would be to use reusable cups, not use plastic straws or silverware, and use reusable bags when shopping! These are not difficult strategies to incorporate into your life, and that is another reason why students need to be educated on the harmful effects of plastic. One of the main ideas is to not purchase items wrapped in plastic. For example, it is better to buy bar soap or paper cartons of milk than the plastic options. Plastic can be something that is hard to avoid, so if you are going to use it, try not to treat it as a one-time thing. The University could get involved by having stores on campus that sell coffee, such as Einsteins or Starbucks, offer a discount to those

who bring their own cups as an incentive ("51 Ways to reduce plastic use or completely

eliminate it!", 2013). When it comes to the amount of coffee students drink, it would be a good

public relations and business strategy for the campus to invest their time in.

Even if people do understand the harmful effects and the recycling process, they still do

not believe they have a direct impact on the world because of where they are located. One of the

main reasons that people tend to think that plastic pollution isn't a big deal is

because they think that it only affects the ocean. In reality, it actually affects basically every

aspect of the planet. The ocean is a major place affected by the issue, though. Stevens, a scientist

with her M.S. in Zoology and a Ph.D. in Ecology, Evolution, and Behavior, states that "the

problem with plastics is that they do not easily degrade" (2015). If they do breakdown, it is just

into smaller pieces that get consumed by things such as plankton or whales (Stevens, 2015).

According to Stevens (2015), scientists are not finding as many plastic bits as they know they

should be. This means that plastic is entering the food chain and can make its way into many

different life forms, including humans. It has been the cause of death of multiple animals,

meaning that we are all at risk. It is very likely to see students on Arkansas State's campus using

many forms of plastic including bottles and straws. This makes us part of the problem despite the

fact that we are a landlocked state, and this is a huge reason we need the education.

Stevens, Keetley, the Ecology Center, and Reef Relief all agree on methods for

alternatives to plastics, and they all compare in the fact that their goal is to educate the public.

Stevens (2015) also states that microplastics are basically impossible to clean up, so the best

solution as of now is to stop more plastic from reaching the ocean. This is why all of these

organizations try to get you to make changes in your habits after educating you on the facts.

They all agree with the method of education being the first step of the process. The main

limitation to all of these websites is getting people to notice them. They can't be effective unless

people read them, and the main people who read them are people who already know that plastic

is a big problem, even though the intended audience would be the uneducated or investors. This

actually just backs up the argument of why students need to be informed even more.

Even though the issue of plastic pollution is proven to be severe, many places around the

world still are not doing anything about it. Authors Xanthos and Walker present plastic pollution

as a global issue by providing an in depth review of international policies that attempt to reduce

the use of single use plastics and microbeads. They found that many countries still don't have the

necessary policies in place to contribute to fixing the issue and recommend continuing or

implementing educational campaigns about plastic in order to see lasting results.

Both of the authors of this piece are involved with the School for Resource and

Environmental Studies at Dalhousie University, Halifax, NS, Canada, giving them authority. The

Wofford 23

politicians who cover policy on plastic bans are the specialized intended audience. This work is important in regards to my research because it shows how many places aren't actually doing anything about the issue of plastic pollution because people aren't informed on the issue the way they should be. Granted that a limitation to this text would be that it isn't actually arguing anything, it is still relevant because it shows just how much the world needs to learn about the problem in front of them.

Knowing the facts and laws about pollution is important, but it can be hard to see how educating students will have any effect. That is why I want to compare it to an experiment that was conducted on children. Tina Davis, Elizabeth Pomba, and Laura Kitagawa are all second grade teachers (as well as the authors of this article) who created a cross-curricular Project Based Learning (PBL) unit for the children. The intended audience would be other teachers in a general sense. The unit they covered was recycling in which they informed the children about the effects of plastic pollution and then had their students develop a fun way to recycle. The students decided on decorating their own recycling bins. The outcome was that the project had a lasting impact on the school and the community as the kids continued to recycle. The only limitation to the text that comes to mind would be the fact that it is a recent article, so you don't really know how long the kids will be impacted about the subject.

Wofford 24

This research is important because it shows how students are impacted by getting involved and are encouraged by faculty. Everyone needs to work together as a team and influence each other in order to see a difference. We would take a different approach than the way it worked with the second graders, but it still works together. This article differs from the others because it shows the process of educating students rather than just presenting facts and statistics.

After providing an example and multiple facts, it is clear that education can be effective, but just how hard should the message be pushed? Authors Kronrod, Grinstein, and Wathieu, are all marketing professors, and in this piece, they claim that assertive environmental messages should not be so assertive if the audience is not already informed about the topic or they won't listen (2017). Their studies include video clips, slogan comparisons, and percentages of clicks on ad links. They have authority to speak on this because of their marketing background. The intended audience would be environmental agencies, which would be considered a specialized audience.

This article is important because it backs up my point in my other sources about how audiences need to be informed or they will not listen. The main limitations in the article would be their assumption that people who aren't majoring in environmental studies care less about the issue. The information provided is useful because it gives insight on how Arkansas State should

Wofford 25

approach plastic pollution on campus. Being pushy and making people feel less intelligent is not the way to go. From a Mass Communications approach, the best way to go about it is with interesting visuals to ensure that the audience is listening and staying interested. In comparison to the other articles, this piece takes an approach that is based on how the audience is affected rather than the process of educating or only stating facts.

There are a variety of reasons in the research discussed as to why the education of students at Arkansas State in regards to plastic pollution is crucial. As you can see with all of the websites reviewed, there are many organizations whose main purpose is to educate and raise awareness about pollution, proving just how important educating the world is. A college is a place of learning and growing, so what better way is there than to educate the people who will make up the future about the fate of said future? Plastic is taking over, and humans need to put a stop to it before it gets to the point of no return. We may not be able to completely solve the problem, but we can definitely keep it from getting worse.

Wofford 26

References

51 Ways to reduce plastic use or completely eliminate it! (2013, January 31). Retrieved March 22, 2019, from https://www.reefrelief.org/2013/01/51-ways-to-reduce-plastic-use-or-completely-eliminate-it/

Kitagawa, L., Pomba, E., & Davis, T. (2018). Plastic Pollution to Solution. *Science and Children, 55*(7), 38–45. Retrieved from https://ezproxy.library.astate.edu/login?url=http://search.ebscohost.com/login.aspx?direct=true&db=eric&AN=EJ1172596&site=eds-live&scope=site

Keeley, A. (2018, July 04). 9 reasons to refuse single-use plastic. Retrieved March 12, 2019, from https://lessplastic.co.uk/9-reasons-refuse-single-use-plastic/

Kronrod, A., Grinstein, A., & Wathieu, L. (2012). Go Green!! Should Environmental Messages Be So Assertive? *Journal of Marketing, 76*(1), 95–102. https://doi.org/10.1509/jm.10.0416

Stevens, A. P. (2015, June 16). Tiny plastic, big problem. Retrieved March 12, 2019, from https://www.sciencenewsforstudents.org/article/tiny-plastic-big-problem

THE PROBLEMS WITH PLASTICS. (n.d.). Retrieved March 12, 2019, from https://ecologycenter.org/plastics/

Xanthos, D. & Walker, T. R. (2017). Review: International policies to reduce plastic marine pollution from single-use plastics (plastic bags and microbeads): A review. *Marine Pollution Bulletin*, *118*, 17–26. https://doi-org.ezproxy.library.astate.edu/10.1016/j.marpolbul.2017.02.048

The Final Project

The final project was by far the best part of the whole semester. At first, my groupmate and I struggled to decide how to approach this. It wasn't until in the middle of a class discussion, I threw out a comment about an ASMR video. This became the basis of our project. At this time, I was going through a lot of personal things and my dog had passed away, so it took a while to get everything started. It was hard to get everything together and worked out, but when we did, we did a good job of executing our message. The video and poster don't work the best alone, but our presentation really pulled it all together to make sense. We worked really hard on it despite not being professional "ASMRtists." I loved presenting it in front of an audience because I am very passionate about the topic.

Use the above QR code to view Sydney Wofford's final project.

Wofford 29

https://youtu.be/_XOh4TO2FkU

Elizabeth Mansfield

April 30, 2019

Reflection & Final Portfolio

Composition II

For this final portfolio, it will contain my rough drafts and my final drafts. This will show how far I have come from where we started within this course.

Final Reflection Essay

Dear Composition II student,

Within this class it is rather easy depending on the amount of effort you are willing to put forth. If you give it your all it will come natural to you. If you give no effort at all then you will realize that you have failed the course. When choosing a topic to research make sure it is one you will not mind reading a lot about. You will be reading about it all semester long. Always utilize your campus resources as well. You never know how much they will come in handy. You're paying for them anyway.

Finding a topic to research can be difficult for some. For me it came rather naturally as I have been interested in this topic to begin with. Our group came up with a few topics and then decided on one. Don't be scared of group work as we all are. For me, my group split a week before presentation and I still put forth all my effort into presenting what I had research all semester. If this happens to you make sure to talk to your professor so that they know what is going on. If you don't communicate with them, they will never know. Since my group left, I talked to my professor all semester about my group and she was extremely understanding as to what had happened. So, make sure that you talk to your professors or your grade could be impacted.

Going into this class I was dreading it because I hate English courses. I put off taking composition II for two years due to this. After being in this class I realized it wasn't too bad. We started small to get to our final project, which was the most helpful part for me. With that being said, I have taken this into my other courses and started small in order to take stress off of myself when writing papers. It has helped me understand different audiences and how to word each paper in order to effectively get my point across.

As I stated earlier, I hated group work. I also hated presenting in bigger groups due to the fact I have moderate to severe anxiety. I am much more comfortable with talking to different groups of people. What really helped me is understanding my topic. Anyone can go out and write a paper, but understanding your paper is a different ball game. I was able to confidently speak to people I had never seen before about my topic. Any other time before this I would have been freaking out and wondering if I was going to make it through.

In this course my professor ensured that we had all of the information we needed to get started on research. The library database will be your best friend. You pay for this too, so might as well use it! In all of the things we needed to research of our topic it helped us understand our topic on a more academic level. It made me aware of how unaware of your topic you can be. My topic was bullying. Everyone thinks they know about bullying but in reality, I was so unaware of what really went on. I had no idea that health care physicians played a major role in noticing if the child was a bully or being bullied. The research the database provides is extremely helpful. Anything you could think of; it will be there.

When I am writing a paper, I just throw it together and hope it comes out nicely. In this course we started with one writing style then led to another and so on. All of these writing styles came together at the end. It was really helpful to see a visual of how far I had come in this semester from a writing perspective. Writing and revising is a major part in every essay you have to do. Sometimes we forget and just put it all together. If you remember and take you time, you can almost guarantee your excellent grade on the paper. I know as college students we get caught up and just hope for the good grade when we write it the day it is due. I can speak from experience. For the most part I got decent grades on papers I threw together. Having a peace of mind that you gave it all you got is what wins at the end of the day.

Overall, remember that writing a paper is not as bad as you think it is. Remember all of the free resources Arkansas State University offers for us. Most importantly remember to understand your topic before you present so you are not scared of what will come out of your mouth. Good luck, give it your all, and you will succeed!

A Former Composition II Student,

Elizabeth Mansfield

Group Proposal on Final Draft

- Types of bullying
- Stages of life bullying
  - Child
  - Teens
  - Adult
- Resources to end bullying
  - Anticipatory guidance
  - Depression Questionnaire for Children (https://doi.org/10.1016/j.peds.2003.09.025)
  - Self administered questionnaire (https://doi.org/10.1136/bmj.323.7311.480)
  - (http://sites.tamuc.edu/bullyingjournal/article/bullies-and-victims-in-higher-edu

        cation/) —this was the group proposal I had put together that Adam & Cassie did not

                                                  do

Thoughts

For the most part I enjoyed the writing process because it helped me learn what I should really be doing when writing. On the other hand, I hated the group work because I did not get the group I expected to get. I got one who did their work when they wanted to and not when I needed them to. Overall, I liked this assignment and it has helped me within my future.

Annotated Bibliography

Topic
    Bullying, Anxiety, and Depression
Research Question
    How does bullying lead to anxiety and depression in college students?
Reflective Introduction

Throughout this research I expected to find information about how bullying leads to anxiety and depression. What I found during research was something that I did not expect. Some of the research explained what I expected to find but the rest were studies on people over the past 30 years. This particular study tried to keep bullying from antisocialness but when the study was concluded it was clear that it lead straight to antisocialness. Throughout my thorough research I also found a study that determines all parties of bullying can have a strenuous effect on their health. For example, poor physical and mental health, anxiety, depression, and poor school performance to list a few. Those enrolled in higher education showed more effects of bullying after enrollment. This concluded that the reason for bullying could be a "rite of passage". Some bullying has went over the top where students could not finish their education and dropped out. Others took a more serious approach to ending their lives. Through all of these studies each of the authors have been in the correct position to formally enter studies and information on how bullying can lead to anxiety and depression.

Annotated Bibliography

Adams, F. D., ED.D., & Lawerence, G. J., Ph.D. (2011). Bullying Victims: The Effects Last Into

    College. *Bullying Victims: The Effects Last Into College, 40*(1), 4-13.

    doi:https://search.proquest.com/central/docview/921231925/fulltextPDF/470B053E698

    8485DPQ/6?accountid=8363

Sample Student Portfolios

Those who were bullied in schools showed effects after they were enrolled in higher education. The study suggests effects of bullying that are long lasting. Also states why bullies do it, which could be a "rite of passage". Some victims in this study became bullies themselves due to it not being large enough to receive notice from teachers. Some performed poorly in school and eventually dropped out and others took it more seriously and commited suicide. Frank D. Adams and Gloria J. Lawrence are professors at Wayne State College who each are involved in counseling and social sciences.

Hutzell, K. L., & Payne, A. A. (2017). The Relationship Between Bullying Victimization and School Avoidance: An Examination of Direct Associations, Protective Influences, and Aggravating Factors [Abstract]. *The Relationship Between Bullying Victimization and School Avoidance: An Examination of Direct Associations, Protective Influences, and Aggravating Factors.* Retrieved February 15, 2019, from http://eds.b.ebscohost.com/ehost/detail/detail?vid=0&sid=6bb87e13-c68a-46a3-9de5-9ebf3226330@pdc-v-sessmgr01&bdata=JnNpdGU9ZWhvc3QtbGl2ZQ==#db=asn&AN=127893880

This study shows the bullying impact of victims. It includes the factors of why students who are bullied are more likely to avoid school involvement. For everyone involved in bullying it states that poor health, anxiety, depression, poor school performance, and many other factors can come out of those involved. Kirsten L. Hutzell and Allison Ann Payne are both

involved in criminology and sociology, making them excellent personnel to discuss the topic of bullying victimization.

Reid, G. M., Holt, M. K., Bowman, C. E., Espelage, D. L., & Green, J. G. (2016). Perceived Social Support and Mental Health among First-Year College Students with Histories of Bullying Victimization. *Perceived Social Support and Mental Health among First-Year College Students with Histories of Bullying Victimization.* Retrieved February 15, 2019, from

https://search.proquest.com/central/docview/1828125387/470B053E698848SDPQ/7?accountid=8363.

The four authors of this journal all are at a School of Education. They each are involved in counseling, child development, or education. This journal states bullying throughout childhood is associated with adult depression. This study identifies factors and has implications for designing interventions that can help adjustment into adulthood. Students completed two surveys over two semesters which reported childhood bullying, current depression and anxiety, and social support. They came to the conclusion of this study that bullying was associated with depression and anxiety later in life.

Thoughts

Within this assignment, it has helped me learn what APA formatting should look like. For one of my class, I am required to write a short summary of the references I use. I did not know this had a name at the time. Through this assignment it has helped me learn what my teacher is expecting from me and my submissions. I really enjoyed the fact that you let us use the writing style associated with our disciplines.

Literature Review

Within the research I have conducted, I expected to find clear and concise articles on how bullying affects mental health. My articles have addressed the severity of mental illness associated with bullying. There were numerous examples of how bullying can result in self-harm, poor academic performance, and mental health disorders as well. Overall, The United States of America has seen an increase in bullying as time has gone on, which has been an important factor in healthcare assessments. Health Care Providers have developed assessments to give them an insight to a child's symptoms without the child noticing they are under assessment. The numerous efforts to examine bullying, causes of bullying, and how to stop bullying have been implemented all over The United States of America, especially within the public-school system.

Healthcare Providers are a major factor of determining mental health among adolescents. In fact, The United States National Library of Medicine has assessed the role of healthcare providers in among the factor of cyberbullying. "A key role that HCP's can play in the prevention of bullying and cyberbullying is by including discussions of bullying as a part of anticipatory guidance." (Moreno & Vaillancourt, 2017) Anticipatory guidance is given to an adolescent to assist parents in understanding what is the expected growth and development of their children. Including bullying in anticipatory guidance validates bullying as a health issue. Moreno and Vaillancourt make parents aware of the symptoms and signs of bullying. They also go on to speak of the clinical settings of the screenings and what to expect. The overall role of

a health care physician is to provide education about bullying. Some parents and adolescents are oblivious to what bullying entails, so it is important to educate them, so they know what to look for. Moreno and Vaillancourt discuss how many opportunities healthcare physicians have to collaborate with schools and families to help develop positive social relationships. Healthcare physicians have realized that bullying puts a toll on students as a whole. They have ultimately made an effort to take the initiative to see the early signs and be able to stop bullying and its effect on mental health.

Yoke Yong Chen wrote an article titled, "Exposure to Bullying Among Adolescents Across Nine Countries." Within this article, authors reported their research to determine the relationship between bullying, post-traumatic stress disorder, and suicide attempts of teenagers across nine countries. This study they discovered that bullying was astronomically associated with post-traumatic stress disorder symptoms and suicide attempts. according to Chen's research, bullying behavior is increasing across nations and is considered as a "leading adolescent concern". (Chen & Eiklit, 2017) Bullying is a very under the radar issue, for the simple fact that people assume it cannot be stopped. Chen goes on to state that there have been numerous definitions of bullying within literature but the most commonly used, "is exposed, repeatedly and over time, to negative actions on the part of one or more other students." bullying is verbal, physical, and social manipulation. Social manipulation would be spreading rumors or isolating an individual. The act of bullying could also be causing harm to another person to fit in. For example, bullying someone else so that you could fit into a particular category. Chen concludes that victims of bullying and the bully them self are more likely to develop mental health problems that could persist to adulthood. Within this article it is clear as to how bullying or being the bully can put a strain on an individual's mental health. After bullying takes place, it can cause a stress on their education as well.

After being bullied it can make some think, why should I try to succeed anymore. Your mental health can play a major role in your education. If bullying were to affect your mental health, this could also affect your education. Adams and Lawrence discuss this in, "Bullying Victims: The Effects Last into College." Throughout this journal article they discuss their study of whether those bullied in schools continued to show effects of being bullied after they enrolled in higher education. They discuss the act of bullying as a "rite of passage". (Adams & Lawrence, 2011) Bullying rarely goes noticed by educators or school officials until a violent act occurs. Adams and Lawrence include their opinions on poor academic work to the people who have been bullied or have not been bullied. People who have been bullied perform poorly in academic work or drop out of school, some choose a more dramatic response such as committing suicide. They discovered that bullying is not just targeted at adolescents, although more prominent, it exists in varying age levels. Adams and Lawrence conducted a short study of about two hundred and seventy undergraduate students. Their study concluded that, youths who are victims of bullying were at an accelerated risk to victimize others as they move from one place to another.

Within the public-school setting children are more likely to witness bullying or be a victim of bullying. Grinshteyn and Yang begin to examine the association between cyberbullying and missing school among students in the United States of America. They conducted a study among a little over thirteen thousand high school students in the United States of America. This study gave them an insight as to why students would want to miss school. They begin to discuss how school attendance is associated with multiple negative consequences such as poor academic performance, higher chance of participating in risk-taking behaviors, and a great risk for dropping out of school. They stated that increased neighborhood crimes are associated with truancy. As a student gets older, their truancy tendency increases. An increase in school days missed can be associated with having a lower-income

family. Also being lesbian, gay, bisexual, transgender, or queer are also at a higher risk to miss high school due to fear of being bullied. The amount of school days missed are not just associated with bullying. It is also associated with illness, being overweight, procedures, or poor oral health. Behavioral health conditions also contributed to school days missed, such as depression, attention deficit hyperactivity disorder, anxiety, and even phobias. Grinshteyn and Yang discuss, "the purpose of this study was to examine the association between the victim of electronic bullying and miss days of school. A recent meta-analysis identified a number of negative outcomes associated with being the victim of electronic bullying including those related to psychological health, physical health, behavior, and social functioning with stress and suicidal ideation as the outcomes with the strongest associations among adolescents. While exposure to violence and traditional, face-to-face bullying, have been correlated with school absenteeism, the effect of electronic bullying has not been examined separately for its association with school attendance." However, electronic bullying is an increasingly common experience among adolescents that has been associated with other negative outcomes. It is important to understand the potential association of electronic bullying with school attendance if it to be prevented." (Grinshteyn & Yang, 2011) The study concluded with the unclear association of cyberbullying and school absences. It did however associate face-to-face bullying with absences.

The association of self-harm and bullying go hand in hand when you ask someone what they think the outcome of bullying is. Karanikola, Lyberg, Holm, and Severinsson state that bullying victimization during childhood is a risk factor of poor physical health, mental health disorders, deliberate self-harm, and suicidal symptoms. They continue to state bullying victims experience severe emotional distress associated with the violence of bullying. Victimization during childhood is a key factor associated with self-stigma. Self-stigma is when an individual internalizes the stereotypes about their status. The studies

Portfolio Compilation

13

they researched show that individuals with personality disorders, depression, psychosis, and conduct disorder are more likely to experience self-stigma. These groups also report more frequent bullying victimization and self-harming behavior. According to the study conducted, exposure to frequent bullying before age 12 was associated with increased risk for deliberate self-harm. Overall, this study was conducted have insight to the associations of bullying, self-harm, mental disorders and plenty of other discussed topics.

Throughout reading each journal article, it is concluded that bullying is closely associated with self-harm, mental health disorders, and academic performance. As discussed, bullying has been addressed with numerous definitions, but one has been vastly used more than others, is exposed, repeatedly and over time, to negative actions on the part of one or more students. Within using this definition, it creates almost an example to what bullying is rather than a definition. Being the bully and being the victim of bullying can create long lasting effects that make bullying, Bullying has been studied time and time again. The effects, types, and numerous other factors that make bullying, bullying. In these articles and the studies, they performed it is clear that bullying is a factor of depression, anxiety, self-harm, and plenty of other mental and physical disorders.

Portfolio Compilation

14

Works Cited

Adams, F. D., ED.D., & Lawerence, G. J., Ph.D. (2011). Bullying Victims: The Effects Last Into College. *Bullying Victims: The Effects Last Into College,40*(1), 4-13. doi:https://search.proquest.com/central/docview/921231925/fulltextPDF/470B053E698 8485DPQ/6?accountid=8363

Chen, Y. Y., & Elklit, A. (2017). Exposure to Bullying Among Adolescents Across Nine Countries. *Journal of Child & Adolescent Trauma,11*(1), 121-127. doi:10.1007/s40653-017-0172-x

Grinshteyn, E., & Yang, Y. T. (2017). The Association Between Electronic Bullying and School Absenteeism Among High School Students in the United States. *Journal of School Health,87*(2), 142-149. doi:10.1111/josh.12476

Karanikola, M. N., Lyberg, A., Holm, A., & Severinsson, E. (2018). The Association between Deliberate Self-Harm and School Bullying Victimization and the Mediating Effect of Depressive Symptoms and Self-Stigma: A Systematic Review. *BioMed Research International,2018*, 1-36. doi:10.1155/2018/4745791

Moreno, M. A., & Vaillancourt, T. (2017, June). The Role of Health Care Providers in Cyberbullying. Retrieved from https://www.ncbi.nlm.nih.gov/pmc/articles/PMC5455868/

15

Thoughts

In the beginning I was a little confused on how this writing process should be done. I don't know what could have been done differently to help me understand it better because you thoroughly explained it. It just was not clicking in my head. By the end of this assignment I now understand what is expected from a literature review.

Final Project

https://prezi.com/view/kXAAgTVFZNGzZuhFG8vD/

I enjoyed getting to research a topic that I wanted to research. It helped me to stay focussed on writing and ensure my paper was filled with information. The only thing I did not like was that my group had bailed on me leaving me to create a project just a few days before the presentation. other than this, it was a great learning experience.

Use the above QR code to view Elizabeth Mansfield's final project.

Megan Knowling

Dr. Airek Beauchamp

Composition 2 Portfolio

Introduction to Portfolio- A Reflection on the Semester

Every Monday, Wednesday and Friday at 8:50am I hear, "get the h*!l out of my face!"

Although this may just be a lighthearted dismissal from class, it was the same reaction I had when being told that in Composition II, the whole semester was spent doing a group project. Despite my initial dread, I ended up in class researching a unique, interesting topic with a generally hard working group (that actually stayed on top of things). With this group, I feel that I grew tremendously as a writer and student, while achieving each course learning outcome.

One learning outcome I felt was going to be personally challenging was revising my writing based on feedback provided by peers, instructors, tutors and other audiences. I knew this would be challenging for me because with my academic work, I don't typically like to rely on other students. I've had previous experiences with peer review that have been unproductive and practically useless, to say the least. But, as we started peer reviews, I found that my group members put in an effort to providing me with effective feedback. I eventually began request that they evaluate certain aspects of my writing where I felt was lacking, and used their feedback to improve not only my actual writing, but the ideas and arguments behind it. I feel as though this was a huge step in my progression as a writer and that I completed this course learning outcome.

Another learning outcome I saw was my group and self potentially struggling with was engaging with a larger ongoing civic, social and academic conversation. I believed this would be a challenge because we have been writing academic essays for so long. There's a handful of topics, such as the legalization of marijuana, that many students choose to write about over and over. Frankly, I was tired of conducting and reviewing research over the same few topics since high school. That said, my group picked a unique topic that I have never written about before. We addressed the overcrowding of animals issue in the Jonesboro Animal Control and NEA

Animal Shelters. Although our topic was uncommon, we did not struggle to find how it contributed to civic and social conversations, as well as our own unique academic conversation within our respective disciplines. Once again, somewhere where I worried I would struggle at the beginning of the semester began somewhere where I believe I was relatively successful.

Despite struggling with a couple of the learning outcomes, I feel as though I was successful in accomplishing each expectation. In addition to this, I wrote my first literature review. I was very nervous about writing this paper because I felt as though what I was writing was wrong. I found myself struggling to evaluate the sources as a piece of writing, not just for evidence, because I was so used to having to mainly focus on synthesizing an argument. No matter how much I evaluated, compared or contrasted the sources, I was constantly fighting back the urge to resort to what I knew and was comfortable with. Regardless of my worries, I successfully completed the literature review of five sources. Not only did I address the main points, strengths and weaknesses of each source, I also compared and supported points I made with evidence, all while synthesizing a larger argument. Overall, the literature review challenged me to accomplish each learning outcome, despite my initial doubt.

In conclusion, Composition II challenged me as a writer and student. The class taught me to rely on my group mates in a group project, explore new topics, and to have confidence in my writing abilities, even if the genre is new to me. Personally, I am content with my growth. I may still dislike group projects, but I overall had a positive experience with my group and this course. Now that the semester is over and I have accomplished what I aimed to do, I will willingly get out of Dr. Beauchamp's face.

Unit 1 Research Proposal

In 2019, animal adoption is an extremely important issue because of the over abundance of animals in shelters, disabling them to perform to the best of their ability. It has gotten to the point that some local shelters are no longer accepting new animal rescues. When someone adopts from a breeder they are more likely to know the animals history. The adopters will be able to see the parents of the animal and they will know the exact breed. On the other hand, when someone adopts from a shelter, they are giving an animal a warm, safe, and healthy place to live. Adopting animals from a shelter may seem like a last resort, but really it should be the first. This is because adopting an animal from a shelter is (usually) cheaper than buying from a breeder. It is also almost always safer than buying from a breeder. We recognize that their are some breeders who are very reliable and reputable but When someone adopts from a shelter they have the opportunity to give an abused and abandoned animal another chance.

Although everyone should be aware of this growing problem, that is not the case. The main people who know about this issue are the workers at animal shelters and pounds. They deal with the consequences of this problem everyday. There are also many animal activists that constantly battle the progression of animal breeders. Other people that are aware and concerned with this issue are animal owners and lovers. The main victims of this problem are the animals, and since they cannot speak for themselves, our project's purpose is to speak up for them.

The amount of research our group has done over the course of this project gives us authority to comment on the difference between adopting from animal shelters and buying from breeders. Through research, we have gathered enough factual information to defend our thoughts on animal adoption. Using this information, we will be able to show why adopting an animal from a shelter is the better option and why it should be the more favorable option. We are able to not only display reliable facts but provide analyzation and reasoning as to why adopting animals and helping out our local animal shelter (Jonesboro) should be more common.

In terms of answers we anticipate finding, we anticipate to statistically see that adopting from animal shelters is financially smarter than adopting from breeders. Looking in terms of animal health, we expect to find that animals adopted from shelters are in most cases healthier than those from breeders, because the shelter vaccinates the animals. That said, we expect to find that it is more socially common/popular to adopt from breeders for multiple reasons. Due to this, we anticipate having to talk about changing the social stigmas around animal shelters. The answer is not in simple "black and white" terms because although people "should" adopt from animal shelters when looking from multiple lenses, the opposite is usually found

When trying to decide where to adopt from, a lot of confusion could be cleared by showing a complete view of the behaviors of animals in shelters and from breeders. Animal Planet conducted a study on this. The organization gathered information from outside sources such as the Humane Society, who using cats investigated why people don't adopt from shelters as frequently in their article over "Adoption Vs. Buying From Breeders". One point made was that people don't trust cats that have been in shelters. This mindset sets people towards buying from a breeder, so that they can select a breed associated with the behavioral traits they desire. Using this, our group may bring attention to the public that not all animals from shelters have unfavorable traits.

When considering the question of adopting from an animal shelter versus a private breeder, the people who will most likely engage with our work the most are going to be the potential adopters. It is a well known fact, adopting a pet is a big decision. People aren't simply looking for a dog or a cat, but a new member of the family, which is why it's so important to

gather all the facts to make an informed decision. Our work will also engage those who care a great deal for animals in general. No matter who you are or where you come from, we all have a soft spot for those furry little creatures who make us smile and steal our hearts.

Works Cited

Cotroneo, Christian. If Everyone Read This, The Shelters Would Be Empty. The Dodo, 2015. Web. 30 December 2015. https://www.thedodo.com/amphtml/dog-shelter-guide-adoptions-1532460278

"Adoption Vs. Buying From Breeder." Animal Planet. 15 May, 2012. www.animalplanet.com/pets/cat-adoption-vs-buying-from-cat-breeders/

Jonesboro, Arkansas. Web. www.jonesboro.org/132/Animal-Control

Unit 2 Annotated Bibliography

Introduction: In recent years, therapy animals have began to become more popular. Due to this recent increase in popularity, I did not expect to find a lot of research on the topic. Despite my expectations, I found a variety of sources researching the benefits and requirements of therapy animals. That said, I did not find research connecting therapy animals to shelter animals. This will make it difficult to connect to my group's question since there is no direct connections stated. Although this was frustrating, it does not make my research a failure, it is still possible to connect the two subjects with some analyzation and creativity. Something positive about my sources are that some of them can be used by my other group members as well because the statistics don't only apply to therapy animals. One question I think could be a 'game changer' if answered in further research is: What difference in behavior do sheltered and breeded animals exhibit? Answering this question will help me piece together an argument that animal shelters should start training therapy animals. Another important question I have left after my research is: Can animal without owners be trained as a therapy animal? Answering this question will allow me to articulate my argument even more. Overall, my research has provided me with qualitative and quantitative data to create an argument for my group and my specific discipline.

Article 1: Puppy brigade reports for duty: A therapy dog program at a children's hospital provides comfort for pediatric patients and families facing the unfamiliar and frightening hospital experience

Hester, Miranda. "Puppy brigade reports for duty: A therapy dog program at a children's hospital provides comfort for pediatric patients and families facing the unfamiliar and frightening hospital experience." *Contemporary Pediatrics*, Dec. 2017, p. 15+. *Academic*

OneFile,

http://link.galegroup.com/apps/doc/A519899770/AONE?u=akstateu1&sid=AONE&xid=72
753e3d. Accessed 14 Feb. 2019.

This article speaks about the benefits that therapy dogs in pediatric hospitals can bring to the patients. Additionally, it highlights that each trained therapy dog has an unmatched uniqueness which helps their patients. Another important point mentioned is that animals other than dogs can be used as therapy animals. Some effective tools the author used were mentioning that other animals can become therapy animals, providing specific examples of therapy dogs and their patients, and including pictures as a visual aid for the readers. One weakness of this article is that the author had limited sources, but the facts taken from each source are consistent in the article itself, which vouches for the validity. Although it would have been better if the author used more sources, the used resources provide useful links for further research. In all, this article provides a good overview of what therapy dogs are, utilized specific examples to further explain why therapy dogs are effective, and provided a great base for further research.

Article 2: Pet Ownership and Cardiovascular Risk

Levine, Glenn N, et al. "Pet Ownership and Cardiovascular Risk." *Arteriosclerosis, Thrombosis, and Vascular Biology*, American Heart Association, 9 May 2013,
www.ahajournals.org/doi/full/10.1161/CIR.0b013e3182920e1.

This article was one of the sources cited in Article 1. It is a scientific statement released by the American Heart Association that summarizes a couple dozen studies from around the world that investigate if pet ownership truly lower cardiovascular disease risk. The ultimate conclusion of

this statement is that yes, owning a pet does lower risk for cardiovascular disease because it lowers the risk for many of the symptoms associated with the diseases. The research could've been broadened to include therapy animals, which aren't necessarily pets. Although therapy animal may not have been included, something important that this article did was evaluate multiple studies covering multiple causes of cardiovascular diseases. They presented variety in sources rather than variety in subjects. Rather than reading, annotating, and using every individual study that this statement summarizes, this source can be used as a scientific base behind my argument. Another place where the article fell short is that it did not state specifically to adopt from shelters. In the future I will need further evidence from another source to prove how adopting from a shelter is more cost effective in order to tie this evidence into my main argument. Even though this may be true, this source did not fail to provide more than enough information to strengthen my article as to why therapy animals should be available to adopt.

Article 3: Therapeutic Interventions- Animal Assisted Therapy Programs

Janssen, Maridith A. "Therapeutic Interventions: Animal Assisted Therapy Programs." *Palaestra*, Fall 1998, p. 40. *Academic OneFile*,
http://link.galegroup.com/apps/doc/A53509918/AONE?u=akstateu1&sid=AONE&xid=147
d45f1. Accessed 14 Feb. 2019.

This article offers a different perspective, in addition to filling a hole that Article 2 left in my research. This article not only looks at the psychological aspect of the benefits of pets, but more specifically looks at the benefits of therapy animals. Something this article did very well was provide specific examples of when therapy animals have been proven to make a lasting impact on the lives of people ranging from children to elders to mental health patients and even prison inmates. These examples will be very effective to use in my writing. Also, providing a psychological aspect to the mixture of evidence vouching for pets/therapy animals will further strengthen my argument. Although this article did do a lot well, a weakness in this article is the almost opinionated conclusions. At the end of each specific example, a brief conclusion was made. The tone was informal and the statement could easily be argued by someone playing Devil's Advocate. That said, some of the points and/or examples in this article could be useful to my overall argument.

Unit 3 Literature Review

An Innovative Solution to Animal Shelter Overcrowding

In the United States, animal shelters are overcrowded. In fact, according to the ASPCA[1], approximately 6.5 million animals enter animal shelters annually (Pet Statistics). Despite this large number of animals in shelters, animal breeders have continued to persistently breed and sell animals. Bred animals hold stereotypes of having good temperment, behaving and being healthier, causing sheltered animals to be stuck with negative stereotypes ultimately preventing their adoption. The overcrowding and considerably low adoption rates of sheltered animals cannot be solved with solely one solution. That said, introducing a new, innovative solution would give shelters another option to get their animals adopted. Animal shelters should train their animals to become therapy animals because of the diverse benefits for both sheltered animals and humans. Therapy animals offer physical health improvements, irreplaceable bonds and improved mental health to humans. Despite typically having substandard reputations, sheltered animals would make great therapy animals.

To begin, one of the unique benefits that therapy animals and pets provide to humans is improved physical health. In 2013, Glenn N Levine and others at the American Heart Association (AHA) released a statement after evaluating a plethora of studies conducted worldwide, which all investigated if pet ownership truly lower cardiovascular disease risk. The ultimate conclusion of this statement is that yes, owning a pet does lower risk for cardiovascular disease. Owning a pet lowers the risk for many of the symptoms associated with the diseases such as systemic hypertension, hyperlipidemia and obesity, while increasing physical activity[2] and mortality of patients of with cardiovascular disease (Levine). This statement provides a

---

[1] American Society for the Prevention of Cruelty to Animals
[2] Physical activity is a preventative measure to avoid heart disease

strong argument behind the physical benefits of owning a pet because it was published by a countrywide acclaimed organization, the American Heart Association, attesting to it's reliability. That said, the research itself focused primarily on actual pets, but it could've easily been broadened to include therapy animals. Although it failed to denote therapy animals, this statement did evaluate multiple peer-reviewed studies concerning multiple causes of cardiovascular diseases. The AHA's analysis of the sources made it clear that owning a pet does indeed reduce risk of cardiovascular disease. Reduced risk of cardiovascular disease could also imply a longer life and less medical bills, adding to the benefits of owning a pet.

While improved physical health may be enough of a reason for some people to start a Google search for breeders in their area, taking a car ride to the local shelter can provide an opportunity for a unique connection that buying from a breeder may not. In fact, Miranda Hester recently published an article in the Contemporary Pediatrics Journal which addressed not only the benefits that therapy dogs in pediatric hospitals can bring to the patients, but how each trained therapy dog has an unmatched uniqueness which helps their patients. Hester provides specific examples of therapy dogs and their patients, such as Tessa Puma, a 6 year old leg amputee, and her therapy dog Rudy who has a prosthetic paw. Rudy and Tessa had a strong connection, which in turn assisted in her recovery, physical therapy, and even finding a prosthetic company. If Rudy had not had a prosthetic paw, he would have still assisted Tessa's recovery, but his condition enhanced the experience and benefited the Puma family in ways they did not expect. Many breeders attempt to breed the perfect[3] dog, cat or other animal for their customers. Shelters do not have that luxury, but that is not necessarily a burden. Animals with disabilities, such as Rudy, are more likely to be found in shelters (Adopt a Less Adoptable Pet

efinitions of perfect & imperfect vary from person to person.

Week 2018), further emphasizing why getting sheltered animals certified to be therapy animals is important. Rudy and Tessa had a unique connection because of their imperfections,[4] one that animals sold from breeders may lack.

Overall, Hester was effective in communicating her message using specific stories of therapy animals/patients, and including pictures as a visual aid for the readers (Hester). This said, there were two major weaknesses in the article. First, the article utilized limited sources. Hester could have had a stronger article had she used more sources. Despite using only a couple of sources, the sources themselves were reliable, the facts taken from each source are consistent in the article itself (vouching for the validity of her argument), and the sources provided additional insight on this topic. The second weakness was that again, the article was not directly connected to animal shelters, leading to the question: Can animal without owners be trained as a therapy animal? Despite this weakness, the question can be addressed with little further research. After reading an article published by One Green Planet[5], it can be concluded that yes, shelter animals can be trained to become therapy animals (Pittman). It is possible to utilize the uniqueness of sheltered animals in order to create a positive, life changing experience for humans. Examining how multiple shelters and organizations train sheltered animals to become therapy animals further proves that local animal shelters countrywide should begin to do the same.

Although it may seem this way, the benefits that training shelter animals to be therapy animals bring are not always physical, or tangible things. Some benefits may be psychological. Despite being published in the fall of 1998, Maradith A Janssens evaluation of some of the psychological benefits of therapy animals still prove true today. Janssen bases her conclusion that the use of therapy animals should be expanded off of psychological fundamentals that all

[4] Refer to footnote 3.
[5] An organization promoting an eco-conscious lifestyle.

good behavior, so it would make sense to adopt from a breeder. On the other hand, it may seem like sheltered animals do not exhibit good behavior, but doctor of veterinary medicine Sheila Segurson D'Arpino argues otherwise. D'Arpino is a qualified individual who not only observed, but conducted many behavioral assessment tests of animals. She noticed that the tests had limitations that could make their results inaccurate. D'Arpino first discusses temperment testing, noting that human psychologists have agreed in the past that people are unable to accurately judge someone's personality based on meeting once, and concluding this applies to animals as well. The shelters do not have the funding to repeat temperment testing, therefore they are basically assessing behavior at one given time, not temperament. D'Arpino also discusses how stressed animals are living in shelters. She points out that most animals react negatively under stress, so animals' behavior in shelters are not true representations of how they will behave at home. She states that reducing animal stress in shelters should be a focus when it comes to improving behavior, rather than blaming the animals current behavior on only the animals. Going along with this, D'Arpino also states that most animals can read body language just as humans can, and will most likely not display kindness until they sense friendliness. She suggests that potential adopters say a friendly "hello" to the dog before making any assumptions about the animal (D'Arpino).

Generally, the most powerful part of D'Arpino's piece is after she assesses each type of test, she proposes her own system of testing. This is the most important part of her piece, because she notes where other testing systems fail: such as being conducted in stressful environments, or by biased testers. Another strength in this article is that D'Arpino noted that there should be a handbook defining certain terms such as aggressive, so that there is not confusion on what aggression really 'is', since individuals have differing opinions. Compared to the other sources,

be loved, all people need to feel worthwhile and that pets can fulfill …ious scientific studies on pets influence things such as loneliness, …xiety and self-esteem. In addition to this analyzation of sources, Janssens …ovides specific examples of how therapy animals have helped people psychologically. One example is an organization called Green Chimneys, which allows children with learning disabilities, emotional disorders, behavioral problems, etc. to connect with animals in order to learn how to develop nurturing relationships and open up (Janssens)

Overall, Janssens' article is a very useful research because it not only analyzes multiple studies, but also provides specific examples of the psychological benefits of therapy animals. A definite strength of this source was that it concerned therapy animals specifically. Neither Hester or Levine's sources did that. This provides a solid backbone to the argument for the expansion of therapy animal programs to shelters because it explicitly mentions therapy animals. Another strength of this article is the examples. Janssens' examples ranged from children to elders, mental health patients and even prison inmates. In comparison to Hester's examples in her article, Janssens' reached a much wider lens of people. This said, one problem with this article is relevancy. As previously mentioned, this article was published in 1998, so some of the examples may have lost their relevance as society changes, or due to events that took place after the publication. Another weakness of this article is that there was a slight informal tone throughout some of Janssens' analyzation, making her conclusions seem slightly opinionated. Despite this, Janssens did not fail to prove that therapy animals do benefit people psychologically by fulfilling humans' innate need for love and to feel worthwhile.

After observing the variety of benefits that therapy animals offer to humans, someone may wonder why sheltered animals typically maintain a reputation of having this piece is the only one that proposes a thorough solution to the system it criticizes while maintaining a formal tone. D'Arpino makes it clear that current behavioral tests in shelters are biased, and may even work against animals. If shelters and adopters realize that the system is biased, they will be able to fix their own mistakes or at least acknowledge where the tests 'fall short'. Many sheltered animals that are labelled unfriendly or aggressive truly may not be.

Expanding upon this idea that sheltered animals are wrongly labeled, in 2018 a group of animal scientists from the Czech Republic researched the behavior of animals 6 months after being adopted from a shelter. Svatava Vitulová, Eva Voslářová, Vladimír Večerek, and Iveta Bedáňová investigated the behavioral differences of animals adopted from shelter before they were adopted and 6 months later. The team investigated multiple variables on both sides of the adoption, including the owners past experience with animals and the animals sociability. One shocking statistic is that 96.2% of participants said that they would adopt from a shelter again, even after a reported 72% of dogs started off with some sort of behavioral issue (Vitulová).

After spending time outside of a shelter setting and taking time to adjust to a home setting, the once sheltered animals were reported to have less behavioral problems and exhibit fewer undesirable traits. The conclusions made in this article support D'Arpino's idea that the behavioral testing system is biased and needs changing. It proved that animals do behave differently in a shelter than they would at home or in a therapy setting. A prominent strength in this article is that the authors cite over 20 previous studies, proving that their data is consistent with the conclusions of others. If there were to be a weakness, it could be that too many variables were investigated. That said, each variable was investigated and prove to have an influence on the overall conclusions and results. Vitulová's study provides numerical data substantiating that sheltered animals poor reputations are not true an overwhelming majority of the time. Although

the animals may display unfavorable personality traits at first, behavior improves tremendously after adoption[6], or in this case after being trained to be a therapy animal.

In conclusion, therapy animals benefit uniquely benefit people in a multitude of ways, physically and psychologically. Sheltered animals would be great fits for therapy animals because of their uniqueness and actual (rather than perceived) personalities. In order to expand the benefits of therapy animals, and solve the issue of overcrowding in animal shelters, local animal shelters should begin to train their animals to become therapy animals. This single change can make a lasting positive impact not only on sheltered animals, but animal shelters and people of all ages, country wide. In theory, shelter animals trained to be therapy animals will solve the issue of overcrowding in shelters and increase the overall physical and mental health of humans. Some animals may even find a future home, and for humans, an overall improved quality of life.

[6] Implying that friendliness and affection are displayed from owners.

Sample Student Portfolios

Knowling 21

Unit 4 Colloquium

Images:

Knowling 20

Vitulová, Svatava, et al. "Behaviour of Dogs Adopted from an Animal Shelter." *Acta Veterinaria*

Brno, University of Veterinary and Pharmaceutical Sciences, 27 June 2018,

actavet.vfu cz/87/2/0155/.

Use the above QR code to view Megan Knowling's final project.

Sample Student Reflections

INTRODUCTION

The previous section provided you with examples of full student portfolios, meant to capture the work in progress as it occurred and to demonstrate the separate assignments both as individual pieces as well as holistic endeavors throughout which the authors' thoughts and sentiments begin to take form, leading to not only clear arguments but clear plans of action. The whole-portfolio samples give you a clear snapshot of a project nearing its end.

This section will provide another view of the portfolios, this time as reflections on the process. The whole portfolios accompanying these reflections can be found online, but we thought it would be beneficial to see how students felt as they were wrapping up, turning it in, and preparing to move on. In some ways, the students in these reflections say the same things most students doing this type of reflection might. They discuss what they have learned about writing and crafting arguments to specific audiences. They discuss things the instructor could do more effectively next time and how the writing required for the course did or did not help them familiarize themselves with their chosen disciplines. As you read through these, we think you might find a sense of exhaustion, but also a sense of exhilaration, and that you might, at least for a few moments here and there, find that same sense of exhilaration as you realize that you are becoming a scholar.

Amber White

Comp II

04/28/19

Reflection

As I look back through the work of this semester I see how much I have learned and how much my writing has changed. This semester I have learned how to make my writing more formal, professional, and research based. I now know how to write for an audience other than myself and my professors. During the end of this semester I have learned how to make writing multi model and how to use Technology to enhance my writing and research.

My writing has become more formal through the assignments in this semester because, When writing based on research, you have to be more formal than usual. I have learned how to give more meaning to my writing. Having one topic for the whole semester gave it a bigger meaning, because it was not just for one grade. Having one topic throughout made us invest ourselves in the topic. My writing started to become more formal in the annotated bibliography due to the research needed for the assignment.

Research was not my strongest skill before this semester. I barely knew what an academic journal was before this class and now I can identify one easily. Being able to be involved in a big conversation and actually feel important in that conversation has been an eye opening experience. I used to believe that I was to young or not educated enough to speak in these big conversations and now I know how to do the research so that I can give myself a voice in the bigger conversations.

White 2

The group aspect of this semester has been amazing, being able to have information based on different disciplines and viewpoints for our topic really helped improve the quality of our final product. I have learned alot about writing even just from being in a group, seeing how different writing styles can really be and how merging them can teach you how to alter your writing style a little bit along the way.

My favorite part of the semester and probably where I had the most improvement is the multi model part of unit four. Learning how to make a website was so much fun. Before this unit I could not have told you where to even start to make a website. Now I have learned that I am really good at website design and I am slightly thinking about changing my minor! The website allowed me to learn how to take our essays and research and compact them into little bits of information that people could look at and understand without reading the entire essays.

This semester has made me a better, more educated, and more confident writer. In my opinion the best writer is educated and confident. I'm not saying that i'm the best writer by any means but I am saying that my writing has definitely changed and improved this semester. I am a more educated writer because I now know how to do more detailed research for my writing and how to articulate that research for an audience who may not have any experience in the topic. I am a more confident writer because I have shown myself that I am a good writer and that I can learn how to adapt my writing for more styles and genres than I could before. I believe that being more confident in my writing and making sure that I educate myself on what im writing about are the two most important things that have made me a better writer.

Laura Bass

Composition II/ Final Portfolio

Dr. Beauchamp

April 29, 2019

Reflection

I've always considered myself a good writer. I know how to properly organize an essay, I know how to use various types of sentences to make the essay flow, and I know how to use words and phrases in ways that grab the audience's attention. These skills carried me through high school English, and up until this point, I thought I had learned all there was to learn about writing. That's when composition II came barreling at me and hit me like a ton of bricks. I remember sitting in class the very first day, looking over the syllabus, reading over the words "rhetoric," "annotated bibliography," and "literature review" and wondering what it is that I had gotten myself into. I took a few deep breaths and told myself that instead of panicking, I was going to remain calm and allow myself to be open to learning something new, no matter how intimidating it seemed.

First off, I had no earthly idea what rhetoric was. Of course I had some experience with dissecting rhetorical concepts such as purpose, audience, and tone, but it was shaky at best. Despite that, I had little to no knowledge about genre in the rhetorical sense. I also wasn't too experienced in the act of engaging in larger conversations about academic and social issues. In my past writing experiences, most of what my peers and I wrote was more about our internal thoughts, feelings, and experiences, or localized schoolwide issues. Not very often were we asked to express our feelings about social or civic issues, whether that be in the community or the world at large. Furthermore, I've never been the type of person to speak up about my personal thoughts, feelings, or beliefs. I've always been very introverted, often keeping things to myself. As for my writing process, I'm more of a "draw up a quick story web and start writing" kind of gal. I've never really done much planning or critical thinking before or during my writing.

As the semester got under way, I quickly realized that my old ways of thinking and writing were going to need some tweaking. To write at this level, I was going to have to learn how to think more critically about not only the task right in front of me, but how it affects the people and the world around me. Through my assignments this semester, I learned just how important it is to think about rhetorical concepts when writing. Having a clear purpose sets the stage for your audience and translates to them the message you are trying to send, and knowing your audience helps you gear your writing in the right direction. Tone sets the mood for your writing, determining whether it's more formal or more laidback, and after that's taken care of, it's time to pick the genre that best encompasses these three concepts and makes the most sense when presenting your finished product.

Learning more about rhetoric also changed the way I write and the process I go through beforehand. Identifying purpose, audience, and tone forced me to think critically about what I was writing. It encouraged me to look at situations and subject matter from different perspectives, and it caused me to constantly be working to improve upon what I had already written. It also helped me when dissecting other people's research, allowing me to better understand what I was reading, for what purpose it was written, and how it could be further used in other situations. Being able to identify these features allowed me to properly incorporate other's research into my own writing.

Lastly, now that the semester is over, I feel more comfortable taking part in larger civic, social, and academic conversations. Through the work I have done this semester, inside the classroom as well as outside the classroom, I've come to realize that it is so important to have opinions about major issues on our campus, in our community, and in the world and to not only have those opinions but to let those opinions be heard. I've learned not to shy away from my truth and to not be afraid of telling others about things that I'm passionate about and things that make me joyful, saddened, or angry. I've also learned the importance of listening to what others have to say, taking into consideration their thoughts and feelings, and understanding their point of view. Moving forward in my academic career as well as my adult life, I hope to use what I've learned this semester to continue to grow as both a writer and a person.

Morgan Richardson

Professor Beauchamp

Composition II

April 2019

Reflective Essay

At the beginning of this semester, I came into Composition II not knowing what we were going to do or how we were going to do it. I have never really excelled in English class or understood how to write the perfect paper. I have struggled many years with writing and seemed to never get taught the things I struggled with. This class has taught me that no one's is expecting my paper to be perfect and there's no such thing as a "perfect paper." I started off very insecure about my writing techniques because didn't want to do or say the wrong thing. This semester has taught me to be comfortable with sharing my work and not feeling constant judgment that I probably wasn't receiving. Making me open up with my group and sharing my opinions pushed me out of my comfort zone, but I'm glad it did because it really opened up my thoughts and learning process in a different way. My groups member taught me so much this semester that I probably wouldn't have been able to understand on my own.

This assignment taught me many things I had not been taught about before or wasn't able to understand. It helped me understand the rhetorical concepts such as purpose, audience, genre and tone. Writing a paper over animal shelters you have to make sure you're getting your point across without sounding like your judging or forcing the reader. I had a hard time with this a the beginning of this project. With our topic, we needed to inform all audiences, so again we had be careful how we said things. I learned that you do have to consider who's reading your work and who it will effect.

At the beginning of this semester I was worried about engaging in larger civic, social and academic conversations, because no one wants to offend the people of your city or say the wrong thing. This mainly concerned me because our topic is such a big issue, and I didn't want to represent our local shelters and embarrass them. Towards the end of the semester, I became very proud of the work and research we all put together. We all worked really hard to make our website as reliable and professional as we could, while making it catch people's eye and interesting at the same time. I am so proud to have helped make such an incredible website and I know my group members feel the same way.

Throughout this semester I believe that my writing and research skills have gotten one thousand percent better. At the beginning, I was constantly asking my peers for clarification about things I probably should've already known. I also resorted to The Pack Prints for questions I needed answered and always felt like I learned a new skill each time. I feel like I have learned so much about research, annotating bibliographies, and how to write a literature review without feeling confused. Before this class I couldn't tell you how to do anything we have done this semester, but now I feel educated enough to help others achieve the same things I was struggling with not to long ago.

Before this class, my intentions when starting a paper would've been to write what my professor wanted to hear rather than what I believed. I learned everyone has different opinions about everything, so I tried not to please a specific audience and looked at the issue from multiple different perspectives. The skills I have learned this semester when writing an essay have been way more effective compared to the other ways I have been taught before. The things I do differently now would be my research process and the way I word my essays. I have gotten better with my writing, but I can improve so much more. After this semester, I plan on continuing improving my writing techniques and learning more about how I can become a better writer.

Alexia Louks

Airek Beauchamp

Comp 2 MWF 8:00

24 April 2019

Reflection

Throughout this semester in Composition 2 I have learned many valuable tools that have allowed me to grow as a writer and researcher. I have expanded my knowledge on important concepts like purpose, audience, genre, and tone. Before I participated in this course I was not interested in partaking in larger civic, social, and academic conversations, but know I have learned that I enjoy it. I know now that I can actually make a difference by sharing my knowledge with the community around me. Since I am going into the science field, the research elements of this course has helped prepared me for other courses in my degree and for my future career. I believe my writing process has pretty much stayed consistent, but the most important process I learned in this course is how to correctly peer review.

During unit one when the class was told we would be working as groups throughout the whole semester I was honestly terrified. I usually do not like working in groups. I always find myself stressing over whether my group is doing their work and whether the final product will be good. However, in this class I found my group members to be very reliable and to work together very well. In this unit, I learned that deciding a purpose for your research was extremely important. Without a purpose there was no where to start. Once my group found a purpose, helping animal shelters, it was difficult to decide who our audience would be. At the beginning we decided the local community would be our audience, but by the end of the semester we changed our audience to the animal shelters themselves.

In unit two when we worked on our own, I learned the importance of peer reviews. Since I had five other people in my group, I received a lot of feedback. I had to gain an understanding of what information to incorporate and what information was not helpful. I found that it also helped me when I peer reviewed my group members, because several times when I found a problem with one of their drafts, it was also a mistake I made. I also learned a lot on research during this unit. It was very difficult to find articles connecting everyone's discipline to our groups chosen topic. Finding the right search words/terms was probably the hardest part, luckily since we did peer review it allowed us to give suggestions to each other. This unit also showed me that I could make a change in the community just by sharing my knowledge and opinion in writing. Since I read many articles throughout the research period, I realized that many other people may share the same opinion as me.

For the duration of unit three I learned the importance of being able to connect all your research and knowledge into one coherent work. You can do tons of research and every article will be completely difference. I learned that if you can find similar topics throughout articles then you can use your own knowledge to connect them to your thesis. However, while writing my literature review I often found myself at a roadblock. I had a difficult time connecting all five articles to my discipline and my groups research question. I had to look at multiple examples and read several guides. In this unit I wrote five rough drafts, and I still know that my final draft could use more editing. With that being said, I am proud of my final draft.

During unit four I was extremely proud of my group and our final project. My group chose to do a website, which I believe turned out really good. Nevertheless, it took a lot of group collaboration and editing to pull it together. Learning to use the website creator was very difficult, especially since there was six people working on it at one time. I believe everyone's work got deleted at least once throughout the process. During this unit I learned the importance of genre and tone. Since a website has the possibility of being seen by many people with different likes, dislikes, and views, my group had to make sure it was as neutral as possible with still supporting our goal.

During this semester I have worked extremely hard to improve throughout my many drafts. I have learned many valuable tools that I will definitely use during the course of my time in college and when I start my career. I have learned the importance of listening to other peoples opinions and being able to suggest quality revision for classmates. Most importantly I have learned that if you want to improve, you have to put in the work.

Sample Student Reflections

Brett Murdie

Professor Beauchamp

Composition II

April 26, 2019

Reflection

Many things can happen in a course of several months, planned and unplanned, and upon reflection of those things you can see a growth in areas you may not have felt like you have grown in. In the months I was in Composition II (Comp II) I felt like I wasn't growing much, if at all, in many areas. However, upon reflection and reviewing some of my early works I began to realize that I have grown and developed in several areas from the work that we have done. I grew to understand more concepts, to be more engaged, to better my research, and to write with a more personalized style.

At the beginning of the semester the only concepts of writing I understood where rhetorical situations and analysis of those situations. In Comp II I learned about more genres that doesn't just involve rhetorical devices like irony or paradox. The genres I grew to learn more about are genres I see everyday on the internet like memes, podcast, infographics, and etc. I also began to think more about who I am writing to and how that audience might react to how I may put things. This helped me build awareness to certain tones and awareness to how to best present and highlight the purpose of what I am writing about.

I also started to engage more over the semester. Since I am a freshman I was really worried that people wouldn't take me seriously, but I quickly realized that all that really matters is that I can get my input

Murdie 2

across. I began to be more active in my group the more time went on and I began to realize how they would react to certain things. This led to an ease of communication over the semester that benefited me tremensely as the project kept advancing through its many phases.

I did a lot of research this semester and I may have done research for classes in the past, I may have never done as much as I did this semester. With all this research I was able to figure out how to find things in a broader approach rather than the specific approaches I have done since early High School. This made finding things to read and use for my research a lot easier and as time went on I was able to go into my mores specific methods as they were more useful later on in the researching process. However comfortable I am with researching will never outweigh me knowing that I will always need to improve and find more efficient methods to do so. However, this class has made me feel like I have made some progress towards more efficient research methods.

My style of writing has started to show more consistently within all the different papers and genres of papers we had to write this semester. I found that I generally have a style that keeps everything more formal. Even writing this reflection I find it difficult to use the words "me" and "I" because of the way I feel I should write. However, like with this paper, I have started changing and feeling able to express myself in my papers even if I try to avoid any informalities in my writing. I may always be working on my style as the years go by and I have to write emails or papers on whatever assignment that I have been assigned, but I feel I have gained step towards a style that incorporates the formality I prefer and the expression I need to improve my writing.

Primary Research

AN INTRODUCTION TO THE PROMISE
AND PERILS OF PRIMARY RESEARCH

Kristi Murray Costello

• • • • • • • •

Inspired by the part of David Bartholomae's article, "Inventing the University," in which he discusses the sheer rhetorical adaptability we ask students to possess, such as writing for anthropology, history, chemistry, biology, and Writing Studies all in the same semester, I consider again the standard research paper, its typical decontextualization, and the ways in which we ask undergraduate students to mimic being "members of the academy, or historians or anthropologists or economists," but how seldom we create assignments that allow them to actually be part of the academy and experience what it means to be a scholar (5).

In his book, *Rhetoric at the Margins*, David Gold writes that in 1930, Arkansas State University was the site of one of the first interracial debates in the US (46). The debate was with Wiley College, which was led by the famous Melvin Tolson (subject of the movie, *The Great Debaters*). Gold explains, "That a team from a small black college could travel so widely—much less successfully—during the height of the Depression is a remarkable achievement" (46).

Wanting to know more about this event, this time in history, and the role of Arkansas State University, my undergraduate Advanced Composition students and I worked together last spring to uncover as much information as we could about the debate as well as the region, the university, and race relations of the time through archival work, research, and interviews. We learned about the price of meat (10 cents per pound) and that lynchings of people of color, mostly men, were public and described in the local newspaper. Sources showed us that money was tight and racial tensions were high. Interestingly, we also discovered that the debate in 1930 actually happened at Arkansas State (short for Arkansas State College for Negroes), which was the common designation for AM&N, the state's first HBCU (Historically Black College or University), now University of Arkansas Pine Bluff ("Arkansas State and Wiley College Debate"). Rae, Lathan, Colby, and Meghan further discovered through searching newspapers that ASU-Pine Bluff and Wiley College faced off again just a year later in Hot Springs to a packed crowd ("Arkansas State and Wiley College Debate"); another group discovered that the two teams faced off again in 1936 to debate world peace "Debate Peace at Arkansas State"). Though our evidence is still somewhat flimsy on this, it looks like Arkansas State University, as we know it, and Wiley College faced off years later, just after desegregation, which would suggest that while A-State Jonesboro did not participate in Wiley's (and the nation's) first round of interracial debates, they were not far behind.

This project allowed the students the opportunity not to act as writers, historians, and researchers, but to *be* writers, historians, and researchers. This project also taught students about their community, how to collaborate effectively, and how to work with others on campus and in the community to gather information. As you will see in Rae, Lathan, Colby, and Meghan's paper, it also helped students experience firsthand the elation and tribulations of primary research.

Works Cited

"Arkansas State and Wiley College Debate." The Chicago Defender (National Edition), 11 Apr. 1931, ezproxy.library. astate.edu/login?url=https://search.proquest.com/ docview/492312147?accountid=8363. Accessed 10 May 2017.

Bartholomae, David. "Inventing the University." Journal of Basic Writing, no. 1, 1986, p. 4. EBSCOhost, ezproxy.library.astate.edu/ login?url=http://search.ebscohost.com/login.aspx?direct=true& db=edsjsr&AN=edsjsr.43443456&site=eds-live.

"Debate Peace at Arkansas State." The Chicago Defender (National Edition), 25 July 1936, ezproxy.library. astate.edu/login?url=https://search.proquest.com/ docview/492518037?accountid=8363. Accessed 10 May 2017.

Gold, David. *Rhetoric at the Margins: Revising the History of Writing Instruction in American Colleges, 1873-1947*. Southern Illinois UP, 2008, pp. 27-45.

COLLABORATIVE SCHOLARLY INVESTIGATION AND PROJECT OVERVIEW
Kristi Murray Costello
Advanced Composition, Spring 2016

· · · · · · · · ·

Overview

David Gold alleges that in 1930 Arkansas State University was the site of one of the first interracial debates in the US. Together, my class and I learned about this debate, research methods, and scholarly writing. And in doing so, as David Bartholomae suggested, we became "insiders" and "work[ed] and participate[d] in a common enterprise" (10-11).

Logistics

The class was divided into four groups and each group was assigned to learn about their particular method well enough, through practice and research, to teach the class.

The Preparation

Group 1: INTERNET AND DATABASES SEARCH: Search the internet and articles from online databases about the debate, the time period, Wiley college, Arkansas State University (hint: then it was called Arkansas State College), and related topics (including Works Cited pages of articles). Be ready to discuss the following questions: Where did you search? What search terms did you use? Where did these searches take you? Be sure to focus on methods, ethics, and tips, process, and findings. Talk to our resource librarian and help develop ideas and tips for other groups' searches.

Group 2: NEWSPAPERS AND MICROFICHE: Check our school and local newspapers, and see if you can access Wiley's school and local newspapers. You might even find it helpful to look at regional and national papers to get a sense of the time period. Engage in internet research about how to search, talk to someone at library about how to search newspapers, and be ready to share this information with your classmates—does all of the equipment work? Do you have to have appointments? Are there some searches the online newspaper works better for and others it doesn't?

Group 3: ARCHIVAL WORK including A-State yearbooks: Look through our university's archives, and any other materials that may be helpful, here and at Wiley (you'll see that they have some archival information online). Also, check the references in "Rhetoric on the Margins." Engage in internet research to see what sites have which materials and talk to professors and/or archivalists about ethics of working with this information, how to find it, etc.

Group 4: INTERVIEWS: Interview people who may know something about the debate and/or debate team here, or elsewhere. Also interview at least one historian who can tell you about the time period, particularly in this region. You should conduct at least four interviews. Think outside the box. Engage in internet research and talk to professors about appropriate interviewing strategies.

The Presentation
(25–30 minutes)

Your group will teach the rest of the class ***how to conduct your assigned method/s, tips for doing so effectively and efficiently here at A-State and in general, and the ethics of doing so.*** You will need to walk your classmates through your process, including who you talked to, what worked, what didn't, what you had access to, what you didn't, etc. You will need to research your method/s through practice, talking to experts, such as librarians and professors, and reading outside sources. All of your practice should entail trying to uncover details about the debate at A-State in 1930 or related information (like what else was going on around that time). In addition to presenting your assigned method, you will also ***present your results (or lack thereof) to the class.*** Keep in mind that the results are only *one* part of your presentation. Be mindful of the fact that sometimes what you don't find is just as important as what you do find and, for this project, learning about the method (and articulating what you learned with your classmates) is just as, if not more important, than the information itself.

The Project
(4- to 6-page group paper in MLA format)

You should have an argument, theme, or main idea that ties this together as a cohesive paper. Then, we will work together as a class to merge the group papers into one scholarly article.

- Introduction (about 1 page)
- Methods: What did you learn about your method in terms of best practices, access, and ethics? What steps did you take? Tell us about your research process. (about 1½ pages)
- Findings: What did you find? What did you learn about the method AND the debate/ time in history? (about 1½ pages)
- Conclusion (about 1 page)

RAIDERS OF THE LOST ARCHIVES: RESEARCHING THE 1930 ARKANSAS VS. WILEY COLLEGE DEBATE

Colby Cockrill, Lathan Garnett, Meagan Hamilton, and Rae Summers-Thompson

• • • • • • • • •

In 1930, Melvin B. Tolson lead the historically black Wiley College in what would become a ten-year winning streak against Southern college debate teams. Initiating the first interracial debate ever in the South, Wiley College took on Oklahoma City University and ended with the University of Southern California, hitting several schools along the way. The Wiley College Debate Team defeated every college they went up against (Beil). According to David Gold in his book, *Rhetoric at the Margins,* Wiley College also debated Arkansas State University (ASU) the same year (46). With this in mind, we, students in Dr. Kristi Costello's Advanced Composition class at Arkansas State University, made it our goal to discover all that we can about this momentous occasion and important time in our region's history. That being said, while today we celebrate the Wiley College debaters for their role in what was a huge step in the promotion of racial equality in North America, factors including racial bias, the Great Depression, and a devastating fire on our campus, left very little information regarding Arkansas State University's early debate teams and Wiley College's trials and tribulations as they traveled down America's southern roads.

In an endeavor to increase the amount of information that could be found, Dr. Costello's class was separated into four groups: interviews, archives, newspapers and microfiche, and internet and online databases. This section of the report contains the archival group's research methods throughout the project, as well as any findings collected through those research methods. Our group also employed other methodologies of research in order to determine direction of archival research.

Method

Our journey began with archives and the goal of uncovering material on the Wiley College debate against Arkansas State College. To this end, first, we decided that we should look in the physical archives on the seventh floor of the Arkansas State University library. We quickly learned that it has its own set of rules: one must sign in, researchers may have a pencil (no pens) and a piece of paper, no electronic devices, and no backpacks or purses. Additionally, materials that a researcher wishes to view must be requested, and those materials may only be viewed in the designated room. Observing all of the strict rules, we looked through the 1930 Arkansas State University ASU yearbook, *The Yearling,* which led us to learning that Arkansas State was then called First District Agricultural and Mechanical College or A&M College, for short, and became Arkansas State College in 1933. We started by going to the section marked, "Clubs and Activities." Next, we read through the information listed beside every senior's picture, looking to find any individual members of the debate team.

Following an attempt to search the archives at the Craighead Historical Society and after scouting through the online archives, found through Google, we turned our attention to the online newspaper databases, having learned that archival research is not only limited to physical preserved items. There are digital archives that often store valuable photographs, advertisements, and newspaper articles. While in the Arkansas State University ASU archives, we attempted to view the digital archives of the *Herald,* the college newspaper and sorted through *Historical Newspapers.* It takes time to go through various search terms and even more time searching through the abundance of newspaper articles from the 1930s, but patience may return rich rewards.

Our first step searching online newspaper databases was to go to www.astate.edu/library. On the Arkansas State University ASU library's home page, there is a link that says, "All Library Databases." Once we clicked on the link, we changed the *database type* to "News" in the dropdown menu, which displays all the news databases We scrolled down to the "H" section and clicked on "Historical Newspapers." Then we typed the search term, "Wiley College." After the results were up, we changed the publication dates, which are located on the left side of the page, to 1930-1939. Satisfied with the articles that made the cut, we scrolled through them in search of something that mentions Arkansas State College and Wiley College. Lastly, we read through the resulting articles with hope of uncovering something that would help us in our journey to find what happened during that debate and glimpses into the time period.

Through conducting archival research, we learned that it is important to be imaginative and to pay attention to every detail, because things that may seem minor have the potential of leading to a more major discovery. We also learned that, when using newspaper or digital archives, it is important to know exact or close approximate dates of the information being sought. Having learned this, we now also know that preliminary research as well as an attempt to acquire necessary resources will help the research process. More broadly, we learned that the degree of successful archival research depends on several factors: it depends on diligent and faithful preservation of documents, photographs, books, and other memorabilia; the preserved materials must be stored in a place that resists destruction (fires, floods, etc.); one must have access (which might depend on time, mobility, and financial resources) to the archived materials in need.

Findings

The dual objectives of this project, to find information regarding a debate between Arkansas and Wiley colleges in 1930 and learn about conducting primary archival research, were resolved more so in the latter methods than in the former. Due to a popular Hollywood film, *The Great Debaters*, which was produced by Oprah Winfrey and directed and starred by Denzel Washington, there is information available (predominantly online and in the Wiley College archives) about the Wiley College debate team. We found the names and photographs of their team members and their coach, Melvin Tolson, on the website *The Great Debaters*. We also found information regarding several other colleges Wiley debated that year, including Arkansas State University-- Pine Bluff, but not specifically Arkansas State A&M College. Realities regarding the social and economic climate of the period possibly contributed to the lack of publicity of the debate.

Archives

We used Google to find and access digital archives from the region, such as Arkansas State University's own History and Heritage, which we cite throughout this piece. In fact, it was through these digital archives, we learned about the "major fire consumed the Administration/Classroom Building in the early morning hours of Jan. 12, 1931, the first day of spring semester classes," which may have led to a lack of materials regarding the debate team (History & Heritage).

We also looked at a physical copy of Arkansas's 1930 yearbook, the *Yearling*, in which there is no mention of a debate team. The title page in the yearbook records the name of what is currently Arkansas State University as then being the State Agricultural and Mechanical College. There are no newspapers, files, photographs, or any other source of information in the Arkansas State University archives pertaining to the 1930 debates. Likewise, we could not find any materials with the Craighead Historical Society. On the other hand, we did find some books that include information about Melvin B. Tolson, the debate team's founder and coach, as well as reviews of his written work (Flasch, Lenhardt). However, there was no information to be found in the books regarding any 1930 debates with Arkansas.

Interviews

We interviewed Dr. Brady Banta, the Associate Director of Arkansas State University archives and faculty member of the Heritage Studies Ph.D. Program. Dr. Banta informed us that there had been a fire in the administration building of the university that would have destroyed any possible materials, including any and all records dating from 1928 to 1932. He also taught us about the social and economic conditions of Jonesboro in 1930. He explained to us that Craighead County, home of Arkansas State University (ASU), was a predominantly agricultural region. Perhaps the most helpful information from the interview was that Arkansas College was segregated in 1930, and it remained so until the 1960s, making it unlikely that the two schools met publicly in the 1930s. If a debate had happened, it was likely that it was not reported to the newspaper for fear of repercussion. Dr. Banta also very graciously offered to comb through a collection of which he told us had belonged to the first principal of ASU, Dr. Kay. Unfortunately, Dr. Banta reported that he could not find anything related to the debates.

We also attempted to gain interviews with Wiley College and author Gary Lenhardt, but received no response to emails.

Internet and Databases

We anticipated that the group assigned to Internet and Databases would exhaust the information that could be found on popular search engines, like Google, so we first gravitated toward published newspapers, which we expected might have been likely to report on community events, such as college debates. In particular, Dr. Banta suggested we explore the database, Historical Newspapers (our process is detailed above). Next, we searched Google and, through it, learned additional information about the social and economic climate of the 1930. Lynchings were not only an acceptable practice in the South, but were the common mode of punishment for any person of color who was accused of any offense (Shipman). Because this area consisted largely of farmers and sharecroppers, so the Great Depression in 1930 critically impacted numerous people and businesses (Arkansas State University).

Primary Research

Interestingly, though people and banks alike were being foreclosed and going bankrupt, Arkansas College actually grew (History & Heritage).

While there is evidence available regarding debates between the two colleges later than 1930, we have naught but rumor and speculation concerning a debate between the two in that specific year. We may also speculate that, due to Jim Crowism and the bigoted ideals that supported those laws, publicity of an interracial debate would have been undesired. Not only would an interracial debate have been distasteful and controversial to many during an already volatile period, but, due to those very reasons, publicizing such an event could have proven dangerous for all those involved. Additionally, as far as news coverage went, debate matches were not considered sellable stories; in other words, it was not common practice to publish news stories about intercollegiate debates, regardless of race.

Conclusion

Our team did locate evidence that supports that Wiley College debated Arkansas State University Pine Bluff in 1931 at a tournament in Hot Springs in a newspaper article found within the Historical Newspapers databases titled, "Arkansas State and Wiley College Debate." The article never mentioned Pine Bluff so we can see how scholars, such as Gold, may have been confused (see the postscript for an additional curveball). And how exciting to aid in better illuminating history. Because of this and our new-found experience with and appreciation of research, we call this research project a success.

We started with little information about the debate, questioning the actual event itself. Through our research, we learned more about our university's rich history, past race relations in our region, and we have even been able to determine that the teams did meet at a later date than the suspected first debate at a neutral location, in Hot Springs, AR, housing multitudes beyond expectations. This is evidence that Wiley College did, in fact, draw attention to their debates. Additionally, we can see that Wiley obviously traveled many miles and this information sheds light on the existence of travelling teams, in general, which means that a debate between the two teams did not necessarily take place at Arkansas State College. In our research we have seen that there are various theories as to why the city of Jonesboro, Arkansas, home of Arkansas State College would not publish information about this debate even if it had happened. At this time, there were social class issues, such as the Great Depression and segregation under Jim Crow laws, that influenced the mindset of many American citizens. The debaters' safety had to be taken into account in regard to both parties. Since lynchings were so common, we can assume that African American students in a rural Southern town were not welcomed with open arms.

As we researched, we witnessed that different types of research are best for different research topics. For example, this debate that happened in 1930 with very little information publicized by local news. Interviews were not a very good avenue of research. All of the people involved in the actual debate are now passed away, any people that would have been young during that time are also probably no longer around, or they did not realize the importance of the event as it happened. Archives and Microfiche seemed to be promising avenues, although they both provided little information. Contrary to our assumptions, internet databases were challenging to find reliable sources and specific information about the debate.

Primary research has proved to us that this practice is many degrees different from secondary research. In primary research we are responsible for the information we gather, and we are responsible for finding reliable resources. This research is unlike most of the research many students conduct; in secondary research there have been previous researchers to compile information. When we are the first researchers, we cannot pull from previously compiled information, because *we* are the ones compiling this information. This is an exciting privilege and should be taken seriously. Further, primary research is a difficult job to undertake and takes skill, hard work, imagination, attention to even the smallest details, and patience. That being said, it should also be mentioned that there is a great deal of excitement and satisfaction in the process itself. Creating theories and tracking down details can be both challenging and exhilarating. Such a journey can take a passive student researcher and turn her into an active investigator.

Post-Script

Since submitting this project, Smithsonian's National Museum of African American History & Culture published a new website. In it, one may view two pages of Henrietta Bell Wells's, one of Wiley's most notable debate alums, scrapbook. The second of these pages contains pressed flowers as souvenirs of her travels. Upon magnifying the page to examine her handwriting, one may see that she has written, "And this is a flower that I stole from Arkansas State College at my very first debate." Scholarly articles, however, suggest that Wiley College's first interracial debate at a Southern venue was in Oklahoma City, so this finding stirs up more questions. Did *she* debate in OK City? If not, did Wiley College, in fact, travel to Arkansas State College for a debate that year, or did they perhaps stop at the campus at some point for some unknown reason? It has been rumored that Tolson, Wiley's coach, was attempting to unionize share croppers in this area. Perhaps while here the two teams defied all odds and went toe to toe in an exchange of ideas. Only further research will tell . . .

?

Copyright Acknowledgments

Booth, Wayne, Gregory Colomb, Joseph Williams, Joseph Bizup, and
William Fitzgerald. Excerpt(s) from *The Craft of Research*
4e. Copyright © 1995, 2003, 2008, 2016 by The University of
Chicago. Reprinted with permission of The University of Chicago
Press. All rights reserved.

Grutter, Alexandra S., Jennifer G. Rumney, Tane Sinclair-Taylor, Peter
Waldie, and Craig E. Franklin. "Fish Mucous Cocoons: The
'Mosquito Nets' of the Sea" from *Biology Letters,* Vol. 7, No.
2, Nov. 17, 2010, pp. 292-294. Copyright © 2010 The Journal
Society. Reprinted with permission. All rights reserved.

Pain, Elisabeth. "How to (Seriously) Read a Scientific Paper" from *Science*
Careers, Mar. 21, 2016. All rights reserved.

Purugganan, Mary, and Jan Hewitt. "How to Read a Scientific Article"
from the Cain Project in Engineering and Professional
Communication at Rice University. Reprinted with the
permission of Mary Purugganan and Jan Hewitt. All rights
reserved.

Ruben, Adam. "How to Read a Scientific Paper" from *Science* Careers, Jan.
20, 2016. All rights reserved.